RED RIVER SETTLERS

Records of the Settlers of
Northern Montgomery, Robertson, and
Sumner Counties, Tennessee

By
EDYTHE RUCKER WHITLEY

CLEARFIELD

Reprinted for
Clearfield Company, Inc. by
Genealogical Publishing Co., Inc.
Baltimore, Maryland
1993, 1995, 1999, 2001

Library of Congress Catalogue Card Number 80-66829
International Standard Book Number: 0-8063-0897-4
Made in the United States of America

TENNESSEE IN 1806

Carter 1777
Sullivan 1779
Washington 1777
Hawkins 1786
Greene 1783
Grainger 1796
Jefferson 1792
Cocke 1797
Claiborne 1801
Knox 1792
Sevier 1794
Blount 1795
Campbell 1806
Anderson 1808
CHEROKEE LANDS
Overton 1806
Roane 1801
Jackson 1801
Smith 1799
White 1806
Wilson 1799
Rutherford 1803
Sumner 1786
Robertson 1796
Davidson 1783
Williamson 1799
Montgomery 1796
Dickson 1803
Stewart 1803

INTRODUCTION

I N 1788 THE GENERAL ASSEMBLY of North Carolina laid off a new district which embraced the three Cumberland counties of Davidson, Sumner, and Tennessee. This district was named the Mero District in honor of Don Estephan Mero, Governor of New Orleans. In 1796 the Mero District was incorporated into the new state of Tennessee, with Tennessee County divided into the counties of Montgomery and Robertson.

This book deals with the northern half of Montgomery, Robertson, and Sumner counties, the area known as Red River. It consists of a collection of county, state, church, and family records, and also contains genealogies of Red River families, developed, for the most part, from a wide variety of sources, including cemetery records, bible records, military records, and private papers, as well as records of deeds, wills, marriages, and court minutes.

The Cumberland River and its tributaries provide the drainage for this section. Red River is a northern branch of the Cumberland. It rises in Kentucky and waters the counties of Montgomery, Robertson, and the northwestern part of Sumner. It flows southwest and falls into the Cumberland at Clarksville—the county seat of Montgomery—after a course of seventy miles. Its principal branches are Sulphur and Elk Forks. The West and Barren Forks have their junction a short distance above Clarksville.

Sulphur Fork, one of the eastern branches of Red River, is in Robertson County. It rises near the road leading from Nashville to Franklin, Kentucky. It took its name from the Sulphur Spring owned by Mr. Archer Cheatham, called "Robertson's Springs," situated near its source, two miles from "Tyree Springs." The creek runs in a northwesterly direction for fifteen or sixteen miles until it passes the town of Springfield, county seat of Robertson County, then turns and flows southwest, falling into Red River at Port Royal in Montgomery County, a distance of some forty miles.

Elk Fork, a large northern branch of Red River, rises near Elkton, Todd County, Kentucky, entering Tennessee in Robertson County, and joins Red River three miles from the northeast corner of Montgomery County.

Montgomery County was named for John Montgomery. Its first permanent settlement was made by Moses Renfroe and his company, April 12, 1780. Renfroe ascended the Red River to the mouth of Carson's Creek where he built Renfroe's Station (sometimes called Red River Station). Among this company were: Moses, Isaac, Joseph, and James Renfroe, Nathan and Solomon Turpin, Isaac Mayfield, James Hollis, James Johns, and a widow named Jones. Some of the others who came soon after were: Francis Prince, Col. James Ford, Martin Armstrong, Anthony and William Crutcher, William Polk, Amos Bird, George Bell, Robert Nelson, Aeneas McAllister, John Easton, Daniel James, James Adams, William Montgomery, Philip Gilbert, Robert Dunning, Hugh McCallum, Benjamin Hawkins, Andrew Snoddy, Isaac Titsworth, Major Evan Shelby (brother of Isaac Shelby), and Dr. Morgan Brown, as well as members of the Nevill, Sevier, Dier, Lindsey, Kittrell, Neblett, and Roberts families.

The first settlers in Robertson County included: Thomas Kilgore (in 1776/1777 he lived for some time in a cave on the South Fork of Red River, near the present village of Cross Plains), Moses Maulden, Ambrose Mauloon, Samuel Mason, Josiah Hankins, Archer Cheatham, Thomas Johnson, William Fort, Jacob McCarty, Benjamin Meneese, William Miles, Isaac and John Phillips, Bazil Boren, Martin Duncan, James Crabtree, and Zebulon Hart, and members of the Donelson, McIntosh, Bell, Randall (Randle), Peebles, Gunn, and Tatum families.

Sumner County was erected November 17, 1786 by the North Carolina Legislature and named in honor of General Jethro Sumner, a gallant officer of the Revolution. In 1779 a settlement of about a dozen families was made at "Bledsoe's Lick," now "Castalian Springs." Forts were built by a number of the earliest pioneers— John Morgan, Major James White, Col. Sanders, Jacob Zigler, Capt. Joseph Wilson. Mansker's Fort was in the lower part of the county. Among the early settlers were: Anthony and Col. Isaac Bledsoe, Robert Desha (ancestor of President Lyndon Baines Johnson), Jordon Gibson, Henry Loving, William Hall, David Shelby, George D. Blackmore, General James and George Winchester, Robert Peyton (ancestor of Hon. Bailey Peyton), Samuel and Joseph Wilson, Michael Shafer, Isaac Walton, David Looney, Benjamin Luylendall, James Trousdale, the Porters, Winters, Lathams, Williams, Hagans, Sheppards, and Bowens.

Many others participated in the founding and settlement of the Red River area. Their records as well as the records of many of those mentioned above will be found in this work. Some records, particularly those transcribed from private papers and family bibles, can be found nowhere else.

EDYTHE RUCKER WHITLEY
Nashville, Tennessee
March 1, 1980

TABLE OF CONTENTS

FAMILY HISTORIES

The year 1980 will mark the beginning of the "Third Century" for descendants of those pioneers who endured many hardships and came into the Red River Country and into the Mero District, or Middle Tennessee.

I am certain that I have not included all the names of the families who found their homes in the Red River Country just north of Nashville, but I have attempted briefly to mention as many as possible in this compilation.

Ayres

Henry and Susan Ayres were residents of Robertson County, Tennessee when he received a pension for Revolutionary service. Henry Ayres died 22 April 1833, and on 4 March 1848 Susan, his widow, commenced to draw a pension based upon her husband's service.

The pension papers show that Henry Ayres was a private in the company commanded by Capt. —— (name not given) of the regiment commanded by Col. Parker in the Virginia Militia — service: three years from 1776.

Susan Ayres made a declaration in Robertson County, 9 May 1848, aged 85 years, the widow of Henry Ayres, deceased, a private in the Revolutionary War who drew a pension at the rate of $80.00 per annum. She would not sign, but made her mark. The declaration was witnessed by John Ayres.

In a letter, dated 23 May 1846 from Springfield, Tennessee, regarding his mother's claim for a pension, Lemuel Ayres stated that Susan Ayres lived with her husband (then deceased) for sixty-five years. The letter bears the signature of W. W. Pepper.

In another declaration before Jesse S. Ellis, a Justice of the Peace, Susan Ayres of Robertson County said that she married her husband in North Carolina in 1781 by the publication of Bonds, as was the usual custom of those days.

On 30 May 1843 before William Seal, a Justice of the Peace, Susan Ayres of Robertson County declared her age to be 81 on 7 August 1843. She further stated that Henry Ayres was a private in the Revolutionary War of Virginia — one year's service in Virginia then home, enlisted three years and served in the Virginia Line. She married him in Surry County, Virginia in the month of January 1781. They moved to North Carolina and later to South Carolina where they remained for fourteen years then came to Tennessee.

Richard James of Robertson County, Tennessee made a sworn statement on 30 May 1842 that he was a citizen of Robertson County, aged 80 years. He spoke well of Susan Ayres and said that he became acquainted with her in South Carolina, in Spartanburg District, in the year 1785 and that she was then the wife of Henry Ayres. Henry and Susan Ayres moved to Robertson County, and Richard James moved also and in the same neighborhood. When he became acquainted with them, they had one child, and he was informed by them that they had previously lost a child or children.

On 30 May 1843 in Robertson County, Martha Head, aged 25 years, made a statement regarding the marriage of Susan and Henry in Surry County, North Carolina in 1781. She had been well acquainted with Henry and Susan since their marriage.

When Henry Ayres applied for his pension, he gave his age as 79 years. The brief of his service shows that he volunteered in 1775 and served twelve months. Later he enlisted for three years. All of his service was as a private. The officers under whom he served were: Maj. Henry Lee, Lt. Col. Richard Parker, Col. Josiah Parker, and Lt. Col. William Davis.

Henry Ayres was a resident of Bedford County, Virginia when he enlisted. He participated in the battles of Red Clay Creek in Pennsylvania, Brandywine, and Germantown.

In the declaration of Henry Ayres, 14 August 1832, he stated that he was 79 years of age. Thomas Gunn, a Minister of the Gospel in Robertson County, made an affidavit as to the character of Mr. Ayres. Henry Frey also made an affidavit regarding the same. James Mitchell said that he knew Henry Ayres in the United States Army and remained three years and believed he was under the command of General Mecklinburg.

Henry Ayres and his family must have been members of the Methodist Church. Thomas Gunn was a Methodist minister at the time the pension claim was pending.

File W-455. National Archives, Washington, D.C.   Rev. Pen. Div.

Bailey

The Revolutionary pension application of John Bailey, on file in the National Archives, Washington, D. C., Revolutionary Pension Division, file R-377, marked "Rejected," shows the name spelled Bailey and Bayley. A letter from Owingsville, Kentucky, 24 June 1825, submitted evidence in favor of Ensign John Bayley and stated that his inability to travel coupled with his poverty prevented him from traveling to Virginia in quest of his officers or some of the men in order to prove his enlistment.

The same letter refers to the cases of John Smothers, Jacob Johnston, Charles Rudder, and Ambrose Jones. Of Jacob Johnston it is stated that he was extremely illiterate, not knowing a letter in the book. He was enlisted in the parish of St. John about 35 miles from Charleston, S. C., and the fort where the battle was fought in June 1775-6 was seven miles east of Charleston on the left hand side of the channel as you go out to sea, "all of which are facts of my own knowledge," said the writer. He was poor and ignorant, and his wife was "Ensane" more than half her time. He served one year in Capt. Horry's Company, commanded by Col. Moulty. The court was decidedly of the opinion that he was entitled to draw. The letter was signed by John Bedall.

At the August 1824 Term court in Bath County, Kentucky, John Bailey, a Revolutionary Pensioner produced in open court and submitted evidence in the original claim of John Bailey on 12 August 1824. From the papers on file it is learned that John Bailey, aged 68, a resident of Bath County, enlisted for a term of one year in August 1775 in the State of Virginia. He was enlisted by Capt. Augustine Willis and was attached part of the time to Capt. Mason's Company and part of the time to Capt. Pelham's Company, Virginia Regiment. He was in the Virginia Continental Establishment commanded by Col. John Ruffin until August 1776 when he was discharged from said service in Yorktown, Virginia. He enlisted again in September 1776 in Brunswick County, Virginia with Thomas Threadgill, commander, for three years. He was in a company commanded by Capt. Isaac Hicks and was attached to the regiment commanded by Col. Glascock of the Virginia Line and the Virginia Continental Establishment and was a first sergeant in said company. He also stated that he volunteered under Capt. Benjamin Hicks against Lord Dunmore. His age at the time of his declaration was 78 years, and he was a hatter by trade. His wife was named Jane, and he had two small boys living with him, none of whom were able to constitute any support.

On 20 June 1825 in Bath County, State of Kentucky, Mary Yarborough made a deposition in which she gave her age as 67 years. She stated that her brother, John Bayley came home in 1775 with a soldier's uniform on and a cocktail in his hat and said to all the family that he was enlisted in the Regulars Service and that he started to the army the next day or so afterwards. Her mother was much grieved. Her brother, John Bayley, frequently wrote letters home from Norfolk while it was beseiged by the enemy, informing his father's family of what was passing. One letter stated that a soldier's head was shot off close to him. Another letter said that he was almost naked. His father, Wm. Bayley, went down to Norfolk with clothes for him.

Thomas Threadgill, a young man who lived in the neighborhood and with whom he was acquainted, visited Wm. Bayley's house and said that he was a Lieutenant in the Regular Army and that he went with John Bayley the second time to the army. Thomas Threadgill frequently wore his uniform to the home of Mary Yarborough's father. When her brother John quit the service, he came home with his uniform. She bought his Aupletts afterwards for ten dollars. She had to plow for her father while her brother was in the army. This concluded the statement of Mary Yarborough.

On 20 June 1825, Bath County, Kentucky, a deponent, Lucy Boyd, aged 59 years, confirmed the testimony of her sister, Mary Yarborough.

The declaration of John Bailey, aged 62 or 63 years, made in Bath County, Kentucky, 22 June 1819, stated that he was enlisted for three years at Brunswick County, Virginia about August or September 1776 by Lt. Thomas Threadgill in the company commanded by Capt. Isaac Hicks.

Robert Bailey and Mark Love stated that John Bailey had a second wife and five small children.

Balthrop

The Balthrops lived in Halifax District, Warren County, North Carolina, in 1790. There was a James Balthrop who died there in 1780, leaving a will in which he mentioned only one John Balthrop.

Francis, also called Frank, Balthrop was in Robertson County, Tennessee before Cheatham County was created. His residence fell in the new county, in which he died and left a will dated 10 February 1849, the same being probated in 1858. In the will he named his wife, J. Media Balthrop, and the following children: Thomas G., Robert, Henry F., William, Jordan R., Patsy Kemp or Patsy Kemp Norris, Nancy R. Everett, Mary Norris, Luary Ann Mose, Sarah B. Gibbs, and Elizabeth Gilmore. Robert Balthrop was appointed guardian of the children who were not yet of age. Henry F. and Jordan R. Balthrop were named as executors.

John C. Balthrop married Nancy White. They were both natives of North Carolina, born in 1810 and 1808 respectively. They arrived in Tennessee shortly before 1830. Their children were William H., Robert F., Mary L., Eliza A., John H., Gustavus J., Julia A., Zachariah T., and Sarah J. Robert F. and Gustavus J. were both killed in the Confederate Army; Robert F. at Alexandria, Louisiana and Gustavus J., at Jonesboro, Georgia. Mrs. Nancy Balthrop died 5 January 1869. Her husband survived until shortly after 1886.

John H. Balthrop was born in Robertson County on 18 August 1841. On 19 January 1862 he enlisted in Company C, 49th Tennessee Confederate Infantry. He was captured at Fort Donelson and taken to Camp Douglas, at Chicago, and held there until September 1862. After being released, he rejoined his regiment and was at Vicksburg, Fort Hudson and Jackson, Mississippi. He then went to Mobile, Alabama where he remained until the battle of Missionary Ridge. From the last mentioned place he went to Dalton, Georgia where he remained until 1864. He then joined the army at New Hope and was in all the campaigns back to Peach Tree Creek where he was wounded in the right thigh which necessitated the amputation of his leg. He remained in the hospital at Macon and Cuthbert, Georgia until the close of the war. After the war John H. Balthrop returned to his home in Tennessee and attended school for two years, after which he attended a commercial college in Louisville, Kentucky. The following few years he was engaged in teaching. He chose Grantsville in 1873 as the place to enter the merchandise business. A short time later he moved to Cheatham County where he remained the rest of his life. He was married on 29 January 1880 to Mary J. Gupton, who was born on 23 November 1855. They had only one child, Eunice F., born 12 December 1880. After locating in Cheatham County, Mr. Balthrop was appointed postmaster at Henrietta, a position he held as long as he was able to work. Mr. Balthrop took an active part in the development and promotion of the Methodist Church at Henrietta.

Some of the descendants of the Balthrop family of Cheatham and Montgomery Counties are to be found at this time in Davidson County, Tennessee.

Cheatham Co., Tenn. Will Book 1, p. 70.
Goodspeed's History of Cheatham County, Tennessee. 1886.

Berry

Logan County, Kentucky is definitely to be considered in the Red River Country. A Revolutionary soldier, Captain George Berry, who stated in his pension application that he was born in 1746 (place not stated), located in Logan County, from which place he received a pension for his services.

Bidwell

Charles Bidwell was born in 1779, a native of Connecticut, of English descent, a descendant of John Bidwell, who migrated from England in the 1630's and died in 1683. The Bidwells were Puritans. When young Charles Bidwell reached manhood about 1810, he came to Tennessee, locating in Robertson County, where he married Mrs. Martha (Binkley) Shaw. Mr. Bidwell became a wealthy planter. He was a Major in the Battle of New Orleans, 8 January 1815. He died in 1848. His wife survived until 1855.

Mrs. Martha (Binkley) Shaw Bidwell was the daughter of Jacob Binkley, an early settler in Middle Tennessee.

Mr. and Mrs. Bidwell were blessed with six children: Charles M., Bell G., Sarah B. (married Mr. Frey), Julia A. (became the wife of Dr. T. P. Crutcher of Nashville), and Arthur F. Bidwell. Arthur F. Bidwell was born 10 October 1839 and was educated at Liberty Academy in Springfield. Later he attended the East Tennessee University at Knoxville. In January 1861 he located on a 400 acre farm on the Cheatham and Robertson County line. In January 1869 Arthur F. Bidwell took as his bride Miss Mary F. Justice, daughter of Jack and Susan Justice of Robertson County. Their children were: Emma F., Buena M., Charles B., John F., Ruth M., Paul B., and Martha M. Bidwell, all of whom were members of the Methodist Episcopal Church.

Bell G. Bidwell, son of Charles and Martha, was born in Robertson County, Tennessee on 19 February 1837. Bell attended Cumberland University at Lebanon and later went to the University of Nashville where he studied medicine, graduating in 1852. He then took up the study of law and received his degree in 1860. Following this he entered practice at Springfield. When the Civil War broke out Mr. Bidwell was commissioned a Captain in a company of the 13th Tennessee Infantry and was promoted later to the rank of Major. After the war he moved to Paducak, Kentucky, where he practiced law and served in the State Legislature of 1873 to 1877. In 1879 he went to Weatherford, Texas.

Major Bidwell was married in 1872 to Ellen P. Flourney, whose mother was a Calhoun of the famous John C. Calhoun family. Her grandfather was John C. Calhoun's cousin. The Flourneys are of French extraction and of a prominent Virginia family who migrated to Tennessee.

Major and Mrs. Bidwell had only two children, H. L. and Nellie, both of whom were reared in Weatherford, Texas.

Goodspeed's History of Cheatham County, Tennessee. 1886. p. 1361.
History of Texas, Tarrant and Parker Counties. 1896. p. 421.

Binkley

Peter and John Binkley came to Pennsylvania in or about 1717 from Herrnbut, Saxony. At least one other brother came with them and remained in Pennsylvania while Peter and John came to North Carolina.

There were several different ways in which the name Binkley was spelled when they first came to America. Among them were Binkle, Binkele, Brinkley, Pinkley, Pinkly, and Binkley, the latter being the most commonly used since 1780.

Peter and John Binkley were in North Carolina in 1727 and were present when a committee met on 24 March 1727 to establish the line between Virginia and North Carolina. Peter Binkley's home had been recommended as a place for the surveyors to stay while at work in that section. The state line ran by John Binkley's property.

Peter Binkley later went to Manakasy, Maryland near Fredericksburg and was connected with the Moravians there. In 1770 he came to Wachovia, North Carolina as a communicant Brother and bought 300 acres of land. In 1771 he bought 309 acres more.

Peter was born in 1704. He spent much of his time preaching and visiting in homes. He had his Memoir written by Sr. Cramer, 12 July 1782. He died in 1793. Seven sons survived him: John, Adam, Joseph, Jacob, Peter Jr., Frederick, and Christian. No daughters were mentioned in his will recorded in Stokes County, North Carolina. He also named Margaretta, his wife.

Of these sons, Adam and Jacob came to Tennessee about 1782. John Binkley's fourth child, Frederick, came to Tennessee with his uncles. John Binkley and two other sons and their families came to Tennessee sometime shortly after 1779.

Adam Binkley settled his family on Sycamore Creek in what is now Cheatham County, and Jacob Binkley went to Robertson County near Springfield. Frederick Binkley bought and built on Stone's River, twelve miles from Nashville. His old home in later years was owned and occupied by the Gleaves family.

John Binkley married Johanna Leedy in Pennsylvania, and they came to Stokes County, North Carolina in 1772. Their children were: Peter, Elizabeth who married a Mr. Childress, John who married Elizabeth Wright, Frederick who was born in 1774 and married Adeline Shackleford in 1804, Jacob who married a Miss Frey, Joseph who never came to Tennessee, Henry who was married in Missouri, Abraham who was married in Missouri, Daniel who married Catherine Moser, George who married Isaac Earthman's daughter, Katherin who married Henry Frey, and Sarah, the youngest child, who married Peter Frey.

The Bible of Joseph Shackleford Binkley provides the following family information:
Frederick Binkley, the son of John and Johanna Leedy Binkley and father of Joseph S. Binkley, was born in North Carolina on 15 February 1774 and died on 18 September 1857. He was married on 24 December 1804 to Adeline Shackleford, daughter of Roger Shackleford and Nancy Carter. She was born in Virginia on 17 May 1789 and died on 5 or 15 September 1868.
Joseph Shackleford Binkley was born 19 November 1810 and died 21 August 1887. He married Martha Buchanan Steele on 18 July 1833. Martha Buchanan Steele, the daughter of Samuel Steele and Patience Shane, was born 9 December 1811 and died 28 July 1859.
Samuel Steele, son of Andrew Steele and Martha Buchanan, was born in Virginia on 13 May 1782 and died 7 March 1864. He married Patience Shane on 19 June 1805. Patience Shane, the daughter of Morris Shane and Phoebe Castleman, was born in Tennessee on 2 September 1787 and died 4 June 1852.
The children of Joseph S. and Martha Steele Binkley were: Mary, born 13 October 1834, died 8 August 1884, married 12 January 1851 to Samuel Steele; Frederick Summerfield, born 22 June 1836, died 23 June 1836; Benjamin Franklin, born 3 May 1837, died 17 December 1903, married 25 March 1866 to Matilda Markham; Malvina, born 1 May 1839, died 12 June 1852; Amanda Rebecca, born 21 October 1841, married 7 January 1862 to Frederick Marshall; Almeda Adeline, born 18 November 1843, died

14 April 1887, married 18 February 1866 to Jefferson Carver; Ann Leady, born 11 November 1845, married 8 April 1868 to Joshua Beadle; Henry Clay, born 25 November 1847, married 16 April 1874 to Ree J. McGee; Martha Elizabeth, born 24 December 1849, died 18 June 1852; Samuel Steele, born 2 October 1851, died 7 March 1883; Joseph Pitts, born 14 May 1854, died 8 April 1921, married 30 April 1876 to Alice Moss; and David Campbell Kelly, born 30 June 1857, died 14 August 1928, married 13 May 1883 to Florence Dickson.

Joseph Shackleford Binkley married a second wife, Elizabeth Ivey Holland, the daughter of Jaret and Elizabeth Ivey. Their daughter, Elizabeth Clark, was born 5 May 1862 and died 6 December 1879. Mrs. Elizabeth Ivey Holland Binkley died 15 July 1879.

Joseph Shackleford Binkley married his third wife, Mrs. Hettie Ellis Young, on 31 October 1885.

Adam Binkley was a private and lieutenant in the North Carolina line and was placed on the pension roll of Davidson County, Tennessee 12 November 1832, aged 94 years.

Daniel Binkley's land division, recorded 28 December 1826 in Davidson County, shows those who received allotments: Ann Strong, Anthony Binkley, Franklin Binkley, Almeda Binkley, Isaac Binkley, Mary Earhart, John Binkley, William Binkley, Mahala Binkley, Milly Binkley, and Martha Binkley.

There is in Davidson County, a record of Mrs. Catherine Binkley's dower, dated 5 April 1826. She is recited as the "relict" of Daniel Binkley, deceased.

Richard Binkley married Celia Hays on 29 December 1806. Frederick Binkley married Adeline Shackleford on 12 December 1804. John Binkley married Elizabeth Hurt on 1 March 1821. David Binkley married Druscilla Shackleford on 30 August 1821. Absalom Binkley married Aggy Page on 15 February 1822. William Binkley married Sarah Cowgill on 28 November 1822. John Binkley married Alenida Binkley on 16 October 1823. Alexander Binkley married Hixey Holt on 10 January 1823. James Binkley married Lucinda Smith on 18 December 1826. Isaac Binkley married Patsy Wilson on 21 March 1828. Adam Binkley married Julia Norris on 30 June 1828. Henry Binkley married Nancy A. Gleaves on 5 July 1828. Eli Binkley married Catharine Swigart on 22 March 1830. Henry Binkley married Mary Bennett on 1 November 1830. And Peter Binkley married Tabitha Norris on 2 April 1831. All these marriages took place in Davidson County. Many later marriages of the Binkley family appear in the Davidson County records. There were also Binkley marriages in Robertson and Cheatham Counties.

Another old Bible from which I have a record in connection with the Binkley family, states that E. G. Binkley was born 6 May 1849, and Mary Melvina Binkley was born 27 June 1851.

The Frederick Binkley graveyard is located on the old Frederick Binkley farm in Davidson County about ten miles from Nashville on a crossroad between Stewart's Ferry Road and Central Pike. There are several very old tombstones with inscriptions.

A number of the Binkleys bought farms in Robertson and Cheatham Counties, on or near the Davidson County line, where they settled and reared large families. Numerous descendants still reside in the locality.

Binkley Bible records.
Davidson County, Tennessee Marriages. Book 1.
North Carolina Wills, Stokes County, by Grimes.
Manuscript data in Whitley collection.
Bible and Tombstone Records of Tennessee, by Acklen. 1933.
Davidson County, Tennessee Will Book 9, pp. 73-105-18.

Bourland

John Bourland was living in Laurens County, South Carolina in 1790 at which time he owned no slaves. In 1812 he was a member of Flat Creek Church, the Red River Association, Tennessee. Therefore we learn where he came from and know that he arrived at Red River between 1790 and 1812.

Brantley

The Montgomery County court record of 28 June 1809 shows that Thomas Brantley was administrator of the estate of James Brantley, deceased. Nothing is shown of the heirs of the deceased.

The will of Charles Brantley, dated 3 February 1803 in Montgomery County, indicates that there were several of that family name in the county at an early date. From the will, Charles appears to have been the father of Sarah, Thomas, and James. Five older children are referred to but not named. A son William was not yet 21 years of age. The inventory of Charles Brantley, deceased, was returned by J. P. Vaughan, Barney Duff and James Hambleton on 24 April 1812.

Montgomery County, Will Book A, p. 72.
Montgomery County, record Old Tenn. Co. 2, p. 180.
Montgomery County Court Min. 1808-1810, p. 266.

Brewer

The name Brewer, especially that of Sterling Brewer, is most familiar in the entire Middle District of Tennessee.

William Brewer of Chatham County, North Carolina and Christian County, Kentucky was one of the Tennessee-Kentucky border families. His activities were as much in Montgomery County, Tennessee as they were in Christian County, Kentucky. His wife was Milly West, and his son William was born 18 June 1803.

National Historical Magazine. July 1938, p. 74.

Brodie

About the year 1813, a family named Brodie came to Montgomery County from North Carolina. Among them was David, born in Granville County on 7 September 1792, and Alexander, born on 13 November 1794.

David Brodie became a physician. His wife, Susan M., was the daughter of William and Lucy Streshley. She was a native of Fayette County, Kentucky, born 28 March 1802. She died in Clarksville on 22 August 1854. Dr. Brodie died 1 January 1871.

When Alexander Brodie grew to manhood, he became a farmer and bought a tract of land. In 1822 he married Miss Mary Oldham, a native of Williamson County. They had six children. He was a member of the Methodist Episcopal Church for between thirty and forty years. He died 19 March 1865, and his wife died 13 November 1869. Of their six children, J. L., born near Rose Hill, became a farmer. In 1866 J. L. wed Miss A. A. Trahern of Christian County, Kentucky, a daughter of William Trahern. Mr. and Mrs. J. L. Brodie had two children, William S. and R. E.

J. L. Brodie enlisted in the 14th Tennessee Regiment under Col. Forbes. After serving ten months, he was discharged on physical disability. He then enlisted in the First Kentucky Cavalry in which he remained only a short time, then joined the Second Kentucky under Morgan. He participated in the Battle of Shiloh and Murfreesboro and was slightly wounded in the Battle of Marian. He remained with his regiment until it surrendered at Washington, Georgia 10 May 1865. He and his family were highly respected members of the Methodist Episcopal Church.

The court of 20 October 1817 proved a deed of conveyance from Thomas Rivers to William O. Roberts, Nicholas M. Gilmer, John T. Gilmer, Edward Taylor, and John Brodie in trust for the Methodist Church of one acre of land. The witnesses were Alexander Martin and Peter H. Cole.

John Brodie was a prominent physician of Clarksville in the early days. He was probably the father of Alexander and David and some daughters (also probably other sons). One of the daughters married Solomon A. Kittrell of Clarksville, who died in April 1818, leaving a wife and children. When his estate was settled, his father-in-law, Dr. John Brodie, was the executor.

Montgomery County, Court Min. 1816-1817, p. 261.
Montgomery Co. Will book 2, p. 389.
Goodspeed's History of Montgomery Co. 1886.
Kittrell Family Manuscript by Edythe Whitley.

Brooke

Dudley Brooke was a Revolutionary Soldier. He migrated to Tennessee and was living in Robertson County in 1833 when he applied for and received a pension for his services. In his application he stated that he was born 3 July 1762 in Chesterfield County, Virginia. He enlisted in 1777 in Capt. White's Company, and in 1778 he again enlisted. In 1779 he enlisted under Lt. Henry Johnson and Col. Anthony New. He again enlisted under Capt. Richard Phillips and in 1781 served seven months in Capt. Robert Cary's Company, Col. Combes Virginia Regiment.

In 1802 he left Louisa County, Virginia where he was then living and moved to Robertson County, Tennessee.

He listed the names of his children in his application: Elizabeth, Sarah, Mary, Harry, John, Frances or Francis, and Dudley Jr.

Revolutionary Pension Records, National Archives, Washington, D.C.

Buck

Samuel D. and Martha A. Buck were both natives of Virginia, from which place they emigrated to Kentucky. They were the parents of three children and were living in Montgomery County, near Clarksville on 9 June 1848 when their youngest son, Henry C., was born. Mrs. Buck died in Christian County, Kentucky when still young. In 1859 Mr. Buck moved to Fulton County, Kentucky and died there during the Civil War.

Dr. Henry C. Buck became a disciple of Aesculapius, studying under Dr. Henry C. Catlett of Hickman, Kentucky. Afterwards he attended lectures in the Medical University of Louisville. Bettie C. Steele, born in Hickman County, Kentucky on 10 April 1859, daughter of John C. Steele, became the wife of Dr. Buck on 27 September 1876. To their union were born Daisy Willie, Henry C., and Mary Annice.

Goodspeed's History of Obion County, Tennessee. 1886. p. 939.

Chewning

This name is found spelled Chewning and Chowning in the early Virginia records. Robert and Jane Chewning appear to have been the emigrants. They were in Middlesex County, Virginia about 1659. The Christ Church Parish Register refers to members of the family frequently.

Robert, son of Robert and Jane, was born in May 1659 and christened on 23 February 1660. The younger Robert appears to have married a lady named Anne about 1680. Their children probably were: Thomas born in 1684, George born in 1688, Samuel born in 1690, Ann born in 1692, Robert born 3-20-1711, and Sarah. Robert, born in 1711, appears to have married Betty Guttery on 24 December 1735.

By the time of the Revolutionary War, the family was well established in almost all the counties of Virginia. After the Revolution descendants became numerous in Kentucky, Tennessee, Georgia, and Alabama.

In 1820 the Robertson County, Tennessee census lists John, Robert, and John Sr., heads of families living in the county. In 1830 John Chowning was over 70 years of age. Little or no effort has been made to trace the Red River branch before their arrival in Tennessee.

Several years ago, I found the following in an old Bible in Springfield:
Wm. T. Chowning, born August 1, 1824, died December 4, 1877, age 53 years, 4 months, 24 days.
Sarah A. Chowning, born February 21, 1826, died October 7, 1892, age 66 years, 7 months, 16 days.
Mary A. Chowning, born September 23, 1845.
John H. Chowning, born September 22, 1846.
Wm. T. Chowning, Jr., born September 5, 1849, died July 9, 1850, age 10 months, 21 days.
Sarah T. Chowning, born June 20, 1852.
Sarah Emma White, born September 15, 1872.
Richard Leander Chowning, born July 6, 1854, died January 1, 1873.
Robert Orlando Chowning, born August 31, 1856, died February, 1886.
Eugene Orville Chowning and Florence Eugenia Chowning (Twins), born April 17, 1859, died 1916.
Crittenden Clay Chowning, born March 2, 1863, died age 1 year, 4 months, 10 days.
John Thomas White, born March 15, 1868.
Mary Ellen White, born February 27, 1870, died November 29, 1907.
Eldred Arthur, son of R. O. and S. A. Chowning, born May 19, 1882.
Edgar Oscar Chowning, born February 12, 1845, died June 18, 1887.
William T. Chowning and wife, Sarah Ann, married 26 December 1844.
J. E. White and Mary A. Chowning, married March 3, 1867.
J. A. Chowning and wife, A. A. McDonald, married February 22, 1872.
Robert F. Richards and Sarah E. Chowning, married August 9, 1874.
R. O. Chowning and Laura A. Murphey, married September 1, 1881.
E. O. Chowning and Sallie White, married February 9, 1888.
Edward Powell and Florence Chowning, married April 15, 1890.

There is an old cemetery, known as the Cole Cemetery, on the John Lee Cook farm, eleven miles from Springfield, which contains a number of unmarked graves. Among those with inscriptions are those of the families of Norman, Cole, Empson, and Rippito. Included among those with tombstones are: Nancy Chowning Rippito, born September 23, 1823, died April 4, 1907; William M. Rippito, born October 16, 1828, died May 18, 1922; Lem Chowning, born April 16, 1817, died January 2, 1895; A. J. Chowning, born May 29, 1831, died April 15, 1911; Susan A. Chowning, born August 10, 1847, died September 9, 1935; and R. L. Cole, born February 22, 1805, died January 23, 1888.

Cobb

Among the earlier wills of Montgomery County is that of William Cobb, dated 9 January 1803. Stephen Thomas and Claudius Hicks were the executors. Hannah, the wife of the deceased was named along with two daughters, Elizabeth and Charlotte. Stephen Thomas was named as guardian to Charlotte and Elizabeth Cobb, heirs of William Cobb, deceased, July 1803.

Dr. Joshua Cobb was born 19 April 1809 and died 7 April 1879. Maria T. Cobb
was born 18 March 1811 and died 7 December 1890. Mary Aurelia, wife of John B.
Tap Scott and daughter of Dr. Joshua and Mariah T. Cobb, was born 28 November
1844 and died 4 November 1869. Edwin B. Cobb was born 29 October 1843. He was a
member of Co. H, 14th Tennessee C.S.A. and was mortally wounded at the Battle of
Chancellorsville in 1863. Mary Norton, the wife of Thomas Cobb, was born 9 June
1813 and died 10 March 1854. All these people lived in Montgomery County.

Montgomery County, Record Book 1. p. 168.
Montgomery Co. W.B. 1797-1810, p. 202.

Connell

According to Mrs. J.A. Esker of Norwalk, Ohio, Giles Connell died in Spartanburg County, South Carolina in 1804. His wife was Elizabeth Gibbs, and among their
children were: William (married Sallie Prince), John Giles (married Jane Tinsley),
Nancy (married John Rossen), a daughter who married William Atkins, a daughter
who married John Yoes, and a daughter who married Nathan Yoes. All these children probably moved to Robertson County, Tennessee, but it is not known whether
they all remained in the Tennessee country.

Jean or Jane Tinsley married Giles Connell, Jr. She was born 3 August 1777.
Her father is said to have been John Tinsley who lived in Southern Kentucky or Nor-
thern Tennessee. Their children were: William who was born in 1797, John Tinsley,
Taletha Morton, Polly, Zellica Foster, Giles, Lucinda, and Thomas Dixon Connell.

National Historical Magazine (D.A.R.) Vol. March 1940, p. 45.
Mss unpub. file, notes on McConnell in Whitley Collection.

Conrad

Nicholas Conrad's estate was recorded in Montgomery County in 1802.

Nicholas Conrad left a will, dated 10 October 1811, in which his body was to be de-
posited in the graveyard amongst the rest of "my family." He wished his property
to be divided between four children: William Coone Conrad, Mary Conrad, George
Coone Conrad, and Sidney Conrad. He devised certain property to Francis Martin
and her daughter, Marilla Whitehead, saying "that is my right in land on Sulphur
Fork being land whereon John Williams now lives and if said taken from Francis
Martin and Marilla Whitehead by better claim then Frances and Marilla have value
in land out of my other land." He appointed James Norfleet and Thomas Johnson and
his son William C. Conrad as his executors.

These two records would indicate that there were two Nicholas Conrads in the
Red River country by 1811.

On the 21st of October 1796, Nicholas Conrad of Robertson County deeded land in
Robertson County to George Sadler of the State of South Carolina.

The will of Joseph Conrad, dated 4 December 1795, is a matter of record in
Montgomery County. In it he made bequests to his two married sisters and to his
brothers, Sampson Conrad and Philip Conrad. He also mentioned Nicholas Conrad
but did not state the relationship. He referred to his mother, who seems to have
been living at the time, and to a sister Peggy. He named his uncle Nicholas Conrad
as his executor.

William C. Conrad, mentioned in the will of Nicholas Conrad of Robertson County, appears to have located in Humphreys County, for in the wills recorded in that
county, I find the will of William C. Conrad, dated 1 June 1837, in which he made

the statement, "my father, mother and sisters graves to be enwalled and marked."
He referred to his niece Elizabeth F.B. Hall, then Elizabeth F.B. Kirby, to whom
he left $5.00. Others named in the will were: his sister Mary Hall, his nephew Tho-
mas Branch Hall, Miles Kirby who was married to his niece, and his sister Sidney
Sugg. Without showing relationship he mentioned Francis A. Williams. He named
his brother, George Coon Conrad, and appointed him executor.

Montgomery Co., Tenn. Record Book 1, p. 165.
Robertson Co. Will Book 1, p. 400.
Robertson Co. Deed Book A, p. 64.
Montgomery Co. Will Book 1797-1810, p. 2.
Humphrey County Will Book 1838-43, p. 246.

Coon

　　　Conrad Coon, who served as a private in the South Carolina Line, was living in
Robertson County, Tennessee on 3 July 1833 when he made application for a pension
based upon his services in the Revolutionary War. His application states that he was
suffering from old age and loss of memory.

　　　The declaration of Conrad Coon from Robertson County, Tennessee, dated 13
November 1832, Town of Springfield, shows that he joined the service in 177— under
Robert Gooden, served in the regiment commanded by Col. Wm. Thompson, and was
in Richland County, South Carolina. It says that he was born in Amelia Township in
the State of South Carolina in the year 1756, according to his father's Bible. When he was
called into the service he was living on the Congoree River, Richland County, South
Carolina. He resided there for several years. He moved to Davidson County, Tennessee in 1795 and remained there for two years, then moved to Robertson County
where he was living at the time he made the declaration. He listed some of the officers under whom he served: General Moultree, General Mason, Col. Horry, regular
officers, and Col. Gooden.

National Archives, Washington, D.C. Rev. Pen. Div. file S-3177.

Copeland

　　　In the National Archives in Washington, the Revolutionary Pension Division, and
in the National D.A.R. Library Vol. 38 Revolutionary Pensioners File W-9395 are
to be found the papers relative to Rebecca Copeland's application for pension on the
service of her husband, Alexander. In these papers William Copeland of Spartanburg,
South Carolina, aged 62, deposed that many years ago he found one of his father's
old books in which were recorded the births of two elder children: James Copeland
born 9-17-1778 and Charles Copeland born 8-24-1780.

　　　Jane McMullen of Spartanburg, aged about 80, deposed that she did not attend
the wedding of Alexander Copeland and Rebecca Copeland, but her two sisters did.
She knew that Copeland served in the Revolution. Jane McMullin also testified that
she knew Lafford French, William French, Simon French, Hugh Moil, William
Moore, all Revolutionary soldiers, and James Alexander, Joseph French, Jonas De-
walt, James Betty also. Alexander Copeland and John Gowin appear to have collected
money for them.

　　　Copies of the South Carolina Indents showing where Alexander Copeland was paid
for his service were presented as evidence.

Rebecca Copeland's claim was allowed.

Curd

The Curd family of Virginia appears to have been founded by Edward Curd who was in Henrico County, Virginia as early as 1704. On 2 October of that year he "purchased of John Woodson for 30 pounds currency, 600 acres of land on the north side of the James River, adjoining land formerly James Blairs' and being part of a greater tract granted John Woodson, Jr. by patent dated 23 October 1690." (Valentine Papers) The following year, 1705, he was assessed and paid taxes on this 600 acres (Henrico Quit Rent Rolls 1705, Va. Hist. Mag. Vol. 28, p. 210).

Between 1716 and 1726 he received various land grants on the north side of the James River in that part of Henrico County that was cut off in 1728 to form Goochland County. On 31 October 1716, 531 acres were granted to him on the north side of the James River and the west side of the north branch of Beaver Dam Creek (Book 10, p. 307).

On 2 February 1724, 1200 acres on the north side of the James River was granted to him (Book 12, p. 130). The same day, 341 acres on the north side of the James River on Beaver Dam Creek (Book 12, p. 131), and on 17 August 1725, 400 acres on Beaver Dam Creek (Book 12, p. 238) were also recorded to him.

In the next few years he deeded most of his Goochland County lands to his children. On 6 June 1726 he deeded to his son John, for "Love and affection," a part of the 531 acre tract on Beaver Dam Creek (Henrico Court Records). On 7 November 1726 he deeded to his daughter Mary McBride, land lying on the north side of the James River (Henrico Co. Rec.). On 16 July 1733 he deeded 200 acres in Goochland County to each of his daughters, Mary Richardson and Elizabeth Williams (Goochland Co. Rec. deeds). On 20 November 1733 he deeded 650 acres in Goochland County to his son Richard (Goochland Co. Deeds).

In his will he gave 100 acres in Goochland County to his granddaughter, Jane McBride, and all of his remaining holdings in Goochland to his son Edward. All of his children, except Edward, eventually went to Goochland County to live. In the vestry book of Old St. John's Church at Richmond, we find the following records (Kith and Kin, p. 17 and records at Alexandria, Va.): "At a vestry held at Curl's Neck Ch. for Henrico Parish ye 17th day June 1735 — Present and elected Edward Curd as one of the vestryman."

Beverley Randolph took the oath as vestryman in place of Edward Curd, deceased, as chosen 2 October 1741. Edward died in 1742. The Henrico County December Court 1742 appointed John Williamson, Thomas Watkins, Daniel Price, and James Young to appraise the estate of Edward Curd, deceased.

Edward's will, dated 4 February 1739/40 and proved on the first Monday in December 1742, named his wife Elizabeth, son Edward, son John, son Richard, Mary Mackbride and her son Edward Mackbride, daughter-in-law (step-daughter) Mary Punch, grandson John Curd, granddaughter Jane Mackbride, daughter Mary Richardson, and daughter Elizabeth Williams. It named wife Elizabeth and Edward as executors. In his will, the elder Edward left the home place to his wife Elizabeth, the homeplace being in Henrico County. His son Edward was to have half of everything during Elizabeth's life and, at her death, the whole of said Henrico estate. The younger Edward was also given the lands in Goochland County, excepting 100 acres which were to go to the elder Edward's granddaughter, Jane Mackbride.

The name of the elder Edward Curd's first wife, the mother of his children is not known. He married secondly Elizabeth Branch, daughter of Thomas Branch and Elizabeth Archer. She was widowed first of Robert Goode whom she married in 1710 and who died in 1718. She was widowed second of Page Punch who died in 1726-7. Elizabeth died on 30 November 1766.

The children of Edward Curd and his wife, as far as is known, appear to have been Edward, John, Richard, Mary, and Elizabeth. Edward married and had issue. John married Elizabeth Price, daughter of Daniel Price. John died in Goochland County in 1752, and his widow married Richard Oglesby on 3 September 1758. Richard Curd married Sarah Downer, daughter of John Downer. Richard died in Goochland County in 1778. Mary Curd married John Richardson and died in Charlotte County, Virginia in 1791. Elizabeth Curd married first a Williams (probably Richard Williams) and secondly, Samuel Allen.

The will of Edward Curd shows that he had two daughters named Mary, both living at the time of his will.

John Curd, son of Edward, died in Goochland County in 1752. His wife, Elizabeth Price, was the daughter of Daniel Price and his wife Mary. Elizabeth's name before her marriage may have been Hughes. The division of John's estate on 16 January 1759 named his wife Elizabeth and the following children: John, William, Joseph, Mary, Charles, James, Elizabeth, and Ann. The younger John Curd was married in Lancaster County, Va. in April 1758 to Lucy Brent and removed to Kentucky about 1780. William Curd was married about 1763 to Mary Watkins and probably a second time to Ann. He removed to Buckingham Co., Va. where he died about 1798. Joseph Curd was married first on 28 September 1762 to Mary Warren and a second time on 6 October 1772 to Mary Truehart. He removed to Buckingham County, Va. where he died about 1811-12. Mary Curd was married on 18 March 1764 to Edmund Curd, son of Richard Curd and Sarah Downer. They lived and died in Goochland County, Virginia. Charles Curd received 800 acres of land in Jefferson County, Kentucky in 1780 and a grant of 1000 acres in Fayette County, Kentucky in 1784. James Curd was married on 20 February 1766 to Mary Graves and lived in Goochland County, Virginia. He died there in 1792. Elizabeth Curd was married in 1764 to John Bowles. Ann Curd was married in 1771 to Richard Sampson.

In the National Archives in Washington, D. C. in the Revolutionary Pension records and in the National D. A. R. Library in Washington, Vol. 18, p. 42 of Revolutionary Pensioners, File No. 8645, there is a record of John Curd and his wife Nancy. John Curd applied for a pension on 20 April 1818, and his claim was allowed. In the declaration filed it is shown that he was living in Logan County, Kentucky at the time of making application, that he was born on 16 September 1761, that he enlisted from Goochland County, Virginia in the summer or fall of 1776, and that he served until 4 October 1777 as a private under Capt. Samuel Woodson and Col. George Matthews. He was wounded in the thigh and taken prisoner at the battle of Germantown, held until the summer of 1778 when he was exchanged in New York State, then "joined the army" and was discharged.

The soldier stated that he married Miss Nancy W. Curd of Goochland County, Virginia on 10 July 1787. She was born 11 July 1763. She was allowed a pension on an application on the service of her husband in Virginia executed 7 February 1839 while she was a resident of Warren County, Kentucky.

The children of John and Nancy Curd, as shown in the pension papers, numbered four, namely: Fanny who was between 21 and 22 years of age in 1826, William, Richard, and a daughter who apparently married a Mr. Slaughter, for there is mention of a grandson, Richard H. Slaughter, three years and eight months of age in 1826.

The Brent Family by Chester Horton Brent. 1936.

Dickson

Simon Dickson was born in England about 1607/8, a stern English Puritan. He was an ardent adherent of Oliver Cromwell and served faithfully as an officer in the parliamentary army during the fierce struggle between Parliament and the King. Simon had a son named Joseph who, in turn, was the father of a Joseph Dickson. The second Joseph had a son Michael, and Michael had a son John Dickson (also spelled Dixon) born in 1704. John Dickson migrated to Pennsylvania and located in Chester County. They were Presbyterians.

After a short time in Chester County, John Dickson, with his wife Ann and his family, moved to Duplin County, North Carolina where they died. They are believed to have lived a short time in Bertie County before going to Duplin.

In 1752 John Dickson was clerk of the court in Duplin, in which capacity he is mentioned several times by Grimes (N. C. Wills). John left a will in Duplin County in which he provided for his children: Michael, William, Robert, Joseph, Alexander, Edward, James, and Mary who married William McGowan.

Michael Dickson, son of John and Ann Dickson, moved to Georgia after the Revolutionary War and there left many descendants.

William, the second son of John and Ann Dickson, was born in 1739 and married Mary Williams who was born in 1749 and died in 1812. Both William and his wife are buried near Kenansville, North Carolina in the Rutledge Cemetery. William was a soldier of the Revolution and a very influential man. He served as a member of the Convention of North Carolina, which met at Hillsboro on 21 August 1775. He was also a member of the Convention at Halifax, 12 November 1776, which framed the Constitution. He was one of the signers of the oath of allegiance and adjuration under the act of assembly of 15 November 1777. He represented Duplin County there. He was in the military service and rose to the rank of Colonel. He lost a leg in the service of his country. At the same time his horse was shot under him when in command at the Battle of Moore's Creek. (Boddie and Allied Families, p. 103)

Robert Dickson, son of John and Ann Dickson, married and left many descendants in Cumberland County, North Carolina.

Alexander Dickson, son of John and Ann Dickson, died in North Carolina, leaving no family. He bequeathed his property as an educational fund, the "Dickson Charity Fund."

Edward and James Dickson, sons of John and Ann Dickson, married and left issue in North Carolina.

Joseph Dickson, son of John and Ann Dickson, was born in 1748. He married Jane Moulton, daughter of Abraham Moulton of Duplin County who died in 1790 or 1791 as his will was proved in January 1791. About 1788 Joseph Dickson settled with his family in Tennessee on land granted to Joseph by the State of North Carolina (by assignment). These lands were largely in what now comprises Dickson County, named in honor of the family. Joseph Dickson lived till 1804. His will, dated 27 December 1803, was recorded in Dickson County, Tennessee and probated in June 1804. In it he named his children: Hugh (prominent in Montgomery County), David (lived in Dickson County), Molton or Moulton (lived in Dickson County), Joseph, Jr. (located in Montgomery, then Tennessee County), Ann (born in 1775, married Mr. Pearsell, and had a daughter, Lucy Jane Pearsell, mentioned in her grandfather's will), Michael (to whom his father left a genteel mourning suit), Abner and Robert (believed to have settled in Dickson County), and William (of whom I have no trace at this time).

Joseph Dickson, Junior, son of Joseph, grandson of John, was born about 1785, as he was hardly of age in 1803 when his father made his will. He married Martha Ann Cowan and resided in Montgomery County, Tennessee. Joseph, Jr. died in 1839 in Montgomery County, leaving a will of record in Clarksville. His family consisted of nine children, namely: James, John, William, Joseph, Abner, Wilson, Martha (who married Mr. Trotter and had Mary Ann, James, Elizabeth, Margaret, and Martha Trotter), Margaret, and Ann.

Joseph Dickson, son of Joseph and Martha Ann Cowan Dickson, was born 20 October 1812 and died 7 January 1858. On 12 February 1835 he married Ann (Sarah Ann) Duvall who was born 31 March 1816 and died 6 July 1862. She was the daughter of Colemore (Colman) Duvall and Martha (Conn) Duvall. Joseph and Ann (Duvall) Dickson were blessed with eleven children: Hugh A. Dickson was born 6 December 1835, died 25 August 1877, and was married 1 December 1868 to Annie E. Mitchell. Mariah L. Dickson was born 22 September 1837 and died 30 August 1885. Rachel M. Dickson was born 13 October 1839, died August 1893, and was married 16 December 1868 to G. A. Gill. Robert C. Dickson was born 6 October 1841 and died 2 September 1862. Mary A. C. Dickson was born 11 October 1843 and died 16 May 1900. James M. Dickson was born 13 May 1845 and died 18 August 1851. Landon W. Dickson was born 23 December 1848, died 17 September 1885, and was married 1 June 1881 to Lillian L. Harris. George Wesley Dickson was born 18 April 1852 and was married 23 Novem-

ber 1882 to Ann Opie Allen, daughter of David M. Allen and Frances Pope. Margaret
J. and Martha V. Dickson, twins, were born 16 May 1854. Margaret J. died young.
The youngest child, Charles E. Dickson, was born 28 May 1851. (Records from Family Bible.)

George Wesley Dickson, born 18 April 1852, and his wife, Ann Opie Allen, were
the parents of six children: Joseph Allen, born in Haywood County, Tennessee, 26
January 1884; Albert Lamar, born 11 April 1886; Frances Emma, born 30 October
1887; Mamie Conn, born 23 July 1893; Landon Frank, born 18 April 1895; and Jesse
Duvall, born 25 January 1898.

The will of Abraham Molton, dated 25 November 1784, is recorded in Duplin
County, North Carolina. Named in the will are his wife Sarah, his children John,
Nuhall, Abraham, Patience, and Elizabeth, and his grandchildren Abraham Hall,
Molton Dickson, and James Hill. The will also names his sons-in-law William Hall,
Joseph Dickson, and Jesse Peacock.

Dickson and Duvall manuscript family history in Whitley Genealogical Collection.

Dikus - Dykus

John Dikus was at Red River about 1800. He died shortly after making his will,
19 May 1812. His wife Sary survived him. His will indicates that he named only some
of his children by name, for he made the statement "Rest of my Children." He does
name sons Hugh, Andrew, John, James, and Edward. The daughters referred to by
name are Mary McNichols and Nancy Watwood.

Montgomery County, Tenn. Record Book A, p. 73.

Dowlen - Frey - Fortune

The Dowlin or Dowlen family and the Frey family were closely connected by marriage. The first of the Dowlins to come to Robertson County, Tennessee appears to
have been Harris Dowlin, Sr. who, according to family tradition, came from the
Waxhaw Settlement on the edge of North and South Carolina. Mr. Dowlin came out
to the "western country" in 1795. He first located in Davidson County, but not long
afterwards he moved to Robertson County, about the time that county was created in
1796.

There is a traditional story, handed down in the family, that Harris Dowlen, Sr.
left home with a brother whose name is thought to have been Amos. Upon reaching
the Cumberland Settlement, Harris decided to remain while his brother traveled on
to parts unknown. Harris was a carpenter by trade. In 1797, two years after arriving in Nashville, in Davidson County, he married Susan Hargrove who died in 1820.
His second wife was Sallie Harrington. Harris Dowlin and his two wives, with other
members of the family connection, are buried at Goodspring Church near Pleasant
View in what is now Cheatham County. I visited the old Dowlin home and graveyard
some twenty years ago. When Mr. Dowlin selected the land upon which he spent his
remaining days, it was in Robertson County, but when Cheatham County was partly
cut off, his property was included in the new county, only a short distance from the
Robertson-Cheatham County line. Harris Dowlen, Sr. died in 1855.

When I visited the old home, at that time still owned and occupied by a descendant, Miss Mary Dowlin, I had the pleasure of examining several family records in
her possession. From these records, which included the Bible of Harris Dowlin, Sr.,
I learned that Harris Dowlin, Sr. had six children by his first wife, Susan Hargrove,
namely: Delaney, Nancy, Jack, Whitman, Susan, and Harris, Jr. By his second wife,
Sallie Harrington, there were seven children, namely: Patsy (who married Will Bennett and had nine children), Rosy (who married Ben Rawls and had five children),
Ursula (who married Martin Fry or Frey and had two children, Huldah and Wiley),
Henry (who married Elizabeth Fortune and had seven children, among whom was Miss

Mary Dowlin, living at the old home), Van (who married Elizabeth Williams and had eight children), and Bill (who married Jane Fortune and had five children).

Nancy Dowlen, daughter of Harris, Sr. by his first wife, married Blaney Felts and became the mother of nine children: Jack, Church, Mary, Sue, Harris, Bettie, Rose, Monroe, and Sara.

Jack Dowlin, son of Harris, Sr., married Susan Shaw and became the father of eleven children: Laura, Martha, Harris, Nancy, John, Monroe, Susan, Ella, West, Alma, and Sallie.

Whitman Dowlen, son of Harris, Sr., married Lucy Harrington. Their children were Jap, Charles, Marilla, Sylvester, Rose, and Sandy.

Susan, daughter of Harris Dowlin, Sr. by his first wife, married Sam Ross and had Samuel and Sue Ross.

Harris Dowlen, Junior, was born in Davidson County, Tennessee on 3 December 1808. He was married on 2 February 1839 to Susan Shaw, born 24 November 1821, daughter of John and Martha (Binkley) Shaw. Her grandfather Shaw was born in Scotland and came to North Carolina from which place some of his descendants came to Tennessee. John Shaw was drowned in a freshet in 1824. The children of Mr. and Mrs. Harris Dowlen, Jr. were: Martha V. (who married a Mr. Sawyer and lived in Kentucky), Laura A., Harris, Jr. (the third Harris in direct line, born 28 September 1841), Nancy (who married a Felts), Sarah (who married a Felts), John S., Cicero, Susan H. (who married a Frey), Leonidas W., Ella, and Alma B.

The third Harris Dowlen, born in 1841, served in the War between the States, enlisting in the Thirteenth Tennessee Infantry. He surrendered with his regiment at Fort Donelson. He was a prisoner at Camp Butler, Illinois but escaped and returned to Tennessee. He was recaptured, exchanged, rejoined his regiment, and served until the close of the war. He was at Raymond, Jackson, Chickamauga, and was with General J. E. Johnson in the Georgia campaign. He was also with Hodd in Tennessee. On 3 October 1867 he married Lucy Fontaine, born 6 January 1846, daughter of Moses A. and Martha (Freeman) Fontaine. To them were born eight children, namely: Earnest F., Willard M., Nancy I., Martha E., Joseph E., Moses B., and John A. In 1873 Mr. Dowlen located on a 310 acre farm where he lived out his remaining years. The entire family were members of the Methodist Episcopal Church South.

Delaney Dowlen, daughter of Harris, Sr. by his first wife Susan, married Gideon Lowe. Their children were: Mary who married Roger Sharon, Scotty who married Bill Gleaves, Kitty who married Dr. Redding, Jennie who married a Mr. Willis, Lishie who married Bud Sloan (the ancestor of the Sloans of Nashville, operators of the Cain-Sloan Co.), Lou, Len, Gideon, Tony, and Sarah who married Jim Cavaret. Sarah and Jim Cavaret were the parents of Mary Delaney Cavaret.

The Fortune family Bible records a number of the family connections as follows: Alexander T. Fortune married Martha J. Williams, 6 September 1835; Thomas E. Hudgens married Mary J. Williams, 23 December 1851; James Rawls married Martha J. Fortune, 23 February 1854; William M. Dowlen married Lavania J. Fortune, 26 December 1862; Henry Dowlen married Sarah Elizabeth Fortune, 21 February 1866; Charles Dowlen married Louella L. Rawls, 28 March 1871; Marvin Dowlen was born 27 February 1898; Martha Dowlen died 16 December 1914; Alexander T. Fortune was born 15 February 1813; Martha J. Fortune, his wife, was born 11 December 1817; Edgar Zollicoffer Dowlen was born 14 November 1862; Alexander T. Fortune died in the thirty-fifth year of his age, 31 December 1843; Sarah Williams died in the seventy-fourth year of her age, 24 October 1851; Abel Williams departed this life in the seventy-seventh year of his age, 12 June 1854; and Martha J. Rawls died 26 February 1857.

The Frey Bible which was in the possession of Miss Dixie Frey of Springfield, Robertson County a few years ago, gives the following: George W. Frey and Sarah B. Bidwell were married at home in Robertson County, 16 November 1848; G. W. Frey was born 17 September 1820; Sarah B. was born 7 May 1831 and died 10 September 1917; Julia Ann Frey was born 7 October 1849 and married P. Anthony, 10 January 1878; Charles B. Frey was born 10 September 1851, died 4 April 1899, and was married January 1880 to G. A. Morris.

Henry S. Frey was born 11 July 1853, died 18 September 1930, and was married 29 November 1881 to M. Clay. Flavins B. Frey was born 27 August 1855, died 18 December 1927, and was married 22 September 1880 to A. E. Clinard.

Emma B. Frey was born 8 July 1857 and died 10 March 1937.

Martha W. Frey was born 11 June 1859 and was married 6 December 1915 to H. C. Murphy; Carrie L. Frey was born 15 October 1862 and was married 4 January 1898 to E. Z. Dowlen; Susan F. Frey was born 22 March 1865 and was married 5 July 1891 to J. J. Dowlen; Edwin R. C. Frey was born 11 February 1867 and was married 25 December 1892 to Annie Carney; and Virginia D. Frey was born 13 May 1869.

Lillie (Edna) Frey was born 10 August 1871, died 10 September 1917, and was married 16 February 1910 to J. T. Gabbert.

H. S. Frey married secondly Annie Jordan.

Ida M. Frey, wife of H. S. Frey, died 11 July 1885.

G. W. Frey died 21 September 1908. J. A. Anthony died 29 April 1913. Carrie Lee Dowlen died 14 September 1916, and S. F. Dowlen died 13 January 1935.

The Rawlses were early residents of Robertson County. Luke Rawls left a will, dated 31 August 1799, proved in July 1800, in which he named his wife Elizabeth executrix and left her 100 acres of land adjoining Luke Rawls, Jr., on the north of Robert Weakley, on the west of John Nichols. He mentioned son Jesse Rawls and heirs, daughter Sarah Simmons, daughter Charlotte Simmons, and daughter Milly Leaner. To aid his wife in the execution of the will he named his friend Rev. Nathan Arneth and his son Luke Rawls.

John Simmons died in Robertson County in 1807. His will, dated 22 June 1806, probated in October 1807, named his wife Margaret and devised to her 891 acres of land "if it can be saved." He named his children Charles, John, Edward, James, Valentine, William, and Thomas. He called James, Valentine, William, Thomas, Mary, and Margaret his younger children. His sons John and Edward were appointed to join Margaret Simmons in the execution of the provisions of the will.

Thomas Simmons, Guthridge Lyons, Adam Harmon, and Isaac Morgan were on the bond of Thomas Simmons who was made guardian of Henry Wells and Morgan Wells, Montgomery County, 1807.

Davidson Co., Tenn. marriage bonds Book 1.
Deeds, Davidson, Robertson and Cheatham Counties, Tenn.
Frey Bible; Dowlen Bible; Fortune-Dowlen Bible.
Misc. data in Whitley collection.
Robertson Co., Tenn. Will Book 1, pp. 244 and 59.
Montgomery Co., Tenn. Will Book A, p. 92.

Downs

The Downs family of Pennsylvania and Virginia appears to be represented in the Red River community by a William Downs. The Montgomery County Court Minutes 1808-1810, 19 June 1809 state that Rebecca Downs, widow of William Downs, filed a petition in court regarding her dower. There are two references to Rebecca Downs concerning her dower.

On 20 May 1793 Hiram Downs of Georgia, appointed Samuel Thornton of Tennessee to sell a house and lot in the Town of Palmyra which was conveyed from Doctor Morgan Brown to Hiram Downs.

Joseph Downs of Montgomery County appointed attorney to sell land at or near the mouth of Bud's Creek on Cumberland River, 8 June 1801.

In Robertson County, Goodloe Warren and John Warren of Person County, North Carolina appointed James Stewart of Robertson County, State of Tennessee to transact business and mentioned a judgement against William Downs which judgement was originally obtained in a court in the State of Georgia and finally in the court held for the District of Miro in the State of Tennessee, 27 May 1801.

A William Downs left a will in Sumner County, Tennessee, dated 3 March 1821, in which "being old and weak," he named his wife Mary and gave one fourth to his son Major Downs, another fourth to his son William, and a fourth to his daughter Elizabeth Tomblin.

It is evident that William Downs, whose wife was Rebecca, was the first Downs who came into the Tennessee County. The indication is very strong and practically conclusive that he came directly from Georgia and not straight from South Carolina. It is also evident that there were two William Downses in the Red River County by or before 1821, the date of the will of William Downs, whose wife was Mary.

Henry Downs, referred to as Junior, was born in 1728 and died in 1798 in Mecklenburg County, North Carolina, leaving a will of record, on or near the North and South Carolina line. He was married in Virginia to Frances Chew who was born in Virginia in 1730 and died on 3 October 1784 in North Carolina. It is strongly indicated that Mr. Downs was the son of Henry Downs, Senior of Virginia. Henry Downs of Mecklenburg County was one of the signers of the Mecklenburg Declaration. Either he or his father, Henry Downs, served in the House of Burgesses in Virginia.

The children of Henry Downs of Mecklenburg are known to have been: Jane who was born on 16 January 1751 and married John Robinson; Joseph who was born on 23 April 1752 and died unmarried in 1774; Henry who was born on 28 July 1754, died in 1774, and married Miss Davis; Thomas who was born on 22 August 1756, died in 1839, and was married in 1788 to Mary Courtney who was born in 1768 and died in 1828; Samuel who was born on 7 May 1758 and married Miss Crockett; William who married Sarah Downs; and Mildred who was born on 22 July 1760 and married James Brewster who was born in 1759 in Virginia and died in 1804 in South Carolina.

Thomas and Mary (Courtney) Downs are known to have been the parents of Francis who was born in 1799, died in 1885, and married James Boyce Griffith who was born in 1797 and died in 1865; and Jonathan who was born in 1803, died in 1845, and was married in 1829 to Mary Theresa Rae who was born in 1813 and died at the age of 82 years.

Jonathan and Mary Theresa (Rae) Downs were the parents of William Henry Downs who married Mary Sue Coffey and had a daughter Minnie; and probably others.

William Downs, whose wife was Sarah Downs, was the father of William Wood Downs who was born in 1802, died in 1882, and was married in 1823 to Harriet Spacks who was born in 1808 and died in 1886.

William Wood Downs and his wife are known to have been the parents of Fernanda Corlla Downs who married Virginia Wilson and had a daughter Ella who became the wife of Samuel Webb, the father of Camilla Webb, the wife of Joe. L. Ward.

William Wood Downs was also the father of William Pinckey Downs whose wife was Martha Fort. They were the parents of Katie, born in 1858, who was married in 1880 to Andrew Claude Hamilton. They became the parents of Elleen Kathleen Hamilton who married a Carothers.

There is a tradition handed down in the family which maintains that the first Henry Downs, called "senior," was a Scotsman born about 1675. He lived for a time in England, came to America about 1730, and settled first on the edge of Pennsylvania. He later moved to Orange County, Virginia. He is said to have married a lady named Jane Douglass, a descendant of James, Earl of Douglas.

The elder Downs was a vestryman and church recorder in St. Thomas Episcopal Church, Orange County, Virginia. He was Sheriff of Augusta County, Virginia in 1746, commissioned to buy the jail in 1746, a member of the court Commission the same year, and Road Overseer the next year. I have not found his will in Virginia. It was his son Henry, Jr. who moved to Mecklenburg and became prominent during the Revolutionary War.

Heitman's _Historical Register of Officers of the Continental Army During the War of the Revolution_ lists Henry Downs, 1776, and adds that he was of "Honor, Md."

Thomas Downs, son of Henry and Frances (Chew) Downs, is listed as a Revolutionary Pensioner having served as a private and Lieutenant, from Mecklenburg County, North Carolina in 1832 at which time his age was given as 78 years.

Alexander tells us, "In looking over the list of early settlers of that portion of the State that was laid off as Mecklenburg County, in that portion bordering on South Carolina and afterwards called Providence, I find that Henry Downs moved from Pennsylvania to this section about 1760. He was elected Captain of Militia for Providence Dist. or 'beat'. He was also made an elder of Providence Church which church was built and organized in 1762. He was also appointed a Civil officer, or a Justice of the Peace. He was one of the signers of this Declaration on the 20th of May 1775 in Charlotte. Mr. Downs was now getting too old for military service, but his son Thomas was young and active and entered the service with alacrity. He was with General Gates in South Carolina in the Battle of Camden, then as bushwhackers hanging on the flanks of Cornwallis' army as he came toward Charlotte, and assisted in giving the British a warm reception around the old log court house that stood in the public square, and on the Salisbury road for five miles. Tarlton must have suffered severely to get and to hold what he captured around Charlotte or he would not have called the place 'a Hornet's Nest'. The Downs family still own and occupy two hundred acres of the original grant that was issued by George the IV. Many of these old places are handed down from sire to son for several generations."

The William Downs who died at Clarksville, Tennessee in 1802 is said to have been born in South Carolina. The Daughters of the American Revolution passed an application, No. 8067, a number of years ago on the record of William Downs who died in Clarksville, Tennessee and whose wife was Jane Douglas. It further says that he entered the South Carolina Line as a private in 1778 and became adjutant of the Second Regiment. For his services he received a grant of land in what is now Mississippi. His daughter Jane married Wm. Caldwell Jamison. It is a matter of record, already referred to, that the name of the wife of William Downs who died in Clarksville, Tennessee was Rebecca. Was she a second wife? William Downs, son of Henry, of South Carolina, is thought to have been the man who came to Montgomery County, Tennessee.

William Downs of Montgomery County Tennessee, has also proved to be the son of Henry Downs, Senior of Virginia. He married Phoebe Hague and reared his family in Wilkes County, Georgia. Nevertheless, your compiler can only agree that William Downs of Montgomery County, Tennessee had a wife named Rebecca at the time of his death and that the William Downs who died in Sumner County, leaving a will, had a wife named Mary in 1821.

Montgomery Co., Tenn. Court Minute Book 1808-1810, pp. 219, 287.
Montgomery Co., Tenn. Will Book 1797-1810, pp. 46, 137.
Robertson Co., Tenn. Will Book 1, p. 74.
Sumner Co., Tenn. Will Book 1, p. 329
History of Mecklenburg County, N.C. by Alexander, p. 291.
Manuscript data in Whitley collection.

Duval

Duval is a Huguenot name and is listed among the French Refugees to America. The family in Maryland, probably the first of the name in America, was founded by Mareen Duvall of "Middle Plantation," Anne Arundel County. Mareen Duval was born about 1630-5 and died in 1694. He came to the province about 1655 and, by the name of "Laval," located on the south side of South River upon a tract of land granted to him by Lord Baltimore. He was a merchant and planter. He contributed to the public cost of an expedition against the Manticoke Indians in 1678 and was appointed commissioner by the General Assembly of Maryland in 1683. He was to purchase sites and lay out towns, etc. He was a prominent and influential citizen of the county and province. At his death he left a will which is a matter of record. I shall not go into his career more fully because there is a very excellent genealogy of the family in print. Mareen Duval appears to have married three times. His first wife's name is unknown; his second wife, Susannah, died in 1692; and the third wife, Mary Stanton, survived him and married a second husband, Colonel Henry Ridgely (also spelled Rodgely). After the Colonel's death Mary married the Rev. Jacob Henderson, Rector of Queen Ann's Parish in Prince Georges County, Maryland.

Mareen Duvall had several children by his three wives: Mareen who was born in 1662/3 and was married in 1685/6 to Francis Stockett; John, a captain, who married Elizabeth Jones; Eleanor who married John Roberts; Samuel who was married in 1687 to Elizabeth Clark; Susannah who married Robert Tyler; Lewis who was married in 1699 to Martha Ridgely; Mareen (the younger) who was born in 1680 ?; Katherine who died in 1703 and was married in 1700 to William Orrick; Mary who was married in 1701 to Rev. Henry Hall; Elizabeth; Johanna who was married in 1703 to Richard Poole; and Benjamine who was married in 1713 to Sophia Griffith.

From the above family descended Colemore or Coleman Duvall of Montgomery County, Tennessee. Colemore Duval's name appears in the Maryland census of 1790 in Prince Georges County. At that time he had a wife and child.

There are numerous deeds to and from Colemore Duval recorded in Montgomery County, Tennessee from 1815 to 1831. He apparently was a man of considerable means when he came to the thriving town of Clarksville.

In the first Surveyors District Book (eye) page 346, No. 20999 made void 18th June 1819, Colmore Duvall by virtue of 45 1/8 acres the residue of warrant No. 1195 issued by the Commissioner of West Tennessee to Colemore Duvall and Barney Duvv, for 410 1/2 acres, entered 45 1/8 acres of land in Montgomery County on the waters of McAdoo Creek, beginning in James McCrory's line at Jeremiah Browns, northwest corner running north with McCrory's line and west, etc., for compt. — 17th June 1819 — Colemore Duvall.

There are numerous certificates which were issued to him, viz., No. 21127, 20430, 20431, and 19986.

An Act appointing commissioners to contract for the building of a Court House, Prison, and Stocks in the County of Montgomery at Clarksville examined J. Cocke, Joel Lewis, J. Conway, received in the Secretary's Office, Wm. Maclin, Secretary (original in Tenn. State Archives, Nashville). The same record is to be found in the Montgomery County Court House, recorded 1822 to 1826 Book D, page 75, which reads, "In obedience to an order of the worshipful Court of Montgomery County, at their April Term 1822, appointing the undersigned Commissioners to examine the accounts between Colemore Duvall and the said County of Montgomery, relative to building the Court House in the town of Clarksville, beg leave to report, that they have examined all the vouchers and accounts now in the possession of one of the surviving commissioners appointed to contract for and superintend said building and also have had a view of the contract entered into, and that the said Duvall undertook the said work for the sum of nine thousand five hundred dollars and from the receipts and orders signed with his own hand, it appears that he received at different times, the sum of nine thousand six hundred and six dollars and sixty cents, leaving a balance in favor of the said county of one hundred and six dollars and sixty cents. Given under our hands this 16th day of July 1822. Signed Jas. Parret, J. B. Reynolds.

Coleman Duvall purchased Lot No.1 in the town of Clarksville in April 1811 (Montg. Co. D.B.1, p. 192). This was probably the first property he purchased in the town. There is another deed regarding this same lot of ground which bears date as early as 1800, which also states that Duval had purchased it.

Another transaction regarding Lot No. 1 in Clarksville is recorded in Deed Book D, p. 663, dated 15 March 1809. Amos Bird formerly of Montgomery County, State of Tennessee but now of the Territory of the Upper Louisiana, to Louisa Ann Duvall, daughter of Colmore Duvall of the Town of Clarksville, State of Tennessee. "Consideration of the love and affection which he the said Amos Bird hath and beareth unto the said Louisa Ann Duvall daughter of Colmore Duvall, as also for the further consideration of the sum of $5.00 to him in hand paid by the said Colmore Duvall," etc., lot of ground in the town in the addition of the Town of Claksville of one half acre, lying and fronting Union and Water Streets, and distinguished by Lot No. 1 in the plan of said addition etc., if Louise Ann Duvall daughter of Colmore Duvall should depart this life before she arrives at the age of maturity, or without legal issue, then the said Lot with all it's appurtenances, shall be the right property and Estate of Eleanor Duvall, daughter of the aforesaid Duvall, etc. June Term court 1809.

Joseph Dickson married Sarah Ann Duvall, Daughter of Colmore Duvall and Martha Conn. Martha Conn was the daughter of Raphael Conn of Maryland who married a lady named Mary.

Zebulon M. Duval must have been a son of Colemore Duvall, although I have no proof. See Zebulon M. Duvall of Robertson County (Rob. Co. Rec. Book 11, p. 86) letters of estate, November term 1841. Zebulon M. Duval died having made no will, application being made by James C. Duvall to have letters of administration granted to him and the estate of said Z. M. Duval, deceased, etc., 1 November 1841.

When Colemore Duvall came to Clarksville about 1800, he was a wealthy and highly respected gentleman. He was called Captain. After his arrival in Tennessee, he became associated with a group of "high living" men and created a festive nature, and by reason of broad hospitality and high life he soon found his little fortune gone, having been consumed in the life he was living. It was not long until he died, leaving his widow with no possessions save seven small children. She was no ordinary woman. Her strong common sense, energy, and faith in God enabled her to meet the situation, and she reared her children, giving them a common school education. One of the sons died in childhood. Colemore, Jr., another son, received the benefit of a higher education. He bore his father's name and was prominent as a teacher of languages. Colemore, Jr.'s son Pitt was a minister and, at one time, was a presiding elder in the Louisville Conference of the Methodist Church.

One of the daughters of Colemore Duvall, Sr. married a Meaddoc (McAdoo) and lived in Cincinnati. She was the mother of at least two sons, one of them named John.

Sarah A., Eleanor, and Louisa Ann were among the daughters, but I have no information on them other than Sarah Ann who is mentioned in my sketch on the Dickson family.

There is an old graveyard in Robertson County, twenty-five miles from Springfield, commonly referred to as the Duval Cemetery. Among the families known to be buried there are Caudill, Stringer, Duval, Eubanks, Cummings, and Gossitt. Four of the oldest tombstones in the graveyard have inscriptions as follows:
Zebulon Montgomery Pike Duval. Jan. 25, 1818. April 1, 1841.
Philadelphia D. Duval. Jan. 18, 1828. August 8 1853.
Sophia, wife of Ben. J. Gossett. Sept. 7. 1832. March 14, 1918.
B. Gossett. April 1819. Jan. 10 1890.

Duvall manuscript and Dickson Family manuscript in Whitley's Genealogical Collection.

Edwards

William Edwards, a Revolutionary Soldier, filed an application for pension while a resident of Robertson County, Tennessee on 12 August 1837, aged 77 years. The papers on file in the National Archives, Revolutionary Pension Division, file R-3263, show that he served from Chatham County, North Carolina. A certificate signed by William Jones, Captain, 27 March 1781 proves service. The claim is marked "Rejected".

Rebecca, widow of William Edwards, made a declaration from Robertson County on 12 August 1837, aged 77 years. She declared that she married William Edwards on 25 July 1775 in Chatham County, North Carolina and that before her marriage, she was Rebecca Brewer. She further stated that they had three children during the Revolutionary War, no names given.

John Edwards of Simpson County, Kentucky, aged 73, declared that he was a brother of William Edwards deceased, and that he was present at the marriage of his brother to Rebecca Brewer.

Her claim is marked "On the rejected list," "She was not a widow at the passage of the act."

Elliott - Louther

Falkner Elliott and his wife Rachel were received by letter between 5 July 1791 and 13 August 1791 at the Red River Baptist Church. A list of members, dated July 1803, states "Faulkner Elliott ... excld." A later list shows, "Rachel Elliott cut off restored."

James McCarrell and his wife Zelpha, Jeremiah Walker and his wife Zebe, and George Elliott, heirs of John Elliott, deceased, were assigned platts by an Act of Assembly, 228 acres of land along the Red River. This assignment was confirmed by the court 1808-1810, Montgomery County.

The will of Lewis Elliott, whose wife was named Nancy, was proved in June 1810 in Montgomery County. The children named in the said will were John, Lewis, Lucy Clark, Nancy Louther, James, and Amelia. The last two mentioned children were not of age. The son Lewis was to have land on Barron Fork of Little Fork of . . . in Kentucky.

Lewis Elliott was made guardian for Merniva Louther and William Lewis Louther on 22 October 1812.

James Elliott's will, dated 3 August 1816, names his wife, Margaret, and children all except heirs of John Elliott, deceased, and daughter, Mary McFadden. The property was to be equally divided among "my children." David McFaddin and Reuben Pollard were named as executors.

On 20 January 1817 the court ordered James Elliott to be overseer of the road leading from Fletcher's fork to the State line in the place of Cadwaller Lucy, and the hands to be William Mann, Glidewell Killebrew, and Prescilla Jeffers' hands, James Lockhart, Cadwaller Lucy, Jarrett McCarty, John Falkner, Joel Marr, and Bayliss E. Prince were to work the same.

Montgomery Co. Record Book 1, p. 435.
Montgomery Co. Record Book 2, p. 82, 267.
Montgomery Co. Court Min. 1816-1818, p. 130.
Montgomery County Court Minutes 1808-1810, p. 245.
Red River Baptist Church records.

Ely

Ely is a New England name. The ancestors of the Ely family came over in the early settlement of that section.

Jesse Ely was born in Logan County, Kentucy on 12 February 1803 and died in Clarksville on 19 January 1847. He was a hatter by trade. He married Charlotte Jamison who was born in the Red River country on 28 March 1809 and died on 17 August 1875. Their son William J. Ely was born in Clarksville on 5 October 1835, the third child of the family which consisted of eight children.

William J. attended private school and later the Clarksville Male Academy. When he was fourteen years of age, he began the printers trade in the Chronicle office where he worked for four years. He then served as deputy postmaster for several years. In 1854 he removed to Peaches Mills where he operated a general merchandising store until 1861. He then returned to Clarksville. When the War Between the States broke out, he entered the Ordinance Department. In 1865 he accepted a position with B. O. Keesee, a hardware merchant. He remained there only one year, and on 1 September 1869 he entered the tobacco business which he continued until 1 November 1876 under the name of Turnley, Ely & Co. From November 1876 to 1 November 1884, the firm name was Turnley, Ely and Kennedy, later Ely & Kennedy, until 1884 when he took the position as bookkeeper with the firm, becoming an equal partner in the business in 1885. He married Fannie Galbreath of Kentucky in 1858. She died in 1860, and about 1869 he married his second wife, Miss Johnie Brown who was born in Kentucky in 1845. By the last wife only one child blessed their union: Edith, born 28 September 1874.

Goodspeed's History of Montgomery Co., Tenn. 1886. p. 1028.

Featherstone

The first mention of the Featherstone family which I have observed was in Hanover County, Virginia. Charles and Edward Featherston paid tax in 1736. Henry Featherstone left a will in Prince Edward County, Virginia, dated 4 April 1760, which styled him "of Chesterfield County". The will mentions Edward son of Charles, sister Mary Foster, and the children of Thomas Jeffress. It also mentions the children of Thomas Sadler but does not call them by name.

Charles Feariston, whose wife was Gean, left a will in Brunswick County, Virginia, dated 3 April 1788. Others mentioned in the will were son Keyer, Fathey Grant, and Charlotte Grant. They are not called children.

In Nottoway County, Virginia, there is the will of Charles H. Featherstone, dated 12 January 1791, in which is mentioned Lewis, son of Elizabeth Featherstone. Elizabeth was under age. Burwell Featherstone and Luke Clarke are also mentioned, the relationship not shown.

There was a Charles Featherstone who was born in 1756 and died in 1840, and who served as a private in the Virginia Militia. He was born in Virginia and died in his native state. He was married in 1797 to Elizabeth Thornton who was born in 1779. They were the parents of William Booker Featherstone who was born in 1818, died in 1878, and was married in 1840 to Amanda Melvina F. Talbott who was born in 1823 and died in 1860. William B. and Amanda Featherstone were the parents of Susie H. Featherstone who was born in 1854, died in 1898, and was married in 1873 to James Neil Long who was born in 1852 and died in 1890. Mr. and Mrs. Long had two known children: Minnie D., who married E. B. Gilliam, and another child whose name is unknown. The Longs lived in Fannin County, Texas.

On the 28th of March 1788, Jesse Featherstone et al. conveyed a tract of land on Leath Creek to John Vaughan of Amelia County. In the deed, reference is made to Jesse Featherstone of Lincoln County, North Carolina and to Richard Featherstone, Burrell Featherstone, Charles Featherstone, Lew Clark and wife Elizabeth, and Jeremiah Little, all of Amelia County, Virginia.

In Nottoway County, John Vaughan and his wife Lucy, Lew Clark and his wife Elizabeth, Burwell Featherstone and his wife, all of Nottoway County, deeded property to Isaac Holmes on 5 January 1792. There is mention of Featherstone Wells of Nottoway County and Jesse Featherstone, Jeremiah Still and Martha Still of North Carolina, to whom the land descended as heirs of William Featherstone, deceased.

William Featherstone was surety on a marriage bond in October 1796, but not the William Featherstone whose will we have, dated 1769. Lewis Featherstone was surety on a bond of Robert Gaines; the name of the bride is not shown; the date is not legible. This was probably Lewis, the brother of the second William Featherstone. In 1827 a Burrel F. Wells was surety on the marriage bond of James D. Connelly and Willie Wells. One Gardner Harwell married Nancy Featherstone on 6 July 1802, and Rolley Harwell is shown as surety. Henry Gaines married Susanna Featherstone on 1 July 1797. Rolley Harwell married Sally Featherstone on 29 November 1890 with Harbird Abernathy as surety. Later Rolly Harwell married Susannah Garnie of Gaines.

The name Burrell or Burwell indicates connection with the prominent Burwell family of Surry and Sussex Counties, Virginia

Elizabeth Short married Charles Henry Featherstone of Amelia County. They were married in Prince Edward County on 15 January 1807. His home was near Chula, Amelia County.

One Burwell Featherstone died in 1856 in Illinois. His wife, Rebecca Adams, was born in 1789 and died in Illinois in 1852. Their children were: Jack who married Patsy Redfearn (Redferren), lived in Tennessee, and had nineteen children; William who was born in 1808, died in 1877 at Exter, Missouri, and married Margaret Pressgrove in Robertson County, Tennessee; Martha America Virginia Louise who was born on 25 March 1832, died on 12 February 1887, and married first a Mr. Smith and second a Mr. McCarrol; John Bedfield who married Mrs. Henrietta Shepard and went to Bonham, Texas; Richard who died in 1853, married a Campbell of Tennessee, lived in Kentucky, and later, in Illinois; Rev. George W. (a Baptist Minister) who was born in 1824 in Robertson County, Tennessee and died in 1923; Marion (a Methodist Minister) who was one time presiding elder at Vicksburg, Mississippi, and moved from Robertson County to Woodville, Mississippi; Joseph Henry Featherstone who located in Meridian, Mississippi; Virginia Sally Ann Elizabeth who was born on 25 April 1817, died on 12 June 1869, and married William Pressgrove on 6 December 1833; Catherine Susan Parthena Adaline who died on 20 May 1867 and was married three times, first to Thomas J. Hightower who died on 11 September 1859, second to William Hussong who died on 19 October 1865, and third to Reuben Allen who died on 20 February 1871. These Featherstones lived in Robertson County, Tennessee.

Burwell Featherstone's brothers and sisters were: Charles Howell, whose wife was Gean and who died in Brunswick County, Virginia; Susannah; Richard; William Griggs; Jesse of Lincoln County, North Carolina; Lucy who married John Vaughan; Lewis; Frances who married Jeremiah Still; and Eliza who married Lew Clark.

There was another Burrell Featherstone, whose wife was named Henrietta, who lived for a time in Robertson County and then moved to Bedford County, Tennessee where he died, leaving a will, dated 17 September 1848 with a codicil dated 17 September 1849, probated 28 April 1868. The will recites the names of three grandchildren: Uncus (Eunice) E. Peacock, Virginia G. Peacock, and Mary E. Peacock. Burrell's daughter Catherine T. married William J. Peacock and lived in Bedford County, Tennessee. Other grandchildren not mentioned in the will by name were Burrill F. Peacock, John W. Peacock, Thomas J. Peacock, and Henrietta S. Peacock. Descendants of these Peacocks are to be found in and around Bell Buckle, Bedford County.

One of the Featherstone branches located in Smith County, Tennessee, namely descendants of Daniel M. Featherstone. He died in 1816, and his inventory there mentions an account against Henry Featherstone, Jr. and an account against Edward Featherstone. He must have been a soldier in the War of 1812, for there is listed in his inventory, money due from the U.S. Government.

The Bible record of Edward Featherstone gives entries of the children of Charles H. Featherstone, as follows; Charles H. Featherstone, born May 3, 1786; Charles H., Jr., born October 13, 1807, died 1833; Richard S., born December 8, 1808; Amanda, born February 9, 1811, died 1859; Edward, born December 8, 1813, died 1853; Mercer and Montgomery (twins), born December 8, 1814; William Booker, born May 25, 1817; Martha E., born 1819; Leadrius M., born January 1, 1820; Everard M., born March 13, 1822.

Edward Featherstone, who was born on 8 December 1813 and died on 1 September 1853, married Mary Howlette of Edenton, North Carolina.

In Amelia County, Virginia in 1786, Burrell Featherstone bought land from Arthur Leath, the land being in Nottoway County. Burrell joined with his brothers in a deed to one Dennis in 1786. This was probably shortly before Amelia and Nottoway Counties were divided. In 1810 Burrell and his wife Rebecca, of Nottoway County, sold 15 acres of land in Amelia County to George Kidd. In this deed he spoke of land adjoining the lands of his brother William Grigg Featherstone and the widow Adams.

Rebecca's maiden name was Adams, and tradition has it that she was a close relative to one of the Presidents of the United States.

There is mention of Richard T. Featherstone and his wife Phebe F. in a deed in 1837. They sold Mill property (near the Nottoway County line) to one John Hughes.

In 1787 Burrell T. Featherstone was security on a marriage bond of Richard Hightower to Sallie Hightower, Joshua Hightower, guardian or parent. The Hightower family was closely interwoven with the Featherstones, and several of the Hightowers came to Robertson and Montgomery Counties, Tennessee.

Rebecca Adams Featherstone died in Illinois on 2 February 1852 and was buried in a family burying ground. Tradition has it that Burrell went to Mississippi and died there, but according to the family record kept by Elias M. Morgan, a descendant of this branch of the family, "Burwell Featherstone, died December 10th 1856, buried at William Featherstones." That is the same place Rebecca is buried. There is no tombstone for Burrel, but the tombstone of Rebecca is inscribed, "Rebecca, wife of B. Featherston, died February 4, 1852, age 63 years."

D.S. Featherstone, born on 6 August 1832 in Robertson County, Tennessee, was the son of William and Elizabeth (Jones) Featherstone. William was born in Virginia about 1773 and moved to Robertson County about 1830, where he died in 1866, aged about 90 years. Elizabeth Jones Featherstone was born in Virginia in 1781 and died in 1864 in Robertson County, aged about 83 years. D.S. Featherstone was married on 29 January 1854 to Susan Crawford, daughter of Charles and Lucy Crawford. Susan was born in the "Volunteer State" in 1838 and died in 1873. D.S. married secondly Elizabeth Dorris, born in 1844. By his first wife, D.S. had Charles, Idella (Mrs. Jno. Ragsdale), and Thomas. By his second wife, there were two daughters, Mattie and Lizzie.

W.R. Featherstone, a merchant at Cedar Hill, Robertson County, was born on 10 April 1845, the son of J.W. and Emily (Jackson) Featherstone. J.W. was born in Virginia in 1821 and came to Tennessee in 1830. W.R. Featherstone was married on 2 January 1878 to M.E. Long and had a daughter, Bertha F. Featherstone.

Rev. S.W. Featherstone was born in Robertson County, Tennessee in 1824, one of thirteen children of Burrel Featherstone, a native of Virginia, born in 1797 (another record says 1778). The Rev. Mr. Featherstone was married in 1842 to Martha Redjarrain who died on 2 December 1885. They had Nancy F. and William Pitt Featherstone. Rev. Featherstone was a Baptist Minister of high esteem in his home county.

It has already been shown that the Featherstones were partly Methodist and partly Baptist, there being ministers of both denominations in the same family. It has also been shown that the Featherstones intermarried with the Pressgroves more than once.

William and Eliza (Featherstone) Pressgrove were the parents of: Franklin, born November 5, 1834; Emily J., born June 15, 1836; George, born August 2, 1838; Adaline, born March 19, 1841; John, born March 14, 1843 d.y.; Andrew, born November 28, 1846; Rebecca Ann, born September 13, 1849; Lorenzo, born November 15, 1851; Sarah Catherine, born September 14, 1854; and William Columbus, born January 31, 1858. These are from the family Bible. Under the deaths, the first one is Andrew Presgrove, died January 19, 1846. The Bible also records the death of Rebecca Featherstone, February 5, 1852.

The Pressgroves must have moved from Robertson County to Bedford County; at least part of them did. A petition of William Galbreath in 1822, to purchase a lot in Shelbyville together with a wood carding machine, September 22, 1825, was signed by approximately three hundred Bedford citizens, including James Pressgrove, George Pressgrove, Andrew Pressgrove, and Jno. M. Pressgrove.

The name Pressgrove is frequently found spelled Prestgrove, Pressgrave, and Pressgreaves.

In a deed, dated 4 November 1812 and recorded in Bedford County, Tennessee at Shelbyville (Deed Book D, p. 526), Andrew Pressgrove sold William Neely some land on Duck River.

William Pressgrove was Sheriff of Bedford County in 1832. William Pressgrove and Nathaniel Wheeler were paid $75.00 in 1849 for making a bridge over the north fork of Duck River on the Lower Nashville Road near Presgrove's Mill.

Some of the Pressgroves and Featherstones went to Illinois about 1850. It is known that others of the Featherstones went south through Mississippi and later into Texas. There are descendants in various sections of the "Lone Star" State. I met a descendant a few years ago, living in Wichita Falls, a very prominent citizen.

Prince Edward Co., Va. Will Book 1.
Brunswick Co., Va. Will Book 1.
Nottoway Co., Va. Will Book 1, p. 25.
D.A.R. National No. 13056.
Nottoway Co., Va. Deeds Book 1, pp. 132, 210.
Peter Jones and Richard Jones Genealogy, p. 187.
Bedford County, Tenn. Will Book 1, pp. 130-134.
Smith Co., Tenn. Wills and Inventories 1814-1816, p. 198.
Amelia Co., Va. deed book 33, p. 197 and other Amelia Co. records.
Goodspeed's History of Robertson Co., Tenn. 1886.
Legislative papers. Tenn. State Archives, Nashville, dated 1822.
Bible records of the Featherstone family.
Misc. data in Whitley collection.

Felts

In the National Archives in Washington, among the files of the Revolutionary Pension Division, under File No. S-2546, I find that Rowland Felts, a Revolutionary soldier, lived in Robertson County, Tennessee. The papers in the file show that he was a private in a company commanded by Capt. Harris in a regiment commanded by Col. Eaton in North Carolina in the Militia, having served eight months in 1779. Among other officers mentioned in the papers were Capt. Harris and Capt. Wren.

Rowland Felts was in the battle of Bryer Creek and stated in his declaration that he marched through North and South Carolina and in parts of Georgia. His declaration shows that he enlisted in Bertie County, North Carolina. His age is given as 76 years on 11 October 1831. He said he was discharged in Nash County, North Carolina and lived in Warren County at one time. He could not sign his name, as his declaration bears his mark as signature.

William Carter, a clergyman of Robertson County, made a sworn statement that he knew Rowland Felts well and that he was of good character. Marvel Lowe also made a sworn statement about the character of Felts. No other family data is shown in the papers on file.

Fiser

R.H. Fiser, son of J.H. and Sally (Pence) Fiser, was born on 24 April 1841 in Robertson County. The grandfather of J.H. was born in Germany, came to Tennessee in 1796 with five sons and settled in Robertson County. His son Joseph Fiser entered land and reared three daughters and five sons, one of them being J.H. Fiser, the father of R.H.

Joseph was a farmer. He lived three miles from Springfield and was an extensive tobacco grower and a Mason. His wife was a member of the Methodist Episcopal Church.

When the War Between the States broke out, R.H. Fiser entered the Confederate ranks in Company C of the Knox City Guards. His first skirmish was at Cheat Mountain. Helm was his regimental commander. After the war R. H. Fiser taught school for two years and in 1868 moved to Humboldt where he purchased land and went into the nursery business and grew fruit for the market. He was one of the pioneer fruit growers of West Tennessee. On 26 April 1866 Mr. Fiser married Miss A. B. Batts of Robertson County, born on 23 October 1843, daughter of Jack Batts. The children of R. H. and A. B. Fiser were Ney, George, Bob, and a daughter who died young.

The family, for several generations, has been Methodist.

Goodspeed's History of Tennessee, Gibson County, p. 879.

Ford

The bond of Joseph Woolfork, Drury Ford, Robert Searcy, Henry H. Bryan, Joseph Robinson, and James Huling was dated June 1808, the occasion being that Joseph Woolfork and Drury Ford were appointed administrators of James Ford, deceased. The inventory of the estate was filed at the same time.

John P. Ford made his will on 20 April 1812 in which he mentioned his late father's estate, i.e. James Ford, deceased. He wished his property to be equally divided between his brothers, Francis P. and Phillip Ford, and his two youngest sisters, Rebecca and Polly Ford. Cordall Norfleet was named the executor.

Judah Ford made her will on 24 April 1812 in which she named a son John P. Ford, daughter Rebecca P., daughter Polly Ford, daughters Cassandra Drake and Sally Boyd. Sons Phillip and Francis P. Ford were mentioned. She also mentioned a granddaughter, Judah A. Drake, and a niece, Polly Norfleet. Cordall Norfleet was named executor.

In October 1801 James Ford was named as guardian to Alcey Pennington, daughter of Isaac Pennington, deceased. The same month and the 28th day, 1801 there was produced in court a record which bears the date January 24, 1794 — to Stephen and Elcy Pennington heirs of Isaac Pennington. The court appointed Jonathan Stephenson executor of the estate, in right of his wife, to settle the estate of Isaac Pennington, deceased.

This might infer that Pennington's widow married Jonathan Stephenson who, in right of his wife, took over the settlement of the estate of Isaac Pennington. The record is not clear as to the relationship.

There appears a deed from John Ford of Davidson County to Anthony Hart of the same place, the date being 20 July 1790, for land in Tennessee County.

Susannah Hart of Davidson County, Territory South of the River Ohio, executrix of the last will and testament of Anthony Hart, deceased, deeded land in Robertson County on 15 August 1797 to Jesse Reed.

In another deed, dated 6 May 1789, John Ford of Davidson County transferred land lying in Tennessee County to John Baker, esqr., of Gates County, North Carolina.

James Ford was one of the most prominent men in the Red River Country and took an outstanding part in the development of that section.

Montgomery County Record Book 1, pp. 45, 102.
Montgomery County Record Book 2, p. 52.
Montgomery Co. Will Book 2, p. 84.
Montgomery Co. W. B. 1797-1810, pp. 143, 149, 347 ff.
Robertson County Deed Book A, p. 68.

Gent

Charles Gent, who had been a private in the Georgia line during the Revolutionary War, moved to Robertson County, Tennessee and was there when he filed for a
pension under the Act of June 7, 1832. In his own statement he said that he was in a
company commanded by Capt. Clark of the regiment commanded by Col. LaMar in
the Georgia Militia for two years from 1776. He was granted a pension at the rate of
$80.00 per year which commenced 4 March 1831. At the time he made application he
was 78 years of age.

According to the brief in his case we learn that he enlisted in 1775-6 as a volunteer and served through the whole war. It would appear that all of his service was
as a private. During the period that he was in service he was at various times under
General McIntosh, Capt. Clark, Col. Coleman, Capt. David Gunnel, Capt. Wilson,
Col. Dooly, and Col. Cunningham.

He made a sworn statement that he was in the battle of Kettle Creek and one or
two Indian fights. He referred to Jacob Patterson's being killed and to Giles Tillet
and Peter Davis who were wounded. He further stated that he was a resident of
Wilkes County, Georgia at the time he enlisted.

Jesse Hooper of Davidson County, Tennessee made an affidavit in regard to
Charles Gent on 1 August 1832. (Pension file S-1903 National Archives, Washington,
D.C.)

Gholson

William Gholson was a Revolutionary pensioner in Caldwell County, Kentucky.
His pension file, No. 35966, is to be found in the National Archives, Washington,
D.C. He served in Virginia. His application for pension, dated 24 July 1820, gives
his age as sixty-two years. There is mention of a son Richard D. Gholson, aged
sixteen years, a teacher in the county school. There is also mention made of other
sons and daughters, but their names are not given. In a letter from Jos. Ficklin,
dated 22 February 1834, Willian Gholson appears to have died on 2 January 1837.

Milton or Mitton G. Gholson was born in Kentucky in 1814 and married Louisa
Rogers who was born in Tennessee in 1816. At the beginning of the war, Milton Gholson was made a Lieutenant-Colonel, enlisting in the 14th Tennessee, Confederate
States Army. His health soon failed, and he returned home and subsequently was
commissioned brigadier-general of militia by Governor Harris. He assisted in rais-
ing two or three regiments of troops in Tennessee and died in Montgomery County in
1883.

John A. Gholson, M.D., son of Milton Gholson, was born in Clarksville on 26
December 1834 and married a Miss Lyle in 1860. She was also a native of the "Volunteer State," born in 1840, the daughter of Thomas and Margaret M. Lyle, both native
Tennesseans, born in 1807. After attending public school, J.A. Gholson went to
Nashville where he graduated in 1861. He enlisted at once in the Fourteenth Tennessee Regiment under Col. Forbes, where he served as hospital steward. He surrendered with Lee at Appomattox Court House in 1865, returned home, and began the
practice of medicine. John A. and his wife had eight children: Alexander R., John
A., Jr., Hugh P., Louisa, Milton G., Lillian A., Lottie E., and Dora I. Gholson.

A.R. Gholson, an attorney-at-law, son of J.A. Gholson, was born in Montgomery County on 26 February 1861. He began the study of law in 1881 and in 1884, entered the law office of Judge Smith and Lurton. From 1881 to 1884, he was a deputy
in the office of the County Trustee and was licensed to practice law in September 1884.
August 1885 brought him an appointment as Deputy Clerk and Master under Polk C.
Johnson, a position he held many years. He was elected a Notary Public in 1885 and
served in that capacity for four years. All the Gholsons I have found related to this
family were members of the Methodist Church.

Gilliam

John Gilliam and his wife Elizabeth were living in Logan County, Kentucky when he filed for a Revolutionary Pension. The papers are in file W-8849 in the National Archives, Washington, D. C., Revolutionary Pension Division. The certificate, No. 13656, was issued on 30 May 1833, based on the Act of June 7, 1832, at the rate of $43.33 per year, beginning on 4 March 1831. Elizabeth Gilliam, the widow of John, was granted $43.33 per year from 4 March 1848. Her certificate, No. 1063, issued on 1 August 1848 under the Act of February 2, 1848 is in the Archives' records and was also filed with the Kentucky Agency.

John Gilliam filed for a pension on 9 November 1832, aged 73 years, while a resident of Logan County, Kentucky, based on service rendered in Virginia as a private. He enlisted in Albemarle County, Virginia. In his declaration he stated that he enlisted at sixteen years of age in 1775-1776 under the command of Michael Wallace, Lt. James Wood, and Capt. Lina Jones. He was discharged at Richmond, Virginia after three months service.

His second tour was under Lt. James Wood, Capt. Nath Garland, and Col. Reuben Lindsay. After three months, he was discharged without a written discharge.

His third tour was as a substitute under Col. Taylor for two months. His fourth tour for six months was under Capt. Slaughter and Col. Chas. Dabney. He was at the seige of Little York and then was detached at Richmond to guard prisoners until the end of the war.

John Gilliam was born in Albemarle County, Virginia on 10 August 1760. On 4 April 1833, Evan Watson, an old fellow soldier, gave an affadavit to prove that he served part of the time with John Gilliam. Thomas M. Smith and Jno. H. Thomas both testified regarding John Gilliam.

On 22 December 1845, Elizabeth Gilliam, aged 79, of Logan County, Kentucky stated that she married John Gilliam on 25 December 1785 in Albemarle County, Virginia and that she and her husband moved to Madison County, Kentucky where they resided until 1821. They then moved to Logan County, Kentucky where they lived until 4 June 1845 when John Gilliam died.

On 26 June 1848, Elizabeth Gilliam stated that she was 82 years of age and that her husband drew $43.33 per year pension.

A certificate of marriage by the clerk of Albemarle County, December 1785, names John Gilliam and Elizabeth Bailey. The application for license was signed by John Gilliam and John Bailey of Albemarle County.

Charles Bailey, aged 78, and Pleasant Gilliam, aged 74, residents of Albemarle County, on 17 November 1845, made statements that they were present at the marriage on Xmas Day, December 25th. They further stated that the deponents had children born previous to 1794 and that before 1816, they had moved to Kentucky.

Nancy Thomas, daughter of the late John Gilliam and his wife Elizabeth, testified that she was born on 10 February 1790 and that the second child was Charles P. Gilliam. A statement made by John R. Aingell also verified the information submitted. On 15 March 1856, Elizabeth Gilliam, aged 90, made application for Bounty land to which she may have been entitled.

Gupton

The Guptons located in that part of Robertson and Montgomery Counties which later became Cheatham County. Abner, James, and Stephen Gupten are listed as living in Halifax District, Franklin County in the census or tax list of North Carolina in 1790.

Abner Gupton, probably the same man as shown in Franklin County, left a will in

Cheatham County, Tennessee which is dated 5 April 1841. There is a peculiar thing abouth the wills of Abner Gupton, for it would appear that he left two wills. In the first he named his wife, Judith, and daughters Mary Hunter, Sarah Perdue (wife of John Perdue or Pardue), Judith Gupton, Elizabeth (wife of Matthew T. Hale), and sons James, Abner, and Robert T. Gupton.

In the second will, dated 11 January 1858, he called his wife Martha A. and went further to state that she was to have all the property she was entitled to from her former husband Samuel A. Powers. The daughters named were Mary Hunter, Sarah Pardue, Elizabeth Hale, and Judith Dozier; the sons were given as James J., Abner, and Robert T. Gupton. In the second will, he stated, "Whereas I have been informed that some years ago my deaf and dumb son Abner Gupton was married to one Jane Batts without my knowledge or consent and since said married and up to death of my son Abner some years ago, said Jane has had several children, some of which I learn are now living and for reason best known to myself, to said Jane and her children 25 acres of land the place she now live on."

Sarah Gupton probably married a son of Thomas Pardue and his wife, Mary M. Thomas Pardue left a will in Cheatham Cheatham County, 18 November 1861, but mentioned only his wife whom he made executor.

Eben and Lydia Gupton, both natives of North Carolina, were in Robertson and Cheatham County along with Abner Gupton. Eben and Lydia had seven children. Their second child, James W. Gupton, was born in Tennessee on 24 January 1844. He was a farmer and blacksmith. In 1874, he erected a gristmill on his farm, which contained about 450 acres of good land. On 6 October 1872, James married Henrietta (Duke) Gupton, widow of Cave J. Gupton. She was the daughter of John E. and Elizabeth Duke and was born on 27 May 1844. Mr. and Mrs. James W. Gupton were members of the Methodist Episcopal Church. They had two children, Minnie and Johnnie.

Cave J. Gupton, the first husband of Henrietta, was born on 17 July 1846. They were married on 18 September 1866, and their children were Robbie E., Samuel D., and Cave D. Gupton. Cave J. Gupton died on 17 April 1871, leaving his widow two hundred acres of land.

Robert T. Gupton, the son of Abner Gupton, was born in 1811 and was married about 1835 to Martha H. Powers, who was born in North Carolina in 1820. They were the parents of eight children, five sons and three daughters. Robert T. died in October 1866, and Martha died on 22 May 1863.

John J. Gupton, son of Robert T., was born in Cheatham County on 19 June 1849. He owned 275 acres of land in 1881. On 9 May 1871, he married Martha G. Gupton, born on 7 July 1853, daughter of Abner and Jane Gupton. The children of John J. Gupton and his wife were Robert A., Essia, Martha H., Charles F., Kendrick, and Dempsey A. Gupton.

It would appear from the records I have found, that Abner Gupton the elder, must have had two wives. After the death of his first wife, he made the second will. His son Abner had died, leaving issue of whom the father knew nothing. It also appears that Robert T. Gupton, son of Abner, may have married his father's step-daughter. This last, however, is conjecture, as the records are not clear.

Cheatham County, Tennessee Will Book 1, pp. 127, 332.
Goodspeed's History of Tennessee, Cheatham Co. 1886. p. 1369.

Harris

The Harrisses are numerous in the Red River community.

Edward Harris of Newbern, North Carolina sold a tract of land on Red River in Robertson County to John Powers on 22 August 1798.

Elias Fort, Jr. was made guardian of Miriah Harris in 1814.

Edward Harris of Newbern, N.C. appointed Col. Thomas Johnson of Robertson County, Tennessee, attorney to convey a tract of land on Red River, 200 acres being part of the tract of 274 acres which was granted to Jesse Cobb on 20 May 1793, the part Isaac Flannery lived on, also another tract of 100 acres including the Big Sinking Spring in the Barrens. The record is dated 31 August 1798, but it was not proven in court until January 1799.

The estate of Edmund K. Harris was returned into the court of Robertson County on 15 February 1802 by Martha Harris, the administratrix.

On 24 March 1808, James Fentress, Esqr., chairman pro tem of the County Court of Montgomery County, issued an order, "an orphan of the deceased to live with said Hugh Harris as apprentice until he is twenty-one years of age, during which time Griffin Mills shall faithfully serve his master." The name of the father of the orphan being bound is not shown in the record.

Abner Harris, Benjamine Whitehead, and William Corlew posted bond when Abner Harris was appointed guardian of Nancy Blanton and Sally Blanton, orphans of Richard Blanton, deceased, in July 1803 in Montgomery County.

John Harriss left a will in Montgomery County, 28 September 1814. In it he named his wife, Frances, and his children, Sally, Martin, John, Jr., Catey, Frances, Jiney, Nelly, Lucy, Peter, and Henry. James Trotter and Willis Jackson were named as executors.

Washington Harris, an orphan boy, aged 13 years, was bound to Jacob Binkley in 1820 in Robertson County. At the same time, Ephraim Roberts was made the guardian of the minor heirs of Richard Harris, deceased.

On 16 April 1816, the Court of Montgomery, on motion, ordered Peter Hubbard to be the guardian of Clementary Harris, Mary Ann Harris, and Bennegay Harris, infants, heirs of Benjamin Harris, deceased.

In the National Archives in Washington, D.C. among the files in the Revolutionary War Pension Division, File S-4307, I have found papers relative to Edwin Harris, a private in the North Carolina line, who made application for pension under the Act of 1832. He received his pension pay in Robertson County, and stated that he had served as a private in the company of Capt. Harris, in a regiment commanded by General Green in North Carolina for a period of six months in 1780. His age is shown as 74 years on 20 August 1832.

It would appear that he served two tours of three months each. Officers with whom he was associated are shown to have been Col. Benj. Sewell, Capt. Edward Clariton, General Green, General Eaton, Col. Haynes, and Capt. Jordon Harris.

He was engaged in the battle of Guilford Court House. When he enlisted for service, he was in Warren County, North Carolina. His application for pension was filed from Robertson County, Tenn. where he resided at that time. William Carter, clergyman, a resident of the same county, made a sworn statement that he knew Edward Harris well. There is no family data shown in the pension file.

Robertson County, Tenn. Court Min. 1820-1822.
Robertson County Will Book 1796-1812, pp. 37, 169.
Robertson County Will Book 1812-1818, p. 122.
Robertson County Deed Book B, p. 196.
Montgomery County Will Book 1, pp. 82, 156
Montgomery County Will Book 2, p. 79
Montgomery County Court Min. 1816-1817, p. 16.
Harris Family Records, Manuscript "Dots and Dashes" by Whitley, unpublished
    Whitley Collection. 3 vols.

Herndon

In the National Archives in Washington, D.C. among the Revolutionary Pension papers, and on file in the National D.A.R. Library, Revolutionary Pensioners Vol. 38, p. 113, SF.13,373, George Herndon's papers indicate that he served in the Revolution in North Carolina. He made application on 13 August 1832, and his claim was allowed. He stated that he was born on 14 June 1762 and that at the time he made application for pension, he was a resident of Logan County in the State of Kentucky.

He enlisted in Chatham County, North Carolina in 1778 for five months ending 10 April 1779 as a private under Capt. Kendrick and Col. Saunders. He stated that he enlisted in the fall or winter of 1779 for three months under Capt. James Herndon (soldier's father) and Col. Lytle.

In 1780-81 he enlisted for three months under Capt. Knight, Col. Lutrell, and Malbry.

He served in 1781 and was captured by a band of Tories under Col. Fleming and imprisoned at Wilmington for four or five months, after which he escaped.

There is no data relative to a wife or to any children other than a son Robert, who was referred to in 1855 as having survived his father.

Herring

The Herrings lived in Montgomery County. James Herring was from Sumner County, Tennessee, and his wife Mourning was from Montgomery County. They had ten children. Mr. Herring died in 1880, and Mrs. Herring died in 1884.

Of their children, Gus M. Herring was born in Montgomery County in February 1845. At the breaking out of the War Between the States, young Gus enlisted in the 47th Tennessee Infantry which was afterwards consolidated with another regiment and known as the Third Tennessee. He remained in that unit until the close of the war.

In October 1879, Gus M. Herring wed M.E. Cowgill by whom he had four children. After his marriage, Mr. G.M. Herring located at Union City, Tennessee.

Goodspeed's History of Tennessee. Obion County. 1886, p. 955.

Hornberger - Haunbarger

As early as 5 October 1789, Joseph Brock of Davidson County sold land in Tennessee County to Phillip Haunbarger of Tennessee County.

On 29 March 1797, Henry Woodson of Greenville County, South Carolina sold a negro woman slave to Philip Hornbarger of Montgomery County, Tennessee.

The court of June 1809 for Montgomery (formerly Tennessee) County described the road leading to Nashville road on the south side of Red River near where McCades road turns off thence the most direct way to Hornbergers old fork across Red River, thence up Jedediah Hall's lane with Watkins and Nelson line to Port Royal road, to and down said road fronting Watkins House, thence, the best and most direct way to White's Mill on Spring Creek, and ordered that Bright Herring, William White, John Davies, Thomas Dunbar, Moses Oldham, Daniel Taylor, Isaac Peterson, James Bailey, John Henderson, Jedediah Hall, and James Lester be a jury to view the same road.

This would certainly establish Philip Hornbarger as living in the confines of Old Tennessee County, later Montgomery.

Montgomery County Minute book 1808-1810, p. 161.
Montgomery County Will Book 1797-1810, p. 22.
Montgomery County Deed Book 1, p. 18.

Howard

Allen H. Howard was born in 1796 in North Carolina and enlisted in the War of 1812 at Clarksville, Tennessee. He was married on 16/17 August 1815 at Charlotte, Tennessee to Elizabeth Wesley Shropshire who was a native of Virginia, born in 1800, and died at Walla Walla County, Washington in 1888.

Allen Howard lived in Dickson and Haywood Counties, Tennessee and in Johnson County, Illinois where he died on 15 January 1840.

He had brothers Stephen, William, and James. The latter moved to California in 1864 and had sons Edward, Warren, and Charles. Charles moved to Benton County, Oregon in 1864 and had sons named William and Charles.

The sisters of Allen Howard were Betsy Ann, who married a Mr. Hill, and Sarah (or Sally), who married Colonel Wm. Henderson, the father of Thomas Jefferson Henderson, the noted soldier and Congressman from Illinois.

The children of Allen and Elizabeth Howard were: Albert, Perry, Joel, Thomas Hill, Drucilla, Nancy (married a Batson or her name was Nancy Batson), and Calvin Batson Howard.

National Historical Magazine, June 1934.

Hubbard

Peter Hubbard applied for a Revolutionary Pension while living in Montgomery County, Tennessee. He was born in South Carolina and served in the Fourth Carolina line under Capt. Samuel Wise and Capt. John Carraway Smith with Col. Wm. Thompson. Hubbard was in the Battle of Sullivan Island. After the Revolutionary War, he removed to Tennessee. He lived for several years in Montgomery County, after which he moved to Bond County, Illinois, where he died.

Peter Hubbard was born on 31 July 1756 in Cheraw District, South Carolina and died on 26 August 1844. He was married in Cheraw District to Mary Ann (last name not known). She was born on 15 May 1767 in the same state and died on 21 May 1826 in Montgomery County, Tennessee.

There were eight children born to Mr. and Mrs. Hubbard while they resided in Cheraw District, and five more were added after they reached Montgomery County, Tennessee sometime between 1790 and 1795. The names of the thirteen children are given here. However, the order of their birth is not certain: John, William, Peter, Francis, David, Manoah, Nancy, Caty, Eli, Philip, James, Trustram, and Lucy Ann.

While in the Red River country, the family lived at or near Palmyra which, at that time, was an important village.

Peter Hubbard was the son of Peter Hubbard, Sr. whose wife was named Agnes.

Descendants of the Hubbard family in Montgomery County intermarried with the Exum family, also early Middle Tennessee pioneers. Arthur Exum's estate appears on the records of Davidson County, Tennessee as being divided from 1819 to 1830. Exum's wife was named Sarah. Their dozen children were: Joseph, William, John, Arthur, Jr., Elijah, Elizabeth (married Adonijah Edwards), Mary (married Wm. Reynolds), Sarah (married Josiah Reynolds), Martha (married Mayberry Walton), Rebecca (married John T. Scott), Margaret (married Abner Champion), and Patience (married Moses Patterson). The Exums and the Reynolds lived in Smith and Dickson Counties as early as 1808.

It is known that William Hubbard died in Tennessee about 1815. His wife, Sallie Johnson, died in 1857. After William's death, Mrs. Sallie (Johnson) Hubbard married a Mr. Ward by whom she had at least two children, Gideon and Rhoda. There were six known children of the union of William Hubbard and Sallie. Mary (called Polly) was born on 7 July 1804 on Meechy Creek on the North side of the Cumberland River, died about 1890 at Rienzi, Mississippi, and was married in 1819 to Reubin Rorie who was born in 1800 and died in 1862. Sallie Hubbard, the second child of William and Sallie Hubbard, married George Steele. Henry Hubbard married Lee Rorie. Betsy Hubbard married first John Steele, second Thomas Phillips, and third Bobby Breedlove. William Hubbard was the fifth child. Nancy Hubbard, the sixth child, married George Cooley.

The family of William Hubbard lived in Weakley County, Tennessee in 1830. George Steele was a resident of the same county and had at least two sons and eight daughters in 1830. George Cooley and his family were living in Stewart County, Tennessee in 1820.

The Rorie family also intermarried with some of the Hubbards in Tennessee. They evidently came from North Carolina, probably from Anson County, for there was a William Rorie who left a will, probated there in 1802, in which he mentioned his wife Judah and his children Reuben, Lucy, Elizabeth, Mary, Judah, Hezekiah, Masy (Mary), and Ann.

In 1820 at the time the census was taken, one Hezekiah Rorie was living in Stewart County, Tennessee.

There was an Ann Rorie who left a will in Anson County, North Carolina, 27 June 1798, in which she named her father, William Rorie, and her brother, Hezekiah Rorie, executors. She also said, "I gave Reuben Rorie's daughter" etc. and left a tract of land to "my daughter Patty Johnston Rorie."

Reuben Rorie, born in 1800 in North Carolina, probably the son of Hezekiah (or Ezekiah), was married in Tennessee in 1818 to Mary (called Polly) Hubbard, who was born on 7 July 1804 in Stewart County, Tennessee. Mr. and Mrs. Reubin Rorie moved to Mississippi about 1836. Mr. Rorie died there in 1863, and Mrs. Rorie died there in 1890. Mary Hubbard Rorie was the daughter of William Hubbard and his wife Sarah Johnson. Sarah's mother is thought to have been Dallie DeGraffenreid. Reubin and Mary (Hubbard) Rorie were the parents of Elizabeth Rorie who was born on 14 March 1821, died in 1881 in Mississippi, and married William Walker, who was born on 16 February 1814 in Kentucky and died on 8 October 1871 in Mississippi. They were married about 1834 in Stewart County, Tennessee and lived for a time in Trigg County, Kentucky. William Walker was the son of William (called Buck) Walker who lived in Kentucky. One of the children of William and Elizabeth (Rorie) Walker was Milbury Jane Walker who was born in Mississippi on 25 October 1845, died on 23 June 1934, and was married on 24 December 1865 to William Franklin Jobe who was born on 14 March 1843 in Mississippi, and died on 28 September 1900. William Franklin Jobe was the son of Joseph Reynolds Jobe, who was born in 1821, died in 1863 in Mississippi and was married on 4 July 1841 in Mississippi to Elizabeth Phillips who was born the same year as her husband in North Carolina and died in Mississippi in 1879. Joseph Reynolds Jobe was the son of John Jobe who was born on 6 June 1801 in Lawrence County, Tennessee, died on 27 April 1889, and was married in 1820 in McNary County, Tennessee to Sarah Farmer, who was born before 1804, as she was aged between 16 and 26 in the census of 1820. John Jobe was the son of Daniel, the son of Samuel. Elizabeth Phillips was the daughter of Lazarus Phillips and his wife, Rachel Saunders. Mrs. Rachel (Saunders) Phillips was born in Chatham County, North Carolina in 1775. She was the daughter of John Saunders of Chatham County, North Carolina, who is believed to have migrated to Tennessee where he resided a few years and then moved to Mississippi. Lazarus Phillips was the son of Jeremiah Phillips of North Carolina who died on 5 September 1805.

One of the most devout families of Methodists in early Robertson County was that of William Hubbard. He was born in Virginia in 1787 and moved with his parents to

North Carolina. His wife, Nancy Qualls, was the daughter of Abner Qualls, a Revolutionary Soldier. Mrs. Hubbard died in Robertson County in 1821, after which Mr. Hubbard married a second wife, Mrs. Elizabeth Gunn, by whom he had three sons and three daughters: Freeman, Richard H., William, Polly Ann, Nancy C., and Lucinda.

Mr. Hubbard arrived in Tennessee in 1813 and lived two miles below Nashville on the Cumberland River. Soon after getting located, he joined Jackson's Army, serving for five years, during which time he took part in the forced march made by the troops to re-enforce the army at New Orleans. But before Mr. Hubbard's company reached there, the battle of New Orleans had been fought, and liberty was secured to the American people.

While Mr. Hubbard was in the army, his family moved to Robertson County and settled near Red River. The year 1846, however, brought a change in the family residence, and they moved to Fayette County and settled eight miles north of Somerville, at which place Mr. Hubbard died in 1850.

By Nancy Qualls, there were two children, James D. and Charlotte W. Charlotte married Joshua Darden.

James D. Hubbard was born in Caswell County, North Carolina on 10 May 1809. On 18 February 1851, before leaving Robertson County, Mr. J.D. Hubbard wedded Miss Elizabeth A. Stoltz, daughter of Capt. J.H. Stoltz, a commissioned officer in Jackson's Army. Mrs. Elizabeth A. (Stoltz) Hubbard was born in the county in which she was married on 13 October 1828. Her father, a native of Stokes County, North Carolina, was born in 1783 and died in Robertson County, five miles west of Springfield in 1862. Capt. Stoltz's wife, Miss Nancy Dorris, was born a few miles north of Nashville in 1796 and died in April 1864. The grandmother of Mrs. Hubbard was Elizabeth Meneese, a sister of James Meneese, who is identified with the early history of Nashville and more especially with the history of the Methodist Episcopal Church in the Cumberland and Red River communities.

Six of the nine children born to Mr. and Mrs. James D. Hubbard are known at this time: Nancy T., James I., William E., Mary Emma, Robert L., and Edward C. Hubbard.

D.A.R. Magazine. July 1951, p. 607.
Revolutionary pension records of Peter Hubbard. Washington, D.C.
Census of Stewart and other counties, Tennessee.
Manuscript records, Whitley collection.
Goodspeed's History of Tennessee. Lauderdale County, p. 860.

Hudgeons

Samuel Hudgeons, a Revolutionary soldier, lived in Robertson County, Tennessee when he applied to receive a pension under the Act of June 7, 1832. His name is spelled Hudgeons and Hudgins in the papers on file in the Revolutionary Pension Division of the National Archives in Washington, file S-1957. He was granted a pension on his application and service as a private of cavalry in the company commanded by Capt. Lucas of the regiment commanded by General Lafayette in the Virginia line, five years from 1776. His pension commenced on 4 March 1831 and was set at $100.00 per year. At the time he applied for a pension, he gave his age as 76 years and stated that his birthday was "May 8th, past." He showed that he enlisted on 9 March 1776, apparently two enlistments as a private. During the five years, he served under General LaFayette, Col. Robert Lawson, Capt. Thos. Lucas, Genl. Scott's Brigade, Col. Baylor, Col. Wm. Washington, and Capt. Church.

Samuel Hudgeons was at the battles of Trenton, Princeton, Brandywine, Germantown, At Stono, Harrington, Lenew Ferry, Timbletown, and other skirmishes.

Sterling Clack certified for Samuel Hudgeons in a sworn statement in which he said he moved shortly after the war into North Carolina, then to Georgia and again to North Carolina and to Tennessee, and to Kentucky where he first met Mr. Hudgins.

The affidavit of Thomas Gunn, a clergyman and resident of Robertson County, and James Doss, a citizen of the same County, certified that they knew Samuel Hudgeons and would give faith and credit to what he said.

Humphrey - West - Whitledge

The three families of Humphrey, West, and Whitledge were closely related after their arrival in Tennessee. Just how they all tie into a single family is not thoroughly worked out.

The 1790 census of Virginia gives a list of the inhabitants and property in the city of Richmond in 1782: Joshua Humphreys, a watch-maker by trade, aged 39 years (who was very likely also an ordinary keeper since he had a license for such an establishment); his wife Anne, aged 36; and the children in the family, David aged 12, Elijah aged 10, Mary aged 7, Charles aged 6, Parry aged 4, and Joshua aged 8.

It would appear that Parry W. Humphreys was in Montgomery County in the early part of 1809. The exact date he came to Red River is not known. On 22 June 1809, Parry W. Humphreys, Esq. and John Cocke, Sheriff, sold lots No. 87 and 88 in Clarksville to Henry Minor. The deed was proved in court.

The same year there was a deed of conveyance executed by Parry W. Humphreys to Frederick W. Huling for lots No. 137, 138, 139, and 140 in Clarksville.

Just what relation Parry W. Humphreys was to the family of John Humphreys, an early settler in the same area, is not definitely known. It is believed that Parry W. Humphreys, a promising young attorney, came from Richmond, Virginia to find his career, which developed into a most outstanding one.

Humphreys County, Tennessee was created on 19 October 1809 out of Stewart County and named in honor of Parry W. Humphreys, a judge of the Superior Court of Law and Equity, 1807-1809, who held the first court in the new county.

In 1816 P. W. Humphreys produced a deed for a tract of land granted to John Granberry, said land lying on Yellow Creek in Montgomery County, containing 722 acres which deed purports to have been made by William Johnson and Mary his wife to George West in 1803 on March 2. This may have been very nearly the date Judge Humphreys arrived in the community, for he is not mentioned in earlier records. He was also thought to have been related to the West family mentioned herein, having married the daughter of the said George West. William Johnson had heretofore acknowledged the transaction referred to, and Mary Johnson, a resident of Bertie County, North Carolina, acknowledged, the court ordering that Whitmell H. Pugh, Lewis Thompson and William Pugh or any two of them of Bertie County, take said Mary's examination.

In his will, George West, of Montgomery County, named his wife, Elizabeth, to whom he left one half of the plantation. His eldest son Robert West and another son George West were left property. Parry W. Humphreys "son-in-law" and "my daughter Mary his wife" were devised certain property by the will. Mr. West was a brother-in-law of William Clements and so identified him in the will. West was an ardent Methodist, for he left a nice bequest in trust to the Bishop and Elders of the Methodist Episcopal Church for the "relief and distress." West may have lived in North Carolina before coming to Red River. Such is indicated in the will by the mention of "a note of Jonathan Jacobs of N. C." He also owned land in Fleming County, Kentucky at the time of his death. He left directions for its disposal in his will. George West died soon after 24 May 1810, the date of his will.

Mrs. Elizabeth West, "the elder," made her will in Montgomery County on 18 July 1815. In it she mentioned her son George, daughter Mary W. Humphreys, granddaughter Martha West, granddaughter Elizabeth H. Humphreys, niece Catherine McKenzie Darlett Clements, and sister Sarah Clements. She named as her executors her sons, Robert and George West, and son-in-law, Parry W. Humphreys.

Thomas Whitledge made his will in Montgomery County on 24 February 1810. In it he named a brother Robert, nephew John (son of brother John, deceased), John Sullivan of Virginia (son of my oldest sister), niece Suckey Humphrey, and niece Ursulla Ford. To them he left land in Kentucky. To his nephew Thomas, son of a brother John, he devised certain property. To his friend Henry Small's daughter, Frances, he left a negro, and to his son, Richard, a colt. He also remembered his friend James Elder. He referred to nieces Sally Oneal, Suckey Humphrey, Ursulla Ford, Elizabeth Whitledge, Nancy Whitledge, and Susannah Whitledge. Henry Small was named as executor.

The estate of Thomas Whitledge, deceased, 1810, Montgomery County, Henry Small executor, named legatees John Whitledge of Kentucky, John Sullivan of Virginia, Thomas Whitledge of Kentucky, Suckey Humphrey of Kentucky, Urcilla Ford of Kentucky, and Francis Small, Robert W. Whitledge, Richard Small, and Henry Small, all of whom, it would appear, were of Tennessee.

Henry A. Humphreys was born in Henry County, Tennessee in 1839, the son of Henry and Susannah (Paschal) Humphreys. The elder Henry was born in North Carolina in 1802, came to Henry County in 1825, and died in 1881. Mrs. Susannah Humphreys was born in North Carolina in 1804 and was living in 1886. Henry A. Humphreys attended school in Maury, Kentucky. He later taught school several years. In November 1861 he enlisted in Company G of the First Tennessee Cavalry as a Confederate soldier. He remained in the service until the final surrender. In January 1868, Mr. H.A. Humphreys married Mrs. Malinda Dumas, a native of Henry County, born in 1837, the daughter of James and Isabella Walker. Mr. and Mrs. H.A. Humphreys had seven children, among whom were Maud, Jennie, Lillie, and Fisher.

John Humphreys, an early settler in the same vicinity, became a resident of Dickson County when that county was cut. He was a man of considerable means. His will, dated 16 September 1826, probated in January 1827, indicates that he owned land not only in Dickson but in adjoining counties. He had a son, John H. Humphreys; a daughter, Clarida, who married Amos Reynolds and who died before her father; a daughter, Sophia, who married Amos Reynolds, the husband of her deceased sister Clarinda; a son-in-law, Edward Holley, who had married Sophia as her first husband, but had deserted her prior to her marriage to Amos Reynolds (Sophia appears to have had children by both marriages); a son, Horatio Humphreys; a son-in-law, John T. Patterson, who was the father of Polly White Patterson; a daughter, Dilly, who was then deceased but had been the wife of John T. Patterson; a daughter, Jenisha Brown, and her children John Humphreys Brown, Asa Madison Brown, and possibly others. To his son Stokley Humphreys, John left considerable property but suggested that he would have obstacles. A grandson Clinton Reynolds, a grandson John Severe Reynolds, and a granddaughter Caroline Reynolds were provided for. Robert Whittledge and B.B. Carbon were the witnesses.

John H. Humphreys of Humphreys County, mentioned in his father's will in Dickson County, made his own will on 20 November 1839. It was proved on 20 November 1839. His children named therein appear to have been David H., Absalom, and William Humphreys. "My children as they married I gave property, namely, George W. Humphrey, Stacy Cole, Martha Doney, Sophia Brigham, and Polly Rushing." John Edwards was named as executor.

Sarah Odneal (Oneal), mentioned in connection with Thomas Whitledge and called "niece," made a deed for "love and affection" to daughter Lucy Grant for a slave on 2 July 1810. On 9 October 1810, James Grant transferred to Zachariah Grant, a slave who was in the possession of Sarah Odneal which negro was given to James Grant and Susannah, his wife.

There is a transcript of a nuncupative will of Lt. Tate Odeneal, dated 4 January 1815, in which he wishes property to go to his mother Sarah Odeneal and to his four sisters and one brother. The will bears the signature of John Donelson, Jr.

Montgomery County Court Minutes 1808-1810, pp. 65, 231.
Montgomery County Will Book 1797-1810, pp. 347-8, 363, 369, 408.
Montgomery County Court Minutes 1816-1818, p. 110.
Humphreys County Will Book 1, p. 620.

Montgomery County Will Book 1811-1818, pp. 57, 387.
Dickson County, Tenn. Will Book 1, p. 54.
Goodspeed's History of Henry County, Tenn., p. 907.
Humphrey Family manuscripts (extensive collection) in Whitley Collection.

Isbell

    Most of the Isbells I have run across were seated in Charlotte and Halifax Counties during the Revolutionary period, yet the name appears early in North Carolina. George Isbell came to Red River from Halifax County, Virginia sometime before 1794. He had not been in the Western county very long when he died, leaving a will recorded both in Robertson County, Tennessee and in Halifax County, Virginia. In his will, George Isbell styles himself "of Halifax County, State of Virginia" thus indicating that he probably executed the will before leaving Virginia. From the will it is learned that he had purchased land lying in Carolina County from John Foster and owned land in Halifax County, lying on the Ridge path adjoining Reuben Pickett, William Adkisson, and others. His wife was named Mary. His sons were John, George, and Thomas D. Isbell. Four daughters were remembered in the will: Sarah, Nancy, Polly, and Agatha. His wife, Mary, and Isaac Oaks, William Collins, and Jacob Faulkner were the executors. The will, dated 15 May 1794, was proved in Halifax County the same year.

    I have not been able to trace the descendants as there do not appear to be any persons by the name in the county at this time.

    In Montgomery County, the court of January 20, 1817 made Daniel Isbell the guardian of Francis Isbell and Betsey Isbell, the heirs of Daniel Isbell, deceased.

Montgomery County Tennessee Court Minutes 1816-1817, p. 131.
Robertson County W. B. 1, p. 313.

Jernigan - Jones

    Thirteen miles from Springfield, in District No. 15 of Robertson County, on property to this day known and designated as the "Jernigan and Jones Heirs," is an old cemetery, sometimes referred to as the Jernigan cemetery and sometimes called the Jones graveyard. This spot represents a community of pioneers. Besides the Jones and Jernigan families, the Empsons, the Durretts, the Esteses, and others may be found. It is more than a family cemetery.

    There are a number of graves which have markers of rock without inscription. Also, tombs with inscriptions of a much later date than those given herein may be found. Time and age are gradually erasing the recordings of the earlier generations. In order to preserve the inscriptions, they are copied as follows:
    Dr. Edgar Jernigan, born December 2, 1860 died December 20, 1935.
    Minnie Brown, daughter of J. G. and V. Armstrong, born October 28, 1874 died November 11, 1880.
    Mary F., wife of W. F. Jernigan, born December 29, 1834 died August 8, 1930.
    W. F. Jernigan, born December 29, 1835 died July 1, 1913.
    Willie, son of W. F. and M. J. Jernigan, born September 10, 1872 died October 3, 1879.
    T. W. Jernigan, born March 23, 1828 died May 2, 1888.
    Eddie Lee Villines, born April 22, 1861 died September 30, 1925.
    Elizabeth Jernigan, his wife, born March 2, 1868.
    Mrs. Josephine E. P. Jernigan, wife of T. W. Jernigan, born September 24, 1837 died June 17, 1867.
    Lucy, daughter of A. G. and J. E. Jernigan, died November 18, 1879, age 11 years, 3 months, 19 days.
    Lunar Jernigan, born March 19, 1887 died July 17, 1887.
    Margaret A. Jernigan, wife of James Barry, born March 29, 1819 died November 12, 1859.

A. C. Jernigan, born March 1, 1837, died March 3, 1921 and Josephine Jernigan, born September 12, 1836 died February 3, 1920. (A double stone)
William T. Jernigan, born 1812 died January 16, 1878.
Thomas V. Barry, born January 28, 1844 died June 23, 1926.
Mary Ella Jernigan born November 27 1861 died August 11, 1880.
Jaun F., son of T. W. and J. E. Jernigan, born January 17, 1867 died October 12, 1867.
J. T. Jernigan, born March 3 1839 died March 18, 1892.
Martha, daughter of J. T. and M. Jernigan born April 10, 1875 died August 1, 1875.
Mildred, wife of J. T. Jernigan, born Sept. 8, 1851 died June 3, 1875.
Susan J., daughter of Braten and Mary Jernigan, wife of John H. Campbell, born January 15, 1844 died November 1 1871.
Braten Jernigan, born August 22, 1807 died May 18, 1866.
Mary G., wife of B. Jernigan, born August 22, 1808 died February 16 1874.
William Jernigan, born June 14, 1777 died March 31, 1865.
Lucy, wife of William Jernigan died December 14, 1844, age about 22 [?] years.
Louisa Deaubra Jones, born April 14, 1830 died September 16, 1905.
Captain Jas. L. Jones, born May 2, 1818 killed in Battle of Chicamauga, September 19, 1863.
Martha A. Rigen, born November 16, 1849 died January 30 1893.
H. H. Estes born Feb. 22, 1841 died April 17, 1900
Victoria, wife of J. M. Wright, born March 31, 1848 died December 26, 1920.

William Jernigan was born in the "mother State" of North Carolina and served in the Revolution. He probably came from Richmond County, North Carolina. There was a William Jernigan in that county, Fayette District, in 1790. There were also Jernigans in Robeson and Johnston Counties, North Carolina at the close of the Revolution. (Jasper Jernigan left a will in 1787 in Johnston County.) After the Revolution but before 1796, William Jernigan migrated to the Mero District where he chose a spot in Robertson County (then Old Tennessee) to seat his family. Even to this day the place is known as the Old Jernigan place. He married Margaret Evans before leaving his native state. To them were born seven sons and two daughters. One of their sons, born before they left North Carolina, 1778, was married in North Carolina and was the father of fifteen children. All but four died young. Those living to maturity were Celia, James A., S. B., and T. W. James A. Jernigan was born on 22 February 1814 and married Miss D. M. Strickland. To them were born Albert, Andrew J., James P., Jane, and Nancy A. Jernigan. James A. Jernigan settled on the place known by the old timers as the Wills farm. Two of Mr. and Mrs. J. A. Jernigan's sons were in the Civil War. One of them lost his right arm and, after the war, moved to Texas where he became a prominent citizen.

T. W. Jernigan was born in Robertson County on 23 March 1828. He was the son of William Jernigan, who was the son of William Jernigan. In January 1857, T. W. Jernigan married Josephine Roney, daughter of William Roney, and had Caroline, Thomas, Mary E., James, and one daughter who died in infancy. Mrs. Josephine Jernigan died in 1867, and Mr. Jernigan married as his second wife, Mary Swan, daughter of Joseph Swan. Caroline Jernigan married Mr. L. Durrett. Thomas Jernigan was in the merchandising business at Cross Plains. James Jernigan was a farmer associated with his father and operated a good 600 acre farm.

David Jernigan was a Methodist preacher. He was born in North Carolina about 1786. He came to Tennessee about 1805 and located two miles from Cross Plains where he lived until his death. His son, William M. Jernigan, was born in Robertson County in May 1817 and married four times, the first time in 1857. His first three wives died soon after their marriage. The fourth wife, Tavia Good, was the daughter of D. and Susan (Cartwright) Good. Her father lived to a ripe old age in Macon County, Tennessee where she was reared. The only child of Mr. and Mrs. Wm. M. Jernigan was named Harry. They were devout members of the Methodist Church as were practically all of the Jernigans of Robertson County.

Another member of the family to come to Robertson County was Elisha T. Jernigan, who was born in North Carolina. He came with his parents from his native state while quite young. He married Agnes Stone in Robertson County. He died on 10 May 1868, and his wife passed away on 12 September 1885. One of their nine children,

Elisha T. Jernigan, Jr. was born in January 1847 and married Malinda Wright in
1867. They became the parents of seven children. Mr. and Mrs. Elisha T. Jernigan, Jr. left Robertson County and moved to Obion County in West Tennessee in 1884.
There Mr. Jernigan purchased a farm of 150 acres. He became one of the most highly respected citizens of the county. Mrs. Malinda Jernigan died on 5 March 1885, and
in July of the same year, Mr. Jernigan returned to Robertson County where he married Molly Dyer. This family was prominent among the Methodists in Obion and
Robertson Counties.

North Carolina Census 1790.
North Carolina Wills by Grimes
Goodspeed's History of Tennessee. Robertson Co. 1886. p. 1162.
Goodspeed's History of Ohion Co., Tenn. 1886. p. 690.
Court Minutes of Robertson County. 1810-1826.
Cemetery Records. Jernigan-Jones Cemetery.

Lee - Chizenhall

Richard Lee deeded property for "Love and Affection and good will" for grandchildren Sinthy Chizenhall, Meredith Chizenhall, Elisha Chizenhall, Lee Chizenhall,
Tersa Chizenhall, Sary Chizenhall, Susannah Chizenhall, Rachel and Elizabeth Chizenhall, the children of his daughter Jane Lee Chizenhall. This record could be
called a deed, and yet it appears to be the will of the said Richard Lee. He mentioned a son-in-law, James Trice. He reserved certain property during his and his
wife Rachel's lifetime. The transaction bears the date April 21, 1814 and was executed in Montgomery County.

The Lee family evidently lived in the Palmyra section of the county, for John
Lee was appointed overseer of the road leading from Palmyra to the Dixon County
line by the court of 1809.

On 23 April 1812, Robert Prince, chairman of the county of Montgomery Court,
according to a court order dated April 1812, and according to the Act of the General
Assembly, bound John Lee, an orphan of Claborn Sims, deceased, to live with John
Lee as apprentice and to remain there until 21 years of age. Francis Sims was also
mentioned at the same time.

The Lee family came from Virginia about 1796-7, locating where Ashland City
now stands (now Cheatham County). Of this family, James M. Lee was born in what
is now Cheatham County in 1803 and married Lotsey D. Maddox. Mr. Lee was a
magistrate for more than twenty years and was a farmer. He died in 1870. Lotsey
D. Maddox, a native of Virginia, was born in 1809 and died in Cheatham County in
1884. Their son, John James Lee, was born near Ashland City, Cheatham County
on 4 February 1850. He began the study of law at Ashland City in the office of S.D.
Power in 1870 and the next year was admitted to the bar. He practiced law until 1876
when he was appointed deputy clerk of the county court, which position he held for
two years. In November 1878 he was appointed Clerk and Master of Chancery Court
of Cheatham County.

Miss Mary C. Wheless of Montgomery County was born on 15 May 1852 and became the wife of Judge Lee in December 1870. To them were born Joseph M., Adri-
an D., Fannie, and Lottie C. Lee. They were outstanding members of the Methodist
Church in Ashland City and attended the church at Clarksville and Springfield frequently.

Goodspeed's History of Cheatham Co., Tenn. 1886. p. 1373.
Montgomery Co., Tenn. Will Book 2, p. 192.
Montgomery Co., Tenn. Court Minutes 1808-1810, p. 160.
Montgomery Co., Tenn. Court Min. and Wills 1797-1810, p. 48.

Lockhart

The Lockharts of Montgomery County came from South Carolina. A Scotch-Irishman by the name of Lockert, or Lockhart, came to America with seven sons and settled in Pennsylvania shortly before the Revolutionary War broke out. Two of his sons, Aaron and another, disliked the northern country, so they moved to Chester County, South Carolina. Aaron and his brother were both in the Revolution. in which conflict Aaron attained the rank of Colonel, and his brother became a Captain. It is thought that the Captain's name was John. There is a will recorded in Chester County, S.C. for a John Lockert (Will Book 1, 1806-1810, Section 10, p. 27).

Aaron Lockert died in South Carolina in 1799, leaving a will. About 1814, his widow, Sarah, moved to Montgomery County, Tennessee, where some of her children had already settled. She prospered there and bought and operated a farm and mill, located seven miles from Clarksville. Mrs. Sarah Lockert was born in 1748 and died in 1834. She lies buried in the Old Riverview City Cemetery in Clarksville, at Second and Spring Streets, about one mile from the court house.

Eli Lockert, the son of Aaron Lockert, was born in 1794 on a plantation near the confluence of the Saluda and Broad Rivers in South Carolina. His father died when he was about four years of age. He came to Tennessee with his mother and assisted her in the operation of the farm and mill. He carried the flour meal and other produce to New Orleans in flat boats, making several successful trips. Growing tired of country life, he removed in 1822 or 1823 to Clarksville and bought the place on which William Daniel later lived. He also purchased land on the square, where the Franklin House now stands, and other property on the square opposite Mrs. Edler's old place.

At about the same time, Richard Cocke moved from Kentucky to Montgomery County, and soon afterwards, his cousin, Martha (or Amy) J. Lacey, daughter of Batt Lacy and Elizabeth Overton, came on a visit. Miss Amy, a noted beauty, remained in Tennessee for a year and then returned to her home near Bloomfield, Nelson County, Kentucky, where she and Mr. Lockert were married in 1823. They came to live in Clarksville where Franklin House stands. Mr. Lockert became deep in debt and lost almost all the property he had acquired in his earlier days. Eli Lockert died in Montgomery County in 1865. His wife, who was born in Kentucky, died in Montgomery County. They are both buried at the same place as Mrs. Sarah Lockert.

Mr. and Mrs. Eli Lockert were the parents of five children. Their son, Dr. Charles Lockert, married and had a son, Lacey Lockert, who became a druggist. James was another son of Mr. and Mrs. Eli Lockert. A daughter, Fannie, married Dr. S.M. Bemiss and moved to New Orleans. One of the daughters married H. M. Doak, and another married a Mr. Stone and had a son, David Stone, of Kentucky.

In the Lockert cemetery plot in the Riverview Cemetery, are tombstones with inscriptions as follows: Amy L. Lockert born 1800 died 1875, Margaret Brown born 1759 died 1837, and Maggie H. Lockert born 1857 died 1861. Dr. Charles H. Lockert, born 1831 died 1865, was also buried at the same place.

In 1816, the court of Montgomery ordered that Eli Lockart be overseer of the road from Poplar Sink to Capt. Jones and that Thomas Blackeney's hands, John Shelby's hands, Samuel Walker, Thomas Walker, William Walker, and others be bound to work said road.

James Lockert (Lockhart) came to Montgomery several years before the rest of the family.

James Lockhart, John Shelby, and Priscilla Jeffries were administrators of the estate of James Jeffries, deceased, 1816. The estate was presented to court at Clarksville on 16 April.

James Lockhart, Esqr. returned a list of taxable property in Capt. Jones' company for the year 1816.

James Lockert was a Justice of the Peace. He resigned on 21 October 1816. The

court of June 20, 1817 ordered that James Elliott be overseer of the road leading from
Fletcher's fork to the State line in the place of Cadwalleter Lucy and that the hands
be William Mann, Gildwell Killebrew, Priscilla Jeffer's hands, Bayliss E. Prince,
James Lockert, John Falkner, Cadwalleter Lucy, Joe Marr, and Jarrett McCarty
all work the road.

James Lockert was County Trustee of Montgomery County in 1817.

Moses Lockart was granted license to keep a house of entertainment in the town
of Clarksville. James Lockert and James Hambleton were on his bond and went security in 1816.

William Lockert (sometimes spelled Lochert), a native of South Carolina, came
to Tennessee and purchased a farm on the south side of Red River, six miles from
Clarksville. He married Elizabeth McFaddin, a native of Tennessee. Their son,
J.W. Lockart, was born in Montgomery County on 11 June 1828. At the age of eighteen years, young Lochert began to learn blacksmithing. In 1852, he married Sarepta Wilson, daughter of Samuel and Polly Wilson. They were the parents of William
S., Charles C., Hamilton E., and Clayton.

Early in 1861, J.W. Lockart raised a company of soldiers for the Confederate
service and was commissioned Captain of the same. The Company joined the 14th
Regiment Tennessee Infantry and was designated Company E. He was elected the
first Captain and soon after the first year's service, was promoted to Major of his
Regiment. A few months later, he was promoted to Lieutenant-colonel, in which capacity he served until the end of the war. Col. Lockert was in all the battles in which
his regiment was engaged, up to and including the Battle of Gettysburg, where he received a severe gunshot wound. He was captured and held prisoner until the end of
the conflict. He returned home and became a farmer, managing his own land on the
bank of Red River.

In 1864, Mrs. Sarepta Lockert died, and in 1867, Col. Lockert married Sarah
Miles, a native of Robertson County, daughter of Andrew and Kittie Miles. One child,
Rebel Lee Lockert, was born to them.

E. Arimenta Lockert, a sister of Colonel Lockhert, was born in 1832 and was
married in 1846 to William H. Rudolph who was born on 3 October 1824.

Aaron Lockert Will. Chester Co., S.C. Will Book 1, Sec. B, 1799-1802, p. 4.
Picturesque Clarksville Past and Present by Titus, 1887, p. 204.
Montgomery Co., Tenn. Court Minutes, 1816-1817, pp. 12, 27 ff., 49 ff., 93-95, 158.
Riverview Cemetery, near Clarksville, Montgomery Co., Tenn.
Rudolph Family Records - file, unpub. Whitley Collection.

Loggin

The name Loggin appears to have been variously spelled Loggan, Loggans, Lo-
gin, and Logan.

On 27 January 1801, William Loggins, a planter, was moving and appointed his
friend, Nathan Land, of the same place as attorney to receive money due him.

In November of the same year, William Loogan sold a slave to David Burney.
On 24 October 1802, William Loggan sold a slave to James Loggan for a consideration
of $200.00. William Loggans made a deed of gift of a slave to James Loggins.

In 1809, a William Loggans was in Maury County, Tennessee, for on 23 August,
he sold 640 acres of land situated on Flat Creek in said county to Andrew Mitchell.

Of the same family, Martin Loggins is shown to have had a bill of sale in Davidson County as early as 21 August 1794, at which time John and George M. Deadrick
of Davidson County and the Territory South of the Ohio, sold a negro woman slave to
Martin Loggins. On the same day, the same parties sold a negro man to William Loggins.

William Loggins is thought to have been from Virginia, probably the son of James Loggins of Charlotte County. He seems to have arrived in Nashville with (or about the same time as) General James Robertson, 1 January 1780. His name is frequently mentioned in the Cumberland Settlement from 1780 to 1788. He appears to have had lands in Lincoln County, Tennessee a little later. About 1805, he was joined by a brother, Reuben, and, about the same time, by another brother whose name was Dixon. There is evidence that William and Reuben Loggins lived in Tuscaloosa County, Alabama at one time.

The North Carolina Land Grants for Tennessee, Book A, p. 230, show William Loggins, Grant No. 357, a purchased grant for 640 acres of land, dated 8 June 1797, based on warrant No. 2117 in the Middle District.

The will of George Logan, dated 18 September 1814, was proved in November of the same year and recorded in Sumner County. In it, George Logan mentioned the name Alexander. Part of the will has been torn off, and the Alexander is believed to refer to a daughter, Peggy Alexander, whom he mentioned in the will at another place, because he did mention his son-in-law, Alexander. His wife was named Hester. He also had a daughter Moriah and a daughter Emeline, who was not of age 18 at the time. From the reading of the will, it is indicated that all of his children were under age.

Samuel Loggins was in Davidson County in 1788, for on 25 July of that year, he sold 150 acres of land on Sycamore Creek to James Mills.

Montgomery Co., Tenn. Record Book 1, p. 122.
Montgomery Co., Tenn. Will Book 1797-1810, pp. 155, 236.
Davidson Co., Tenn. Records.
Maury Co., Tenn. Records.
Tennessee Land Grants. State Archives, Nashville.

Lurton

Dr. L. Lurton, the son of a leading physician and native of Kentucky, was born in Scott County, Kentucky in 1820 and died in Tennessee in 1877. His wife, Sarah Harman was born in Scott County in 1824 and died in Tennessee in 1881. Her father, Zebulon Harman, a Virginian and a Methodist minister, was one of the early pioneers of Kentucky and organized what may have been the first Sabbath school in that state.

Horace H. Lurton, a banker of Clarksville, the son of Dr. L. and Sarah Lurton, was born in Campbell County, Kentucky on 26 February 1844. In 1861, he joined Col. Ben Hill's Regiment of troops and became Sergeant-major. He was discharged in February 1862 on account of ill health. In the latter part of the same year, he joined the Second Kentucky Regiment and, at the surrender of Fort Donelson, was sent as a prisoner-of-war to Camp Chase, Ohio where he succeeded in making his escape the following April. Two months later, he joined Dortch's Cavalry (afterwards Co. G, 3rd Kentucky Cavalry of Morgan's Brigade) and in July 1863, was again taken prisoner and remained such until the close of the war.

In September 1865, he entered the law department of Cumberland University and graduated from that school two years later. He was licensed to practice in 1867 and the following year became a law partner of the Honorable Gustavus A. Henry, the leading Whig orator and politician of his day. Ten years later he became associated with the Honorable James E. Bailey in the practice of law, and upon the resignation of the Honorable C. G. Smith as chancellor, he was appointed to fill that vacancy. At the election of 1876, he was chosen without opposition. In 1878, Judge Lurton became a law partner of C. G. Smith and gained wide spread reputation. Judge Lurton was married on 17 September 1867 to Fannie Owen, who was born in 1845. Their children were Leon O., Mary, and Horace H., Jr.

Mantlo

Little is known of the Mantlo family before they arrived in Robertson County, Tennessee. The name is so similar to that of the Croatoan Indian, Manteo, that it is only natural to wonder if the Mantlo family traces through Indian blood.

In 1933, there was an old Bible in Springfield, Tennessee, in the possession of a descendant, which contained the following entries:

Richard W. Mantlo, born May 11, 1779 Louisa County, Virginia.

Rebecca Mantlo, born 1772 married Moses Roe in 1792. Both lived in Louisa County, Virginia. She died 10 June 1825.

Martha Burnette Harris, born September 29, 1782 in Louisa County, Virginia.

Sylvanus T. Mantlo, son of Richard W. and Martha, born September 11, 1800.

Lewis F.M. Mantlo, born 12 June 1802 died September 28, 1815.

Amanda M. Mantlo, born 16 June 1804.

Sarah B. Mantlo, born 13 June 1807.

Robert D. Mantlo, born 22 April 1809.

Regenia Maria R. Mantlo, born 6 November 1811.

Richard D. Mantlo, born 8 December 1813.

Benjamin R. Mantlo, born 6 November 1816.

Martha Louisa Mantlo, born 13 April 1819.

Lynch T. Mantlo, born 18 March 1821.

Frances Cornelia C.W. Mantlo, born 10 January 1824, died 21 August same year.

William W. Mantlo, born September 7, 1826.

Richard W. Mantlo, married Martha Burnette Harris in 1799.

Augusta Mantlo, born September 29, 1832.

Lucretia Mantlo, born January 17, 1834.

Franklin Mantlo, born October 16, 1835.

Cornelius Mantlo, born October 4, 1839.

Cineinnatus Mantlo, born March 26, 1843.

Gustavus A.H. Mantlo, born October 11, 1847.

Albert G. Mantlo, born March 30, 1847.

Leander Mantlo, born 27 August 1849.

Licander Mantlo, born 27 August 1849.

Peter Mantlo, born 27 August 1853.

Mary Mantlo, died 7 April 1850.

A second old Bible in Springfield, Tennessee contained the following entries in 1933:

Franklin Mantlo, born October 16, 1835 married November 1, 1863, Emily A. Mantlo, born May 3, 1841 died July 19, 1889.

Mollie W. Mantlo, born July 3, 1866 died October 25, 1866.

James Irving Mantlo, born September 2, 1867 died October 3, 1868.

John R. Mantlo, born September 25, 1871 died October 5, 1890.

Mattie M. Mantlo, born Feby 18, 1875.

George F. Mantlo, born May 30, 1877.

Ann L. Mantlo, born December 5, 1879 died November 22, 1897.

Henry F. Holland, born October 16, 1895.

Vernita Gladys Holland, born February 28, 1900.

Winnyfield Holman died Oct. 1874.

James Calvin Holman died October 1876.

Sarah F. Powell died July 1872.

Emily A. Mantlo, mentioned above, was Emily A. Holman before her marriage to Franklin Mantlo.

Descendants of the Mantlo family of Robertson County are to be found around Clarksville, Springfield, and in the vicinity of Columbia, in Maury County, Tennessee.

Linch T. Mantlo married Sarah Zech in Robertson County, Tennessee on 21 October 1840.

Manuscripts, unpub. file on Montgomery Co., Tenn. in Whitley Collection.
Mantlo Fam. Notes - file unpub. Whitley Collection.

Matthews

Richard Matthews, Sr. left a will which is recorded in Robertson County, probated 11 October 1799. In it, he named his wife, Ellinor, and mentioned granddaughter Jane Matthews, granddaughter Ellinor Matthews, and sons John, Sampson, and William. The executors were Charles Colzen, Sampson Matthews, and Wm. Matthews.

William Matthews of Green Co., Kentucky sold his part of the land inherited from his father Richard to his brother, as recorded in Springfield.

Sampson Matthews was in Robertson County on 23 August 1806, when he witnessed a deed between Richard Kinney and James Sawyers.

Benjamin and Elisha Owens sold 100 acres of land in Robertson to Isham Matthews in 1796.

The grand jury of April 17, 1797 included John Matthews, Sampson Matthews, William Matthews, Elias Fort, William Lusk, Barton Coats, James Lockart, James Walker, Johnson Kilgore, and Jesse Martin.

Sampson Matthews of Robertson County sold land to John McShehee of Perquimans County, North Carolina on 29 January 1803.

The case of Mathew vs. Hughes, Admrs., a chancery suit begun 23 July 1767, Sampson and George Mathews orators, was recorded in Augusta County, Virginia in June 1769. James Hughes, deceased, made a will leaving his wife, named executrix, and three small children: Euphremia Hughes, Jane Hughes, and Mary Hughes. However, the wife refused to prove the will, and administration was granted to Sampson Matthews. James Hughes owned lots in Staunton, sold to him by William Preston by order of the county court, being property of the county. The wife and Euphremia Hughes answered for the children.

In the case of Sampson Matthews vs. John Archer, commissioners to North Carolina in 1768 took the deposition of Ephremia Wilson.

Regarding John Stewart vs. Sampson Matthews, in Chancery, Sampson Matthews was a brother-in-law of Randal Lockhart. There were no further details.

Sampson Matthews, a Magistrate for the County of Augusta, certified that he had administered the oath prescribed by law to be taken by a Governor, unto Thomas Enlson, Jr. Esq., on 19 June 1781.

At the request of Col. Sampson Matthews to disqualify him from serving as Senator at the end of the next session in and of the Assembly recommended by coroner.

See the case of Richard Mathews vs. Campbell. John Campbell was a merchant in Philadelphia in 1781 but of Drunmore Township, Lancaster County, Pennsylvania according to his 1788 letters. Campbell was related to Richard Mathews according to the answer of John Campbell, sworn to before John Kean of Frederick County on 6 August 1787. A letter from Campbell, dated 4 October 1781 in Philadelphia, says, "Mrs. Campbell joins me in love to you and Mrs. Mathews." A letter from Matthews to Campbell, dated New Glasgow, 10 October 1783, says, "My brother Joseph officer's certificate, the interest of which is punctually paid annually and warrants on the Treasury are almost the only circulating medium we have here. John Carclay is going to Georgia. Col. Geo. Matthews and a number of others, officers set off to Georgia about 15 Nov." Some years before 1788, Richard Mathews lived at New Glasgow in Rockingham County. A letter of Richard Mathews to John Campbell, dated New Glasgow, 11 Sept. 1781, so states.

MSS unpub. notes file, Matthews fam. Robertson & adjoining Counties, Whitley Coll. Robertson Co., Tenn. Deed Book 3, p 272; Deed Book A, p. 169.
Robertson Co., Tenn. Minute Book 1, pp. 20, 171; Will Book 1, p. 42.
Chalkley's Augusta Co., Va., Vol. 1, pp. 217, 359, 364, 389, 527.

Maulding

Among the earliest families to appear in the Red River settlement were the
Mauldings. They lived in Virginia as early as 1636. The name appears to be spelled
in various ways, most commonly: Maulding, Maulden, Moulding, Mouldin, Malding,
Mauldin, and Madlen.

According to the land patent office in Richmond, Virginia (patent book 1, pp.
400, 494) Captain John West, Knight, Governor of the Colony of Virginia, patented 400
acres of land in Nansemond County on 26 November 1636 to Francis Maulden, the
same being due him for the transportation, at his own expense, of eight persons into
the colony, including himself and his wife, Katherine. Apparently Francis Maulden
was the emigrant to Virginia. He seems to have located in King William County.

Richard Mauldin received 400 acres of land in Mattapony River in King William
County, Virginia on 15 July 1717. The patent by George I was signed by Alex. Spot-
wood, Governor (Ibid. Book 10, p. 320). He received 200 acres in King William
County from George I on 13 November 1720 (Ibid. Book 11, p. 72). He received 387
acres in King William County through two grants, near the same time, 9 July 1723
(Ibid. Book 12, p. 52). On 11 April 1752, he received 387 acres in Caroline County,
situated in St. Margaret's Parish (Ibid. Book 14, p. 400).

George the Second, etc. "Whereas there was granted unto John Mauldin Sept. 7,
1727, a certain tract of land situate on the Upper Fort of the Robinson River in Spotsylvania County, which said land is now in the county of Orange, containing 1000
acres and known as Mauldin Fork bordered by the lands of Richard Mauldin. The
said John Maulding failed to cultivate the same, and the said Richard Mauldin, hath
made suit to possession and to whom it is now granted, March 24, 1734." (Patent
Book 15, p. 455, Va. Land Office, Richmond.)

Three hundred acres more were granted to Richard Maulding on the same date
as above, as well as a grant for 1000 acres on the same day. Both were situated on
the Forked of the Rapidan, viz. what is now the Robinson River (Ibid., p. 406-8).

Richard Mauldin, Junior received 2000 acres in that part of Orange County called
Augusta, situated on Peaked Mountain, from Governor Goode on 30 January 1734
(Ibid. Book 20, p. 510).

Peaked Mountain lies west of Staunton in the out range of the Alleghanies. It can
be viewed plainly from the Chesapeake and Ohio Railway coaches between Staunton and
White Sulphur Springs.

It seems evident that there was a Richard Mauldin, Sr. and a Richard Mauldin,
Jr. and a John Mauldin at the same time and at the same place in Virginia.

According to a Bible record, Richard Maulding was born in 1765. James Maulding appears to have been a son of Richard Maulding, Jr. of Peaked Mountain in Augusta County, Virginia.

The name Mauldin appears in the 1790 census of Maryland in Cecil County, with
heads of families, Benjamin and William. In 1790, the name Mauldin does not appear
in the census of Virginia, but several by that name are found in North Carolina in
the first census reports. John, Joseph and two Thomas Mauldins were in Perquimans
County; Tucker Mauldin was in Dobbs County; and Richard Maulding was in Moore
County.

South Carolina had several Mauldings in 1790. Capt. Blake Maulden was in Pen-
dleton County, 96th District. Harris, Joab, and John Mauldin were in 96th District.
Laban Malding and Herod and Benjamine Malden were in Laurens County, 96th District.

Jacob Maulden left a will in Stafford County, dated 1704 (Torrence, Virginia
Wills).

On 3 April 1733, Richard Mauldin of St. Mark's Parish, Spotsylvania County,

deeded 1774 acres in St. Mark's Parish to Nicholas Battalie, Gent., of St. Mary's
Parish Caroline County. The land was part of a tract bought of Mauldin out of another tract granted to James Taylor, deceased, by patent, 21 July 1722. Jane, wife
of Richard Mauldin, acknowledged dower.

Richard Mauldin of St. Mark's Parish, Spotsylvania County, sold 100 acres of
land from the above mentioned tract to Zachariah Gibbs, 3 April 1733. Jane, wife
of Richard, acknowledged.

In another transaction on 3 April 1733, Richard Mauldin of St. Mark's Parish
transferred 184 acres in St. Mark's Parish to John Barnett. Jane, wife of Richard,
acknowledged.

William Edins of St. Mark's Parish deeded 248 acres in Spotsylvania to Richard
Mauldin and Nicholas, both of the same place. It represented the whole of a
patent granted to Edins on 28 September 1728. Rebecca, the wife of Wm. Edins,
acknowledged.

On 27 March 1734, Richard Mauldin of Spotsylvania deeded 120 acres in Spotsylvania to Edward Tinsley of King and Queen County, 2 April 1734. Jane, wife of Richard, acknowledged dower.

Richard Maudlin, Gent. of St. Mark's Parish, Spotsylvania deeded 300 acres
(part of Col. James Taylor's tract) to William Daniel, Jr. of St. Ann Parish, Caroline County, 30 March 1734.

James Taylor of King and Queen County sold 1000 acres of land to Richard Mauldin of King William County, 4 March 1727.

On 21 January 1734, Richard Mauldin was one of the Commissioners of Peace of
Orange County, Virginia.

The Mauldins were prominent in Augusta County, Virginia at the time that county was created, 21 May 1747. The following abstracts are loosely quoted from Chalkley's Chronicles of the Scotch-Irish Settlement in Virginia: Extracted from the Original Court Records of Augusta County, 1745-1800.
        William Burk deeded to Henry Downs, Gent., for 85 pounds current Virginia mo-
ney 350 acres of land on Shenandoah River at the upper end of 2000 acres that did
belong to Richard Malden near Peaked Mountain; corner to Paul Long; Selzer's line.
Witnessed by Adam Muller, Barbary Miller, Jno. Edwards.
        Philip Long, eldest son and heir-at-law of Paul Long, deceased, who was eldest
son and heir-at-law of Philip Long, deceased, of Frederick County, Virginia, to Jacob Campbell, 150 acres purchased by Philip the elder from Richard Mauldin and
deed recorded in Orange County, corner of Jacob Coger.
        Philip Long and Katherine, 15 May 1765 sold to Henry Long brother of said Paul,
and Uncle to said Philip Jr. for 100 pounds, 240 acres sold by Richard Mauldin, to
Philip Sr., 22 Sept. 1743 descended to Paul and from Paul to Philip Jr. on Shenandoah River. Henry Long's other land.
        Richard Mauldin had 2000 acres patented 30 June 1743 on Picked Mountain. Hen-
ry Long and Barbara to Henry Julias delivered Jacob Julias, 13 June 1788.
        Another patent of 2000 acres to Richard Mauldin, 30 June 1743 corner to Henry
Eulias [Julias].
        Mathias Long Vs. Henry Long, Ejectment, Rockingham County, August 29, 1797
Original patent to Richard Mauldin, Jr., for 2000 acres on Peaked Mountain south
River Shenandoah, 30 June 1743, 240 acres sold by Malden to Philip Lung surveyed
for Henry Lung, 1753. Copy of will of Henry Lung, dated 16 January 1779, probated
27 April 1779. Barbara was the widow. Eldest son, Henry, and other minor children.
Sons Paul, Mathew, and Nicholas. Grant to Henry Long, 100 acres on Shenandoah,
1768.

There is mention of a patent to Richard Malden, Jr. for 2000 acres of land in that
part of Orange designated to be called Augusta, Peaked Mountain, South River, dated
30 June 1743, and a patent to Henry Long for 100 acres in Augusta on Shenandoah, 20
September 1768. The will of Henry Long, Sr., farmer of Rockingham, dated 6 January 1779, recorded in Rockingham on 27 April 1779, mentions his wife Barbara and

infant children, eldest son Henry, Paul, Mathias, and Nicholas Long.

Nicholas Long and Melinda, his wife, of Green County, in the New Territory, conveyed to Mathias Long of Rockingham County, one third interest in 127 acres in Rockingham on South River bequeathed to Nicholas by his father Henry. The instrument was recorded in Rockingham in July 1794.

Henry Long and Elizabeth, his wife, of Rockingham, sold their interest in the land to Mathias Long on 22 July 1793.

On 7 October 1740, William (x) Malding witnessed a deed (Book C), dated 4 October 1740, from Hugh Sanders of St. George Parish, Spotsylvania, planter, to Decley Gatewood of said Parish and County. Hugh's wife was Catey.

Henry Goodloe of St. George Parish left a will, dated 25 November 1748, proved 2 May 1749, and witnessed by John Minor, Diana Goodloe, and John Wallace. In it he mentioned a granddaughter Elizabeth Maudlen and also Jane, wife of John Mauldin.

Elizabeth Goodloe, widow and relict of Henry, of Spotsylvania, left a will, dated 25 February 1750 and proved in 1761, in which she mentioned Elizabeth Maulden. Also, one of the legatees named was "grand-daughter" Elizabeth Maulden.

The North Carolina branch of the Mauldings first lived in Perquimans County. Grimes, in his North Carolina Wills, p. 243, lists Thomas Maudlin, September 16, 1758, January Court, 1759 — son Edmund, wife Sarah, brother Edmund Chancey — executors, John Clayton (father-in-law), Richard Clayton (brother-in-law), and Wm. Trumbull. The will of Ezekiel Mauldin, dated 25 March 1732 and proved 17 April 1732, mentions son Jeremiah, son Joshua, son James, and wife and executor Hannah. The last mentioned will bears the seal (coat-of-arms) of the Mauldin family. In 1775 in Perquimans County, Gideon Mauldin left a will in which there is mention of Zebree, Nathan, Samuel, Gideon, Mary, Deborah, Margaret, John, and Silas. These appear to have been the children of Gideon, the testator.

There is a deed between Richard Mauldin of Cumberland County, North Carolina and Thomas Beal of Chatham County which bears the date 1785. In Orange County, North Carolina, there is on record, a law suit in which James Sheperd had a conflict with Richard Maulding in 1765.

The Tennessee Mauldings scattered all over Middle and West Tennessee as well as into Western Kentucky. Each branch of the family had many children, some of whom married into some of the most prominent families of the Red River section. The men in the Mauldin family were keen sighted and made money rapidly. They acquired vast landed estates, moving with the progress of migration of their day. Ambrose Mauldin is found mentioned many times among the earliest records of Davidson, Montgomery, and Robertson Counties in Tennessee, and Logan County, Kentucky. In January 1784, Ambrose Mauldin made a motion to the court that Fanny Tramel (also spelled Trammel) be admitted to administer the estate of Nicholas Tramel and that she be granted letters accordingly.

On 16 May 1801, Ambrose Mauldin of Logan County, Kentucky deeded a tract of land in Sumner County to James Roaney of Sumner County, Tennessee for $1000.00.

West Mauldin was Sheriff of Logan County and was paid for traveling from Logan County to his home in Harrodsburg to compare polls for members of Congress on 15 November 1792. Martin Maulding was paid for the gubernatorial election in Logan County before 1798.

Molton Mauldin was granted a tract of land in Montgomery County, Tennessee: "May 20, 1790, North Carolina, Know ye that we and in consideration of the sum of 10 pounds for every hundred acres hereby granted paid into our treasury by Molton Maulden have given and granted and by these presents do give and grant unto the said Molton Mauldin a tract of land, containing 640 acres lying and being in the said County of Davidson on Sulphur Fork a branch of Red River, beginning at a hickory west 320 poles to a hickory and popular south 320 poles to a black oak and dogwood and hickory east 320 poles crossing Clay Lick Creek to an elm thence north 16 poles to the beginning as by the plat next to the grant doth appear together with all woods, waters, minerals, hereditaments and appurtenances to the said land belonging to or appertaining. To hold to the said Moulton Mauldin his heirs and assigns forever." By virtue of preemption, the land was surveyed for Molton Mauldin on 5 November 1785, Warrant No. 311, registered in Montgomery County, Tennessee in deed Book A, p. 32.

Mauldin's Station was built in 1780 or 1781 and was located one mile west of the present Louisville and Nashville pike and four miles east of Kilgore's Station or fort. It was the second settlement in what is now Robertson County, Kilgore's being the first. Mauldin's was near the present Kentucky-Tennessee line. Therefore the Mauldins were active both in Tennessee and Kentucky.

Richard Mauldin was born in 1765 and died on 24 May 1835 in Madison County, Tennessee. His wife, Elizabeth, was born in 1762 and died in 1810. They were the parents of Pressley, Daniel, Claiborne, James, and Sarah, who was born on 5 March 1791, died in 1840, and married Bartholomew G. Stewart.

As the settlement of West Tennessee continued and pushed forward toward the Mississippi, some of the Mauldings and their connections followed in the path of migration. They located in Madison, Haywood and other West Tennessee counties. In Madison County, we find them quite prominent. On 21 March 1823, Bartholomew G. Stewart appeared in court and made oath regarding one wolf scalp which was proved also by Richard Maulding.

Between 1821 and 1832, Pressley, Daniel, and Claiborne Maulding lived in Madison County. Daniel Mauldin was there as early as 1819, for in that year he made purchases from the estate sale of George Mizles, deceased.

Bartholomew G. Stewart was born on 5 January 1786 and died in Madison County in 1840. He had lived for a time in Hickman County, Tennessee. His wife, Sarah or Sally Maulding, was born in Tennessee in 1791   They were married on 19 March 1809, according to the family record in the possession of a descendant. Mr. and Mrs. Stewart were the parents of nine children: Elizabeth, who was born on 15 May 1810, died on 25 May 1835 (1855), and was married on 7 February 1828 to Joseph C. Snodgrass; Mary Stewart, who was born on 2 June 1812, died on 6 March 1878, and was married on 1 September 1831 to Silas Goodrich; Montgomery B., who was born on 14 January 1814 and died on 22 August 1847; Henry Taylor, who was born on 28 August 1815; Frances (called Franky), who was born on 9 October 1817, died on 18 February 1888, was married first on 9 February 1837 to John C. Jackson, and secondly to Alexander Tomlinson, who was born on 18 April 1818; Joseph Nepoleon, who was born on 19 December 1821, died on 24 December 1898, and was married on 29 April 1847 to Sarah E. Matthews, who was born on 14 February 1830 and died on 7 August 1904; William Arnold, who was born on 13 July 1824 and died on 19 December 1891; B.G., Jr., who was born on 16 August 18— and was married on 19 December 1839 to Mary A. Goodrich, who was born on 30 July 1821; and Robert Weakley, who was born on 21 November 1817 and died on 4 April 1849 in Haywood County, Tennessee.

Elizabeth Stewart and her husband, Joseph C. Snodgrass, were the parents of Adolphus E., who was born on 5 January 1831, and Elizabeth, who was born on 11 March 1833.

Franky Stewart and Alexander Tomlinson were the parents of seven children: Virginia Ann, who was born on 18 May 1840, died on 18 April 1875, and married a Mr. Holland (children: John N. and Fannie D.); Mary, who was born in 1856 and married James A. Tomlinson, her cousin; Lizzie, who was born in 1852, died in 1886, and married Jno. Webb Timberlake, Sr. (six children); Alemdia, who was born in 1850, died on 2 December 1885, and married Dr. Newt Williams (five children); Ida, who married William Long; Ike, who married Sally Pope; and John.

Joseph Nepoleon Bonapart Stewart and his wife, Sarah Evans Matthews, were the parents of fourteen children: Noble, who was born on 21 September 1848; Evin, who was born on 25 February 1866; Everett, who was born on 21 July 1850; Truly, who was born on 9 October 1851; Emma, who was born on 23 February 1853 in Mississippi; Nepolean, who was born on 29 November 1854; three babies, who were born on 6 May

1856 and died; Tobias, who was born on 20 June 1857 in Arkansas and died on 28 June 1907; Tally, who was born on 30 June 1859 in Arkansas; Blake, who was born on 15 February 1862 in Arkansas; Oren, who was born on 22 September 1864; and Rodney, who was born on 22 February 1869 in Mississippi. This family moved from Madison County, Tennessee to Mississippi, then to Arkansas, and later back to Mississippi.

Virginia County Records by Crozier, Spotsylvania County, pp. 11, 101, 124, 130, etc. (Deed Book B, 1729-34).
History of Orange County, Virginia by W.W. Scott, 1907, p. 26.
Chronicles of the Scotch-Irish Settlement in Virginia: Extracted from the Original Court Records of Augusta County, 1745-1800 by Chalkley, 1912, Vol. 3, pp. 259, 429, 531, 537 and Vol. 2, pp. 14, 269.
History of Russellville, Logan Co., Ky. by Finley.
Virginia County Records by Crozier, Spotsylvania County 1721-1800, pp. 9, 11, 153.
Cumberland County, North Carolina, Deed Book C, p. 442.
Orange County, North Carolina Court Minutes 1762-1766, p. 252.
Davidson County, Tennessee Minute Book A, p. 9.
Sumner County, Tennessee Deed Book 3, p. 153.
State Archives, General Expenditures 1792-1798. Kentucky Historical Society Register (1934) Vol. 32, pp. 54, 129.
Madison County, Tennessee Minute Book 1, 1821-1825, p. 129.
Madison County, Tennessee Tax List 1822-1832.

McCue

According to family records, Bridget McCue was born in Lancaster County, Pennsylvania on 23 December 1798 and died in Clarksville, Montgomery County, Tennessee on 12 September 1859. She is said to have married first a Mr. Ferrell and second Joseph Reynolds, who was born in County Antrim, Ireland and died in Montgomery County. Bridget had a daughter named Ellen Farrell or Ferrell who lived with her in Clarksville and was married there on 12 April 1853 to David Gorrell.

By her second husband, Bridget had a daughter, Mary Jane Reynolds, who was born at Germantown, Pennsylvania on 17 October 1836 and was married at Clarksville on 5 July 1855 to Stephen Oliver Wright Brandon.

D.A.R. Magazine, April 1949, p. 336.

McFarlen

William McFarlen, who was born on 20 May 1818, came from Granville County, North Carolina. He married Lucinda Jacobs, a native of Robertson County, who was born on 26 September 1819. Mr. McFarlen was a blacksmith by trade. After living in Robertson County for a while, he moved to Gibson County, West Tennessee where he died on 20 April 1873. His wife died there on 26 September 1881.

J.G. McFarlen, one of their eight children, was born on 13 May 1851 after the family had moved to Gibson County. On 1 December 1870, J.G. McFarlen married Miss M.F. Hart, a native of Madison County, Tennessee, who was born on 14 September 1854. Like his father, Mr. McFarlen was a blacksmith and a farmer. He was a member of the Cumberland Presbyterian Church and a Mason. Mr. and Mrs. J.G. McFarlen were the parents of four children: Robert N., William W., Abraham, and Malinda E.

Goodspeed's History of Gibson County, p. 899.
Unpublished Manuscripts file, McFadden Notes, Whitley Collection.

McGinnis

John S. McGinnis, a North Carolinian born in 1799, was one of the early cabinet makers in Montgomery County. He found an excellent field open in his trade in Montgomery, where he worked until 1841 when he moved to Dyer County. There he purchased 150 acres of land upon which he resided until his death in 1856. His wife, a native of Montgomery, died in Dyer County in 1859 at the age of forty-five. They had seven children, all born in Montgomery County.

John M. McGinnis, a son of Mr. and Mrs. John S. McGinnis, was born on 15 November 1840. Like his father, he was a cabinet maker, a trade in which he was engaged for many years.

In May 1861, John M. enlisted in Company K, 4th Tennessee Infantry, Confederate States Army and took an active part in the battle of Chickamauga, Franklin, and other engagements of minor importance. After serving some time, he had a severe attack of rheumatism and was compelled to return home. In the winter of 1862, he rejoined the army, serving in the 9th Tennessee Cavalry, and remained in the field on active duty until the surrender of Richmond. He was captured twice and taken to Alton, Illinois, where he was detained for seven days the first time and thirty days the second.

At the time of his entering service, he was residing in Dyer County. After the war, he returned to Dyersburg. On 22 December 1870, he wedded Miss Carrie Doughety, who was born in Nashville in 1852. They had six children: Mattie Bell (died young), Katie, Michael, Willie Lee (died on 12 July 1886, aged 7 years), Ethel May, and Lucy Alice.

After returning from the army, Mr. McGinnis went into the undertakers business in Dyersburg. He also operated a blacksmith shop. He was a Mason and a member of the Methodist Episcopal Church South.

Goodspeed's History of Tennessee, Dyer County, p. 1049.

Mitchell

Robert B. Mitchell was born in Kentucky on 5 January 1798, the son of an early settler. When Robert B. was about twelve years old, his father moved to Tennessee, locating in Robertson County. Young Robert was a fine mathematician and served as surveyor for many years. He lived from time to time in Robertson and Weakley Counties and, in 1849, settled in Obion County. Robert was a magistrate in Robertson County for twelve years and also served as postmaster at Mitchellville. He was of a progressive nature and owned the first portable thrasher in Robertson or Weakley Counties and the first steam mill in Weakley. He operated a distillery in Robertson for nearly thirty years and a water flouring mill.

Margaret C. Linebaugh was born in Russellville, Kentucky on 23 December 1815 and died in Robertson County on 15 April 1846. She married Robert B. Mitchell and was the mother of four children, the third of whom was Robert H. Mitchell.

Robert H. Mitchell was born in Robertson County on 8 January 1844. He was left without a mother at the age of two. His father was a great believer in education, so when young Robert was old enough, he was sent to school in Trenton where he attended Andrew College.

Robert H. Mitchell enlisted in the Confederate Army at the age of 18 years. He joined Company H, 7th Tennessee Cavalry under Colonel, later General, W.H. Jackson. He served during the entire war and was in thirty-three engagements. He was wounded at Sulphur Springs, Alabama and took the Oath of Allegiance at Paducah, Kentucky under the terms of the general surrender. On 23 November, Robert H. Mitchell married Margaret O. Major, daughter of Rev. J.M. Major. Mrs. Margaret O. Major Mitchell was born in Graves County, Kentucky on 18 July 1844 of a Methodist family. Mr. and Mrs. Mitchell were the parents of four children: Maggie J., who was born on 11 October 1866 and died on 14 October 1884; Bertie E., who was born on 3 August 1868 and graduated from Wesleyan Female Institute at Staunton, Virginia; Lizzie H., who was born on 27 December 1869; and Ophelia, who was born on 11 January 1872.

Goodspeed's History of Tennessee, 1886/7, Obion County, p. 964.
Mitchell Manuscripts file unpublished Whitley Collection.

Murphey - Murphy

George and Elizabeth Murphey are believed to have been the parents of at least one branch of the Murpheys in Robertson and Montgomery Counties. It is apparent that more than one family of the name appeared quite early in the Red River Country.

Little is known of the elder George. His son George, Junior was born about 1771 and died in 1867. He was evidently married twice. The name of his first wife is missing. By her he had two daughters, Elizabeth and Nancy. Nancy married Joshua Elliott. George Murphey, Jr. married, as his second wife, a Mrs. Raibourne (also spelled Ryburn), a widow whose maiden name was Huntley. Their children appear to have been Bob, Ired, Melinda, Tom, and Robert Huntley. Ired lost his life by falling off a footlog and drowning. Tom went to California, and nothing more is known of him. Robert Huntley was born in 1824, died in 1880, and became a Lieutenant Colonel in the Civil War. He served as Sheriff of the county and as County Court Clerk at various times. He was married twice, first to a Miss Greenfield and second to a Miss Braden. It is not known by which wife his children were born. They were: Robert H., Corn, Lizzie, Minnie, Georgia, Braden, and Samuel. Samuel was a captain in the army during the Phillipine Insurrection.

Robert Murphey, another son of George Murphey, Senior and his wife Elizabeth, married Polly Lawrence. He died in 1826. Their children were: Elizabeth, Elias, Joseph, Carroll, Rhoda, and Robert. Elizabeth married a Blankenship. Elias died in 1862, aged 60 years. Rhoda was born in 1824, died in 1862, and married a Mr. Whitehead. Robert, the younger, was born on 20 May 1827 and died on 17 March 1882.

There was at least one daughter of George, Sr. She married a Mitchell. It is believed that there were other children of Mr. and Mrs. George Murphey, Sr. The record is not clear.

Robert Murphey, a native of Virginia, came to Middle Tennessee quite early, remaining the rest of his life, which ended in 1823. His son, Robert, was born in 1824 and lived in Robertson County. He was married twice. His first wife, Rebecca Winters, was born the same year as her husband and died in 1859. Robert's second wife, Elizabeth Head, was living in 1886. Robert died on 2 April 1881.

J. C. Murphey, a prominent merchant of Adams Station, was born on 30 April 1851. He was the son of Robert, Junior and the grandson of Robert Murphey, Senior, the settler. In 1872, J C. and his brother W. C. Murphey established a general merchandise store in Adams Station. After one year, J. C. sold his interest and started to school. In 1876, he again opened a mercantile business at Adams Station. On 20 December 1876, he married Mettie Fuqua, who was born on 25 July 1856 in Robertson County, the daughter of Samuel and Eliza Fuqua. Mr. and Mrs. J. C. Murphey were members of the Methodist Episcopal Church.

About 1934, I found an old Bible in the possession of Mr. J. T. Murphey, living near White House. The following data was taken from it:
   J. C. Murphey and England married 15 February 1855 at the residence of J. F. England, by James Cook, esqr., Robertson County, Tennessee.
   J. C. Murphey was born January 21, 1824 and died October 31, 1907.
   Mary E. England was born July 4, 1836.
   James T. Murphey was born January 5, 1856.
   Eliza J. Murphey was born August 6, 1858.
   Laura A. Murphey was born March 10, 1861 married R. O. Chowning, September 1, 1881.

William E. Murphey was born June 19, 1863 died January 5, 1884.
John W. Murphey was born July 16, 1865 and died August 27, 1918.
Susan Ida Murphey was born August 7, 1868 married Charlie Covington, December 25, 1885.
Mary W. Murphey was born March 3, 1871 died May 22, 1895.
Seamore L. Murphey was born March 29, 1877.
Monroe Seal married Eliza J. Murphey, November 9, 1880.
Laura A. Treadway died September 17, 1900.
Ida Covington died February 28, 1907.
Mary Murphey died January 4, 1914.
Monroe Seals died August 29, 1914.
Emma White died March 2, 1924.

There was an E. G. Murphey who married Nancy G. Williams on 9 August 1841 in Robertson County. I have not discovered to which branch of the family he belongs.

Mathew Mills Murphey died in Montgomery County prior to 1818. He probably left only one child, also named Mathew Mills Murphey, who was left an orphan and was apprenticed by the court in 1818.

The Covingtons and the Murpheys intermarried. There was a Henry Covington in Robertson County before 1815, for in May of that year he wrote his will, proved the following August, in which he mentioned his wife, Winny to whom he left 350 acres of land. His sons appear to have been Leroy, Nicholas, Henry, Lawson, and the child "wife pregrant with." The daughters named in the will were Susanna, Elizabeth, Lucy, Polly, Charlotte, and Harriett. He also mentioned the property coming from his father's estate, amounting to about $400.00. His wife and Stephen Cole were named executrix and executor.

On 30 July 1800 in Montgomery County, Morgan Brown, Esqr., chairman of the county Court, and George Oldham, by order of the court, apprenticeshipped William Murphey, orphan of Patrick Murphey, deceased. At the same time, Margaret Murphey, an orphan of Patrick, deceased, was bound to Thomas Keefe.

Montgomery County, Tennessee Will Book A, pp. 83, 119.
Robertson County, Tennessee Will Book 1812-1818, p. 229.

Neblett

The Neblett and Roberts families did not live on Red River but were prominent in the settlement of Montgomery County. They came from Virginia to Old Tennessee County. The name Neblett is spelled in various ways, the most commonly used are: Noblett, Niblet, Niblett, Neblitt, and Noblin.

The first mention of the name which I have found in Virginia is of a Richard Neblitt who came over and settled in Accomac County. There is a record of a grant of land there for the transportation of persons to the colony, given in a certificate granted to Capt. Danl. Jenifer for eight hundred acres of land, rights underwritten: Rich. Barlock, Jno. Muncke, Marg. Martin, Enoch Rugge, John Luke, Rose Gossiss, Dorcas Grinsden, John Albon, Roger Wolford, Joseph Amos, Edw. Brockhouse, Geo Russell, James Ganson, Mary Presitly, Richard Niblett, and Hen. Peacke.

As early as 1636 there were persons by the name of Neblett in Virginia, but whether they are connected with Richard is not definitely determined. Richard Neblett's will is recorded in Accomack County, dated 16 March 1699 and proved 6 August 1700, in which he devised items to his wife Elizabeth (100 acres "I now live on"); to his granddaughter Margaret, daughter of Abraham Banks by Sarah, my daughter; to his grandsons, Richard and Burnell Neblett, sons of Burnell Neblett and his wife Margaret; and to his son-in-law (name not given).

The direct line of Nebletts herein is definitely known from Francis Neblett of Sussex County, Virginia. Francis and his wife, Elizabeth, were attendants of the Albemarle Parish Church in Sussex and Surry Counties at a very early date. The births of their six children are recorded in the parish register: John, born September 4, 1744; Elizabeth, born November 23, 1746; Sarah, born October 21, 1750; Sterling, born October 23 1753; John, born September 1, 1755; and Lucy, born November 21, 1758. In part of the entries, the name is spelled Niblet and in part, Neblet.

Old Free State by Landon C. Bell lists the children of Francis Neblett in a sketch of the Neblett family of Lunenburg County, Virginia, but Mr. Bell, in corresponding with me, stated that he could not find what became of the descendants at the time he compiled his book. His information was somewhat limited. There are a goodly number of deeds and other documentary material which refer to Francis Neblett in Lunenburg County, and the records are rich with data regarding the children and grandchildren of the progenitor of the family.

Francis Neblett apparently left no will. His inventory, dated 7 July 1778, with other documentary evidence, gives definite details as to the children.

Sterling Neblett, son of Francis and his wife, was married twice. first to Mary Chappell and second to Betsy Coleman. He appears, from the material in Sussex, to have owned land in that county and to have been a most prosperous citizen. His descendants are found scattered throughout Southside Virginia. His son, Dr. Sterling Neblett, became a prominent man in his day.

There were evidently two sons named John among the children of Francis Neblett. The first died in infancy or before his tenth birthday. In 1755, a second son was born, who was given the name of John. He became a local Methodist minister and resided in various places in Southside Virginia during his career in that state. He was married before 1779 to Susannah Hightower, daughter of William Hightower of Amelia County, Virginia who died in 1764, before his daughter reached maturity. Rev. John Neblett preached the Methodist doctrine in Lunenburg, Brunswick, and adjoining counties before migrating to Tennessee and locating in Montgomery County.

Elizabeth, daughter of Francis and Elizabeth Neblett, married Sterling Orgain. Their descendants are numerous in Montgomery and Stewart Counties in Tennessee.

Sarah Neblett, daughter of Francis and his wife, married a Mr. Allen. It is thought that many of their descendants located in the same community in Montgomery County, since many Allens are associated with the Nebletts at that place.

Lucy Neblett was unmarried at the time of her father Francis' inventory.

Rev. John Neblett lies buried in Montgomery County, Tennessee, and his tomb, although standing, is in a very delapidated condition. It is situated in a barn lot on the farm owned in 1933 by Mr. Andrew Lyons, near the Palmyra road nine miles south of Clarksville. The inscription on the tombstone shows that he was born on 10 September 1755 and died on 11 March 1830. These dates check with the family Bible of his son Edward, and with the entries in the Albemarle Parish Register. There is one other tomb standing in this same plot, that of Sarah Vance Neblett, who was born on 19 March 1790 and was married twice, first to Asahel Brunson, Jr. and second to John Neblett, Jr.

The Revolutionary manuscripts in Richmond, Virginia, in the State Archives, list John Noblock as having served from the 27th of February to the 27th of March 1781. It is well established that here the name has been spelled differently but that the record refers to John Neblett. The Lunenburg County records show the name so spelled in several transactions.

From the will of John Neblett and various other sources, we have the issue of Rev. John and Susannah Neblett as follows: Francis, who married a Miss Ferguson; Sterling, who married Miss Daly; Elizabeth, who married a Mr. Whitehead; Edward, who was born on 9 August 1779, died on 11 October 1845, and was married on 5 December 1805 to Ann H. Roberts; Lucy, who married Peter Givin; John Neblett, Jr., who was married first to Sarah Vance, the widow Brunson and second to a Miss Roberts; William, who married three times, first to Sally Love, second to Amey Williams, and third to Elizabeth Carney; Benjamin, who married twice, first to an unknown party and second to Miss McAllister; Susan, who married Richard H. Adams;

Stephen, who married Miss Allen; Mary, who married John Martin; Henry, who married Miss Bosley; Sally, who married Mr. Daly; and Daniel. (Mrs. Mary Bell Neblett Weaver gives Daniel as the son of Rev. John, but I find him mentioned in no other place.)

Edward Neblett, son of John and Susannah, was married on 5 December 1805 to Anna H., daughter of Samuel and Bedee Roberts of Prince Edward and Amelia Counties, Virginia and later of Montgomery County Tennessee. Anna H. was born on 9 December 1786 and died on 15 February 1875. After moving to Tennessee, Mr. and Mrs. Edward Neblett lived their entire lives in Montgomery County. Their home was located on the Salem Road about nine miles from Clarksville. In 1933, I visited the place. A portion of the old house was still standing and was owned by Mr. Boyd Neblett, a descendant.

Edward Neblett died in 1848, and his estate is a matter of record. The twelve children of Edward Neblett were: Samuel P., who was born on 10 November 1806 and died on 20 June 1813; James Hightower, who was born on 22 May 1808, died on 7 February 1875, was buried in the Neblett Graveyard, and was married on 2 December 1830 to Mary Thompson; David H., who was born on 22 January 1810 and died on 8 November 1813; Edward W., who was born on 8 April 1812 and died on 8 November 1815; Benjamin Roberts, who was born on 12 January 1814, was married first to Miss Hatcher, and was married second to Miss Barbee; Bedee Ann, who was born on 1 November 1815 and married Allen Neblett, a relative; John E., who was born on 31 July 1817 and was married first to Miss Browde and second to Miss Milligan; William Henry, who was born on 30 March 1819 and was married on 4 December 1846 to Sally Elizabeth Richardson; Edwin Cannon, who was born on 25 January 1821 and died unmarried; Susan Rebeccak, who was born on 6 June 1823; Virginia Emmely, who was born on 25 August 1825 and married W.D. Dillard; and Peter Pincham, who was born on 2 April 1828 and was married on 30 June 1857 to Laura A. Lowe.

William H. and Sally (Richardson) Neblett located in Dickson County, Tennessee. Their family consisted of nine children: Aurelia Augusta, who died young; Richard Henry, who died young; Julia Virginia, who was born on 20 August 1852, died on 3 July 1924, was buried in Greenwood Cemetery, Clarksville, and was married on 11 March 1885 to the Rev. Benjamin Hinton Johnson; Benjamin Edward; James Richardson, who married Miss Grimes; Mary Bell, who married Rev. J.L. Weaver (she was living at Charlotte, Dickson County, Tennessee in 1933); William Harrison, who married Maggie VanLear Stone; Sallie Adaline, who was unmarried and living at Charlotte, Dickson County in 1933; and John Walter, who married Elizabeth Marr.

Julia Virginia Neblett and her husband, Rev. Benjamin Hinton Johnson, were the parents of Sarah Richardson Johnson, who married Newman Cheek of Nashville, son of Joel Cheek, Sr., founder of the Maxwell House Coffee Company.

In 1933, I visited the Roberts graveyard, situated about eight miles from Clarksville on the Salem Road. There I found a number of tombstones:
James H. Roberts, born October 1, 1796 died September 17, 1870.
Polly, wife of Wm. H. Eldridge, daughter of Sterling and Ann Neblett, born November 22, 1806 died May 4, 1862.
Peter Laird, born October 25, 1792 died November 2, 1850.
Elizabeth, wife of James H. Neblett, born November 22, 1802 died June 13, 1859.
David Harrison, born March 16, 1774 died June 17, 1821.
Collin C. Roberts who departed this life April 9, 1812 age 22 years.
Peter P. Roberts, born February 3, 1788 died February 16, 1833 age 46 years.
Robert, husband of Lucy T. Edmondson, born November 23, 1813 died March 7, 1885.
John Thomas Richardson, born March 5, 1820 died October 30, 1897.
S.A. Laura Wyatt, wife of J.T. Richardson, born February 15, 1826 died October 24, 1872.
Sally Truitt Richardson, born Worcester County, Maryland, March 27, 1800 died December 22, 1875.
Katherine Clifton, born February 2, 1812 died December 1842.
Samuel Roberts departed this life July 15, 1822 age 63 years.
Bedee Roberts consort of Samuel Roberts, departed this life April 9, 1831 age 66 years.

Lucy Ann Edmondson, born September 23, 1824 died August 30, 1862.
James H. Richardson, born in Worcester County, Maryland, November 1833
died November 27, 1857.

William Neblett, son of Rev. John and Susannah Neblett, was first married on
18 April 1792 in Lunenburg County, Virginia to Sally Love. He was married the second time on 5 October 1803 in the same county to Amey Williams. After William
moved to Tennessee, he married his third wife, Elizabeth Norfleet Carney, an heir
of Richard Carney. William Neblett came to Montgomery with his father about 1806
or 1807. The Montgomery records mention him several times.

Lieutenant Richard Carney of Montgomery County is also called General Richard
Carney in the April court of 1833. He was formerly of Norfolk County, Virginia and
of Bertie and Halifax Counties, North Carolina. He died intestate. His heirs included William Neblett and his wife, Elizabeth Norfleet (Carney) Neblett, of Montgomery
County, Tennessee.

William Neblett died about 1851 in Montgomery County. Among the records there
is mention of some minor children including a daughter, Jane.

The issue of William Neblett and his wives were: William Neblett, who was born
on 10 April 1797 and married Miss Cheely; Sterling, who married and left a son Sterling and probably other children; John; Robert Caldwell, who was born in 1795 and
was married (probably in Mississippi) to Maria A. Powe; and Rebecca, who married
Dr. John W. Ussery.

The old Ussery farm is on the Salem road leading from Dickson Road only a few
miles from Clarksville. It is in the same section in which the Roberts, Edmundsons,
Nebletts, Lowes, and Hatchers lived.

John W. Ussery married Rebecca Neblett and located in Montgomery County.
Their son, John R. Ussery, was born on 3 July 1826 and married America Smith in
1853. Mr. and Mrs. John R. Ussery were the parents of Ida, George, William,
Sarah E., Maud H., Robert L., Edwin M., Eugene E., Frank, and Norman Ussery.
Mr. John R. Ussery was superintendent of the Sabbath-school of the Antioch Metho-
dist Episcopal Church for many years.

A number of the descendants of William Neblett are found in the vicinity of Na-
vasto, Texas.

Accomack County, Virginia Certificates and Rights 1663-1709, p. 50.
Accomack Tithables or Tax List 1663, 1695 by Stratton Nottingham, p. 4.
Virginia Historical and Genealogical Magazine Vol. 30 (1922) p. 343.
Wills and Administrations of Accomack Co., Va, 1663-1800 by Nottingham, pp. 24, 118.
Albemarle Parish Register, Sussex and Surry Counties, Va., Va. State Library,
    Richmond, Va.
Vestry Book, Cumberland Parish, Lunenburg Co., Va. by Landon C. Bell, p. 511.
Old Free State by Landon C. Bell, Vol. 2, pp. 319-327.
Sunlight on the Southside, Lunenburg County by Bell (1931).
Lunenburg Co., Va. Will Book 3, p. 9 (Inventory of Francis Neblett).
Lunenburg Co., Va. deeds. Book 15, p. 249; Book 18, pp. 171, 172; Book 19, p. 214;
    Book 20, p. 53; Book 21, pp. 16, 17, 18.
Goodspeed's History of Tennessee, Montgomery Co., p. 111 (1886).
Montgomery County, Tennessee deeds. Book D, p. 57.
Montgomery County, Tennessee Will Book B, pp. 240, 444; Will Book C, p. 322;
    Will Book D, pp. 89, 99; Will Book K p. 1; Will Book 1826-7, p. 225 and nume-
    rous other references.
Montgomery County, Tennessee Record Book H, pp. 3, 74, 635; Record Book F,
    p. 117 (1826).
Amelia County, Virginia Will Book 2, p. 73 (Will of Wm. Hightower 1764).
Neblett Family Bibles, copies in Whitley files.
Cemetery records copied by Whitley and in Whitley files.
Neblett Family Manuscripts by Whitley, filed in the National D.A.R. Library, D.C.
Virginia Soldiers of 1776 by Burgess p. 603.
Roberts Bible records, in Whitley collection.

Misc. family records in Whitley collection.
Hist. of Neblett Fam. of Montgomery Co., Tenn. by E. Whitley. (Unpublished manuscript in Whitley Collection)

Newsom

Green B. Newsom was born in 1796 and came to Tennessee when he was young. He was in the War of 1812 and filled the position of regimental quartermaster. He was a teacher by profession and taught in Columbia, Franklin, and Lebanon. He died in 1859. His wife, Malinda Dickerson, a native of Tennessee, was born in 1798 and died in 1845.

Their son, Dr. W. R. Newsom, a physician of McLemoresville, was born in Springfield on 14 February 1831. He was educated at Andrew's College, Trenton, graduating in 1856. He then entered the University of Nashville and graduated in 1859. In 1858 he was elected Trustee of Bethel College, which position he held until 1872 when the school moved to McKenzie.

On 7 July 1859, Dr Newsom married Mrs. M A. Roach, a native of Jackson, Tennessee, born in 1825, the daughter of Jones Newsom. She had a daughter Eliza J. by her former husband the Rev. J. N. Roach, the founder of Bethel College and its first president until his death in 1852.

Two children blessed the home of Dr. and Mrs. Newsom: W. R. and N. D. The latter became a physician.
_____
Goodspeed's History of Tennessee, Carroll County, p. 876.

Outlaw

The Outlaws came from North Carolina to Red River. They were a large and prominent family. They had close relatives in East Tennessee. This name is found among the earliest settlers in Montgomery, Robertson, and Sumner Counties.

A motion made by the court of April 16, 1816 ordered that Prudence Outlaw be appointed guardian to George, Sally, Leorance, Right, John, Prudence, and Louise Outlaw.

The will of Wright Outlaw, 28 June 1815, mentions sons Wright W., John A., George R.; wife Purdence; and daughters Sally V., Levinia M., Prudence, and Louisa L. Outlaw.

On 18 March 1809, David Outlaw, for love and affection, gave a negro slave to his son William Watkins Outlaw.

On 17 April 1813, Wright Outlaw conveyed certain negro slaves for "love and affection" toward his children which he had by his wife, Prudence, namely George Reddie Outlaw, Sally V. Outlaw, Lavinia M. A. Outlaw, Wright W. Outlaw, John A. Outlaw, and Prudence Outlaw.

John C. Outlaw was reared in Bertie County North Carolina. He was married in his native state in 1808 to Cynthia Redit. They came to Sumner County in 1812. Mr. and Mrs. Outlaw were the parents of thirteen children: M. R. T., Emily E., H. H., Julia A., Almeria, Nathaniel S., J. C., Drew A., J. F., Sallie, Cynthia, Lycurgus, and John J. John J. Outlaw died on 5 August 1845.

Mr. John C. Outlaw followed the carpenters trade. He was a member of the Baptist Church for a number of years. In 1832, he left Sumner County and went to Obion County where he died. Mrs. Cynthia Outlaw died in Obion in 1845. She was a strict member of the Methodist Episcopal Church for more than forty years.

J. F. Outlaw, one of the sons of John C. Outlaw, was born on 24 June 1821 while the family resided in Sumner. After a fair education in the country schools, he went to Mississippi to study medicine under Dr. Cocke. He graduated from the Medical University of Louisville, Kentucky in 1848. He began the practice of medicine in Montgomery County. On 21 September 1848, Dr. Outlaw married Agnes H. Smith of Montgomery. Dr. and Mrs. Outlaw had three children, two of whom died in infancy. They were members of the Methodist Episcopal Church.

George and Frances (Belotte) Outlaw, both natives of North Carolina, were reared in their native state and came to Montgomery County in 1804. George was in the War of 1812. He was born in 1780 and died in 1843. Frances Belotte was reared an orphan and died in 1869. Mr. and Mrs. George Outlaw were the parents of a dozen children. One of their children, George W., was born on 20 March 1823 in Montgomery County. In March 1880, George W. Outlaw moved to Danville and built a large brick house and ran a hotel He also had an interest in the merchantile business of S. W. Jelly & Co. At one time, George W. owned upwards of 2000 acres of land. He married Elizabeth Outlaw in 1849, and they had three children. Their daughter, Elmira T., became the wife of J. S. West of Houston County Tennessee. Mrs. Elizabeth Outlaw died in 1854. Mr. Outlaw was married a second time in 1858 to Mrs. Anne (Tomlinson) Kelly. They had Mattie D., Eddie, Johnnie J., and Roda D. Outlaw.

Quite a few Outlaws are buried in Hopewell cemetery at Hopewell Baptist Church in the Second Civil District, about eight miles from Springfield.

Montgomery County, Tennessee Will Book 1, pp. 143 158; Will Book 2 p. 134.
Montgomery Court Minutes 1816-1817, p. 12.
Goodspeed's History of Montgomery County, p. 1082 (1886).
Goodspeed's History of Houston Co., Tenn., p. 1397 (1886).

Payne

The Payne family figured conspicuously in the early history of the United States. The family claims relationship with Robert Treet Payne, one of the Signers of the Declaration of Independence. William Payne was in the Indian Wars and also in the War of 1812.

William Payne was born in North Carolina and emigrated to Tennessee when he was young In 1821 or 1822, he married Margarette Brown of North Carolina. They had six children: Greenwood, William, R. S., Melvina, Pattie, and Priscilla. Mr. Payne was a farmer. He died at his residence in Sumner County in 1861. His wife died in 1850.

R. S. Payne, son of William and Margarette, was born on 12 October 1823 in Davidson County, Tennessee. He was a farmer and lived in Montgomery County. In 1852, R. S. married Susan Gold or Golden of Montgomery County, a member of the Methodist Episcopal Church. They had nine children, six of whom were living in 1886: Eugene, Earnest, Maud, Blanche, Ida, and Anna.

When the war with Mexico broke out in 1846, Mr. R. S. Payne enlisted in Campbell's First Tennessee Regiment under General Taylor and participated in all the engagements of the war. During the Civil War, he was appointed captain of the Home Guards and was in the battles of Shiloh, Vicksburg, and Baton Rouge. After the war, he returned to his farm.

On 30 Januay 1871, Mrs. Susan Payne died. In 1876, Mr. Payne married his second wife, Narcissa Bryant. They had two children. One died in infancy, and the other, Robert, became a well known and highly respected citizen. The Paynes were instrumental in church work in the Methodist churches of the county.

The name Greenwood in this family indicates a close connection with the Paynes of Davidson County, some of whom were also in Sumner County.

There were at least three Josiah Paynes in Middle Tennessee by 1810. They have frequently been confused as one and the same.

One Josiah Payne of West Nottingham Township, Chester County, Pennsylvania, was a Quaker, 1716-1744. He moved to Fawn Township, York County, Pennsylvania about 1744. Some of the next generation went to Pittsburgh, Pennsylvania, while others went southwest to Hopewell, Berkeley County, Virginia and later to Washington County, Tennessee, arriving there prior to 1800. The children of this Josiah Payne appear to have been Josiah, born in 1716; Matthew, born in 1719; George, born in 1728; and Joseph, born in 1730.

Josiah Payne, the son of Josiah Payne of Chester County, Pennsylvania, died in Blount County, Tennessee, 1823-25. His wife was named Sarah. He lived in Nottingham Township until 1751. Quaker Minutes say, "He lived far distant."

Matthew Payne, son of Josiah Payne of Chester County, Pennsylvania, married twice. The name of his first wife is not known. His second wife was Sarah (widow Green). This family came early to Davidson County, Tennessee. In 1787, Matthew sold land on Clinch River, Russell County, Virginia to his son Josiah. He was on Mansker's Creek in Middle Tennessee in December 1784. Josiah Payne executed a power of attorney in Davidson County to Matthew Payne. There are other documents which clearly establish the connection of Josiah and Matthew Payne in Middle Tennessee. Matthew Payne's children were Matthew, Jr., Josiah, George, and John. Matthew Payne, Jr. married Amelia Cooper on 17 June 1791. John Payne married Polly Cave.

Josiah Payne, son of Matthew of Davidson County, lived in Davidson County in 1813, leaving a will. His wife, Sarah Green, was the daughter of Lewis Green of Washington County, Tennessee, who died in 1781. Sarah died by 1823. Her inventory is a matter of record. Her estate, reported by Flowers McGregor, was divided among the following: Ann Payne, wife of Gideon Pillow; Greenwood Payne, who was born in 1789 and was married on 14 December 1805 in Davidson County to Martha (called Patsy) Payne; Spencer Payne; Squires Payne, who was married in 1815 to Sallie Hannah; William Payne, who was married on 10 June 1796 to Elizabeth Payne; Zachariah; George W. Payne, who was born in 1793 and was married on 4 August 1812 to Mary Iredell; and Minerva Payne, who was married in 1807 to Robert Booth.

The deposition of Sarah Payne, dated 1785 in Davidson County, sets out that she was a step-daughter of Josiah Payne; her mother-in-law was Mary, wife of Matthew Payne, Sr.; her brother-in-law was George, son of Matthew Payne; Zachariah Payne was her brother. It further states, "Lewis Green went to the Cumberland settlement," as did also her "husbands family," Matthew Payne, Sr.'s wife and children. The deposition infers that John Payne was a brother-in-law.

George Payne, the son of Josiah Payne of Chester County Pennsylvania, died in Virginia in 1801. He had a son named Jesse, who was born at Hopewell, Virginia and died in Washington County, Tennessee, 1823-34.

Joseph Payne, the fourth son of Josiah Payne of Chester County, Pennsylvania, was born in 1730 and died in Smith County, Tennessee, leaving a will, dated 1822. His wife was named Martha, and their children were: Molly, who married a Mr. Stewart; Joseph; William; George; and Matthew, who married a Miss Rowland.

Another Payne family in Middle Tennessee was from Goochland County, Virginia.

George Payne died in Virginia in 1744. He married Mary Woodson in 1705, and they were the parents of Josias (often taken for Josiah), George, Jr., John, Judith, and Robert Payne.

Josias, the son of George and Mary, was born in 1705, died in December 1785, and was referred to as of Pittsylvania County, Virginia. In 1732, he married Ann Fleming. Their children were: William, who was born in 1733 and was married first in 1755 to Mary Barrett and second to Susanna; George, who was born in 1734, received land from his father in 1757, was High Sheriff in 1759, and was married in 1754 to Agatha George of Goochland; Josias, Jr., who was born in 1735, died in 1804 in

Davidson County, Tennessee, was commissioned a Lieutenant in 1779, and was married first in 1755 to Elizabeth Fleming; Anna, who was born in 1743 and was married in 1763 to William Harrison; Susanna, who was born in 1745 and was married in 1761 to William Heale; Agnes, who was born in 1740 and married William Mitchell; John, who was born in 1740, died in 1783 in Philadelphia, was clerk of Cedar Creek Monthly Meeting, moved from Goochland to Hanover County, Virginia, then to North Carolina, then to Philadelphia, and was married about 1761 to Mary Coles.

George Payne, the son of Josias and Ann, married Agatha George. They were the parents of Jesse, who was married in 1779 to Sally Lewis; Anne; Mary Watts; Susanna Woodson; and William George Payne.

Josias Payne, Jr. and his wife, Elizabeth Fleming, had children: Tarleton, who was born in 1758 and married Elizabeth Winston; Sally, who was born in 1759; Josias, who was born on 25 April 1761; William, who was born in 1764; Fleming, who was born in 1766; Charles F., who was born in 1768; and Elizabeth C., who was born in 1769 and married first to John Blakemore and second to Henry Bradford, who was born in 1758 and died in 1815.

After Elizabeth Fleming Payne died, Josias, Jr. was married in 1789 in Davidson County, Tennessee to Mary Barnett, by whom he became the father of Anne Payne, not the Ann Payne who married Gideon Pillow.

Descendants of these Paynes scattered all over Middle and West Tennessee.

The will of one John Payne, Sr., dated 9 October 1805, in Robertson County, Tennessee, proved April 1807, states, "To George Pool cow and calf;" "To John Chewning money I lent him for his land;" "To Augustine Cook;" "To Josiah Payne, books," etc.; "Daughter Clary Cook my BIG BIBLE;" "Granddaughter Cloe Cook;" "Son Josiah Payne and Geo. Pool executors."

Goodspeed's History of Tennessee, Montgomery County, 1886, p. 1083.
Davidson County, Tennessee Deed Book A, p. 217; Deed Book B, pp. 159, 168, 215; Deed Book D, pp. 147, 513; Deed Book F, pp. 42, 256, 297; Deed Book K, p. 185; Deed Book Q, pp. 729, 770, 771; Deed Book R, p. 83; Deed Book S, p. 575; Deed Book U, pp. 15, 469, 634; Deed Book X, pp. 318, 573; Deed Book Y, pp. 96, 377.
Davidson County, Tennessee Will Book 1, p. 53; Will Book 7, p. 51; Will Book 1805-16, pp. 253, 257, 318, 363; Will Book 1821-26, p. 284.
Smith County, Tennessee Will Book 1, p. 178.
Robertson County Will Book 1, p. 233.

Penrice

Francis Penrice was in Montgomery County quite early. He was made constable by the Court of September 26, 1808. About 1810, he was appointed guardian of Jency Channell, James Channell, and Henry Channell, infants, heirs of Elisha Channell, deceased, all under 21 years of age.

A marriage contract was perfected between Joseph Penrice and Sally Allen on 9 January 1811. Sally made her mark to the agreement. The agreement sets out that at Sally's death, her property was to revert to her four daughters, Lucy Allen, Elizabeth Epps, Sally Mathew, and Patsey Allen. Thus we are informed that Sally Allen was a widow at the time she married Joseph Penrice.

William Penrice, Francis Penrice, and Robert Penrice posted bond on the administration of the estate of Joseph Penrice, deceased, 20 April 1812.

Montgomery County Court Minutes, 1808-1810, pp. 136, 316.
Montgomery County Will Book, 1811-1818, pp. 20, 44.

Pitt - Pitts

The earliest information I have of the Pitt family, dates back to Nicholas Pitt of Blandford, Dorset, who was living in Blandford in 1545. The arms were "Sable, a fess chequey argent and azure between three bezants."

William Pitt, son and heir of Nicholas, married Helena, daughter of James Haveland of Isle of Guernsey.

The Reverend John Pitt, eldest son of John and Priscilla, was born in 1641 and died in 1672. He was Rector of Blanford, St. Mary's. His wife, Sarah, was the daughter of John Jay. The second son of John and Sarah Pitt was Thomas, afterwards Governor of Fort St. George, East Indies. While there, he became possessor of the famous Pitt diamond which founded the fortunes of the family. He died in 1726, and his wife, Jane, daughter of James Innes, died in 1727.

Robert Pitt of Coconnor was the son of Thomas. Robert married Harriett, the third sister of John Villiers, Earl of Grandison, and represented the famous borough of Old Sarum in Parliament. He died in 1727, and his wife died in 1736. They were the parents of William Pitt, Earl of Chatham, Prime Minister of England, who was born in 1708, died in 1778, and is buried in Westminster Abbey.

The Pitts of Isle of Wight County, Virginia descend through Thomas Pitt, second son of William Pitt and his wife, Helena Haveland. Thomas was a merchant of Bristol and Chamberlain of the city. He made his will as Thomas Pitt, merchant of Bristol, on 1 May 1613, and the same was probated on 5 August 1613. In his will, he mentioned son William; Robert Pitt, the son of his son William; William and Robert, sons of his son William; daughter Alice Northan; daughter Anne Merrick; son-in-law John Merrick; Anne's three children: Ann Waters, Mary Waters, and Robert Merrick; daughter Mary Owen; son-in-law Robert Owen; daughter Mary's three children: Robert, Mary, and Jane Owen; cousin Matthew, Maryland alderman; kinsman William Pitt; kinsman Edward Batten; friend Samuel Davies; daughters-in-law Mary Marlowe, Cicely Gunning, and Elizabeth Batterten; and kinsman Mary Robinson. He named his son William Pitt as executor of the will. His wife was evidently married before, for he mentioned three daughters-in-law (step-daughters) in his will.

The above William Pitt, son of Thomas and executor of the will, was also a merchant and ship owner. He was engaged in the Turkey and East Indies trade. He died in 1624, and his will was that of a wealthy man. It is abstracted as follows: William Pitt of Bristol, Merchant, 12 March 1622, proved 4 February 1624; wife Mary; son William; son Robert; son Henry; son Thomas; daughter Mary Pitt; mentions a house built by his father Thomas Pitt; mentions nephew Robert Merrick; daughter Ann Pitt; daughter Mary Pitt; daughter Martha; "To my son William my best Turkey ring which was my great grandfather's Mr. Roger Cookes;" brother-in-law Richard Davis; sister Mary Davis; sister Marlowe and sister Sunning; cousin Mary Robinson; sister Alice Knight and brother Knight; cousin William Pitt, draper; and cousin Nicholas Pekes.

Mrs. Mary Pitt made her will on 25 November 1634, and her son Robert was executor. The children of William and Mary Pitt were William; Mary, who married Andrew Newell; Thomas; Anne; Maud, who married Dr. Richard Russell; Martha; Col. Robert Pitt of Isle of Wight, Virginia; and Captain Henry Pitt of Isle of Wight, who married Anne, widow of Robert Watson about 1655.

The Pitts of southeast and southern Virginia are believed to be the progenitors of the Sumner and Robertson County, Tennessee Pitts, through the branch which went into North Carolina and later into the Western Country.

The earliest record of these Tennessee Pitt or Pitts families, who are represented in Robertson and Sumner, appears in Sumner County where Lunsford Pitt left a will in 1813. He must have been a very old man when he died, for it is known that he had grandchildren and probably great-grandchildren at the time of his death. In his will, he stated, "I have long since given unto my beloved son Burton H. Pitts one horse" and "in August or September last lend him and his brother Henry Pitts and Lunsford C. Pitts for benefit of my said son Burton H. Pitts children, a negro woman," etc. "I will and bequeath to the children of my said son Burton and then their heirs namely to his son Lunsford Pitt and son George Gains Pitts and his daughter Rebecca Pitts," etc. "Further I have lately paid Henry Fetherson interest." He goes on to say, "I have long since given to my beloved daughter Lucy Featherson one negro girl," and "I have long since given to my beloved daughter Fanny Black one feather bed." The next item in the will sets out, "I have long since given to my beloved son Henry Pitts one roan horse." The will also provides for "beloved daughter Betsy Yandall;" "grandson Lunsford Pitts Yandall;" daughter Judith Yandall; the heirs of son Burton H. Pitts; and son Lunsford Pitts. Trusty friends Samuel P. Black, Charles Fetherson, Wilson Yandall and John Yandell were to be executors. Charles Featherstone was the acting executor of Lunsford Pitt. The will was recorded in Sumner County and also in "Wise County, Kentucky."

Henry Pitt, aged 75 years, was a pensioner living in Sumner County in 1840. Thus he was born about 1765.

In the census of 1820 for Sumner County, there are five Pitt or Pitts families enumerated: John, Winifred, Henry, William, and Robert.

The Sumner inventories and settlements, 1808-1821, mention Richard Strother, Lunsford Pitt and Stephen Pitt heirs, also James Hollis. In his will, Richard Strother, Sumner County, named his wife, Susannah, and daughter, Susannah Pitt, along with others.

Susannah Strother married John Pitt on 12 March 1808, and William Pitt married Jane Robertson in 1813. Both these marriages were in Sumner County.

The Pitts and Yandall (Yandell) families were closely associated and intermarried. It is believed that they came to Tennessee together. William, Samuel, William and David Yandell were in Sumner County by 1820.

It has been established that Lunsford Pitt was in Sumner County by 1805 and probably much earlier. In that year, he purchased land from Fanny Sanders and sold land to William Yandell. William Yandell's land was on Drakes Creek of Barren River. In September 1807, Lunsford Pitt sold land adjoining Pitts and Yandell to Wilson Yandell, the same being witnessed by Samuel P. Black. There are numerous deeds in Sumner in which Lunsford Pitt, probably the younger, and the Yandells are associated.

The Blacks, Yandalls, and some of the Pitts went to Rutherford County, Tennessee to live. They were in Smith County for a short time before going to Rutherford and settling prior to 1830.

Wilson Yandell, mentioned in the will of Lunsford Pitts in 1813, was a physician and was honored with a degree from Johns Hopkins University for his skill in medicine without ever having attended a lecture. This branch of the family has produced a number of outstanding physicians of Tennessee and Kentucky.

All the Yandells I have found left Rutherford County, moving to Kentucky and Gibson County, West Tennessee.

Wilson Yandell died in Rutherford, leaving a will, dated 8 November 1826 and proved in January 1828. In it, he made provisions for his son, Dr. Lunsford P. Yandell, whom he had educated abroad at a cost of $1400.00 and to whom he had provided a shop at great expense; a daughter Eliza Becton; wife Betsy Yandell; and son-in-law Dr. Frederick E. Becton. He named his affectionate brother John Yandell as one of his executors. Sons Henry and Burton Yandell were to receive good English educations.

John Yandell married Judith Pitts (or Pitt) on 13 March 1809 in Sumner County.

Joseph Pitts' will was recorded in Robertson County on 25 January 1818. In it, his wife, Patsy, is named. Milly and Joseph Pitts were to divide with their mother. His wife and Bartley Pitts and George Barber were executors. The will was proved in 1819.

There is also a division of land of Joseph Pitt, dated 12 February 1820. Lot No. 1 was drawn by James Lynn; Lot No. 2, by Bartley Pitts; Lot No. 3, by Major Gregory; Lot No. 4, by Joseph Pitts; and Lot No. 5, by Robert Gordon.

The Pitt burying ground is located on a farm on the Cross Plains road, owned by Thomas Pitt of Springfield, Robertson County. There I learned that J. Pitt died in 1837. Wilson Pitt was born on 20 March 1814 and died on 14 April 1880. William Pitt was born on 5 August 1807 and died on 25 August 1877. Mary, wife of G. W. Walton, Sr. was born on 5 May 1837 and died on 21 May 1862. She was the daughter of William and Nancy Pitt. Jeremiah Pitt was born on 18 July 1811 and died on 28 January 1855. Mrs. Susan Pitt, wife of Jeremiah Pitt, was born in March 1817 and died on 1 June 1855. Nancy Pitt, wife of William Pitt, was born on 6 December 1813 and died on 27 December 1889. Mary A., wife of Wilson Pitt, was born on 22 February 1824 and died on 14 May 1883. Allie Pitt, wife of W. H. Huddleston, was born on 17 November 1841 and died on 10 September 1885. Alonzo Pitt was born on 5 May 1856 and died on 4 October 1909.

The Yandalls who died in Rutherford County are buried on the banks of Stone's River, on land adjoining where my great-grandfather lived.

O. G. and Elizabeth E. (Yandall) Pitt, both natives of the Bluegrass State (Kentucky), lived in Montgomery County for over forty years. Their son, Guthridge L. Pitt, was born in Montgomery County, Tennessee on 15 July 1860.

The Rev. Fountain Pitts, the venerable Methodist minister, who preached in both Tennessee and Kentucky, descends from the above family.

There are some members of the family buried in the Gideon Cemetery at Gideon Church, twelve miles from Springfield, in the 12th Civil District of the county of Robertson. At the same place are found the graves and tombstones of such families as Hollis, Shannon, Crawford, Sanders, Warren, Parker, Adams, Cole, Morgan, Gober, Drake, Darke, Pitt, Coke, Cook, Jones, Darrah, Grubbs, Williams, Mayes, Hinkle, Webster, England, and others associated with the Pitts. The oldest of these tombstone inscriptions are:
Peter Warren born March 2, 1797 died October 21, 1877.
Lovina, wife of W. M. Darrah, born May 18, 1823 died January 29, 1896.
W. M. Darrah born August 27, 1823 died August 9, 1901
Mary Frances England born April 30, 1838 died January 27, 1910.
Martha T. Williams born August 17, 1834 died February 18, 1911.
Elizabeth, wife of Peter Warren, born January 19, 1838 died May 22, 1881.

History of Isle of Wight County, Virginia by Boddie.
Sumner County, Tennessee Will Book 1, p. 168.
Sumner County Census 1820.
Sumner County Census 1820.
Robertson County Census 1820.
Revolutionary Pension list, Robertson and Sumner Counties, 1840.
Sumner County, Tennessee Marriages, Book 1.
Sumner County, Tennessee Deed Book 4, p. 206 and other Sumner County deeds.
Rutherford County, Tennessee Will Book 7, pp. 284-5.
Smith County, Tennessee Deeds.
Gibson County, Tennessee records, deeds, marriages, wills.
Robertson County Will Book 3, 1819-21, p. 65.
Unpublished Pitt family data, Whitley Collection.

Poston

John Hammill Poston, probably the first merchant in Clarksville, arrived about 1806 or 1807 with a stock of goods furnished by a wealthy merchant of Virginia, named William King. Poston was born in Charles County, Maryland on 15 April 1786. He was the son of William Poston, whose wife was Sarah Hammill. William's father, John Poston, emigrated from London to Charles County, Maryland. At one time, John H. Poston owned a large portion of Clarksville and considerable real estate in Mississippi. His home was known as Poston's Spring, and later as the Ice factory.

He owned all the land on Red River between the two bridges and up to Main Street in Clarksville.

In a suit before the Court of April 24, 1817, John Smith, Poston and his wife Nancy, William B. Nelson, Robert Nelson, George B. Nelson, Adaline Nelson, Horatio Nelson, and the heirs of Robert Nelson, deceased were involved regarding the estate of the deceased Nelson.

John H. Poston married Nancy L. Nelson. They were the parents of thirteen children. Hugh Hammill Poston of Nashville was one of their sons, and Benjamin F. Poston of Clarksville was another. Richard and William Poston, two other sons, settled in Memphis. They were lawyers. One of the daughters of Mr. and Mrs. J. H. Poston married John F. Couts, as his first wife. All the family that I have learned about were Methodist. Mr. Poston died at the old brick homestead on 2 October 1848.

The court of 1809 for Montgomery County proved a deed from John H. Poston, conveying Lot No. 58 in the town. In the same year, Poston was made a Justice of the Peace and was among those to receive the list of taxable property for the year 1809.

Montgomery County Court Minutes, 1808-1810, pp. 158, 161; 1816-1817, p. 206.
Picturesque Clarksville by Titus, 1887, p. 274.

Power

S. D. Power, Sr. was born in North Carolina in 1799, and his wife, Martha Ward, was born in the same state in 1798. The Power family arrived in Davidson County, Tennessee in 1820. In 1824, they moved to that part of Montgomery County which is now Cheatham County. S. D. Power died in January 1832, and his wife, Martha, died in February 1867.

Samuel D. Power, the son of S. D. and Martha Power, was born in Montgomery County on 7 October 1841. S. D. Power, Jr. was educated in the country schools and at Wirt College in Sumner County. When he was eighteen years of age, he began to teach school. In 1866, Mr. Power moved to Clarksville and went into the grocery business. At the same time, he worked at the trade of carpenter. He was elected recorder of Clarksville in 1868 and held office for one term. During his term as recorder, he studied law. In 1869, he was admitted to the Clarksville bar and in 1870 moved to Ashland City, where he began the practice of his profession. He was soon made County Attorney for that county. He was a prominent attorney of Montgomery and Cheatham Counties. In 1853, he married his first wife, Fredonia M. Major, who died in 1857. His second wife was Sallie A. Duff. Mr. and Mrs. Power were active members of the Methodist Episcopal Church in their community.

Priestley

Sarah Priestley's will, executed on 13 February 1829, was recorded in Davidson County, Tennessee on 14 May 1829. In the will, Mrs. Priestley devised certain property to her daughter Sarah Ann Hoover and husband, and called Philip Hoover, her son-in-law. She also mentioned sons Philander and Joseph, to whom she left specific bequests. She also made provision for the children of her son, Dr. Jno. Priestly, deceased. The executors named were sons James, Joseph, and Philander.

Dr. John Priestley was of English descent and was born in Davidson County, North Carolina (now Tennessee) in 1790. He studied medicine under Dr. Butler, after which he finished his education in Philadelphia. After graduation, Dr. Priestley practiced in Sumner and Robertson Counties. He died in the prime of life in Robertson County in 1824. His widow married Beverley Nelson about 1829 and died in Haywood County, Tennessee in 1872.

John T. Priestley, one of the four children of Dr. and Mrs. Priestley, was born at Springfield, Robertson County, in 1824. He acquired a good education and, on 12 November 1846, married Eliza B. Williams, who was born in 1828, the daughter of John M. and Ann Williams of Rutherford County.

John T. and Eliza B. Priestley had ten children: William, James E., John M., Robert Walter, Joseph L., Anna, Eveline (who married Wm. C. Deuberry), Emmett D., Thomas P., and one other child.

In 1848, Mr. J. T. Priestley moved to Weakley County, where he purchased 170 acres of land. He added to it from time to time until he possessed about 850 acres. He was a Mason and stood high in the minds of Weakley citizens.

Davidson County, Tennessee Will Book 8, p. 303.
Goodspeed's History of Tennessee, Weakley County, p. 1012.
Manuscripts unpublished file, Notes on Priestley family in Whitley Collection.

Prince

It would be impossible to write about the early settlement of Red River without referring to the Prince family in numerous ways.

Some historians have stated that the Penrice and Prince families of the Red River Country are one and the same. I have found little or no evidence to prove this.

There is a power of attorney from Thomas Suter and Nancy, his wife, for Molly, Nancy Channell to Richard Whitehead to receive in the State of Georgia or elsewhere, all money which may have descended to him and her from Matthew Channell of the State of Georgia, now deceased, July 16, 1816.

Of course I can see from the above, where Penrice and Prince could be confused in the old script. I have seen a transcript of this record, and the name Prince is not mentioned therein so far as I can find.

Priscilla Jeffries and Bander E. Prince were appointed guardians of Nathaniel Jeffries, Sally S. Jeffries, Lucinda Jeffries, Evan and Priscilla Jeffries, Jr., infant heirs-at-law of James Jeffries.

The following would indicate a connection between the Prince and Pennington families: Joseph Woolfork was appointed guardian of Francis Prince Pennington, heir of John Pennington, deceased.

The inventory of James House, deceased, shows that he possessed little. However, among the items listed was a pair of saddle bays. Was he a Methodist? Rachel House, Brian Whitefield, and Robert Prince were bound as trustees for the children. Rachel House was appointed guardian of the orphans of James House in 1797.

Montgomery County Court Minutes, 1816-1818, pp. 52, 96, 287.
Montgomery County Will Book, 1797-1810, pp. 17, 19.

Rice

Rev. J. G. Rice, Sr. was born in Lincoln County, Tennessee on 17 January 1830. When he was about three years old, he moved with his parents to Lauderdale County, Alabama, where he remained for two years. Then, with his widowed mother, he moved to Warren County, Tennessee, where he lived until he was twenty-one years of age. In October 1850, he joined the Tennessee Conference of the Methodist Episcopal Church and was appointed to travel the Richland Circuit in Giles County, Tennessee. At the next session of Conference, in 1851, he was appointed to the Savannah Circuit in Hardin County. At the Conference held in Pulaski in October 1852, he was ordained by Bishop Soule and appointed to Frankfort Circuit in Alabama. At that time, the Tennessee Conference embraced part of North Alabama.

The next year, the Conference ordained Rev. Rice as an Elder and sent him to the Winchester Station. He was later removed to the Sparta Station. On 24 January 1856, while at Sparta, he married Josephine D. Plumer of Nashville. The following May, he was transferred to Kansas as a Missionary and stationed at Atchinson. He attended the Conference held for Kansas in September 1856. He was then sent to the Lecompton Station, where he remained for twelve years. In the winter of 1856-7, Rev. Rice was Chaplain of the Kansas Legislature. In September 1857, he returned to the Tennessee Conference and was appointed to the Franklin circuit. After that time, he served in Hickory Creek, Berford, Antioch, Duck River, Chapel Hill, Spring Hill, and Cedar Hill Circuits. In 1886, he was pastor of the Antioch Circuit in Montgomery County. Rev. Rice was a member of the Tennessee Conference for about forty years. He had a large family.

There was another Rice family in Robertson County much earlier than the date of arrival of Rev. J. G. Rice.

The Honorable James E. Rice was a native of Robertson County, born on 17 September 1815. His parents lived near Adairville, Kentucky, yet they were actually in Robertson County, Tennessee. After reaching manhood, James E. Rice moved to Springfield where he studied law. When he was about thirty-four years of age, he moved to Dover, Stewart County. There he joined in partnership with Judge Herbert S. Kimble and began the practice of law. On 7 May 1844, Judge Rice married Julia A. Dawson at the home of her parents in Montgomery County. It was at Judge Rice's home in Dover that the historical surrender of Buckner to Grant was made. Espousing the cause of the South, Mr. Rice gave his all and followed the flag until there was no flag to follow. After the war, he returned to Montgomery and permanently located in Clarksville. He became attorney general of the Judicial Circuit, and at the first general election for county officers, he was a successful candidate for Circuit Judge. After being re-elected, he was succeeded by Judge Stark. Judge Rice then returned to the practice of law, which he continued until his death on 2 March 1884. His son, James W. Rice, was born in 1851 and became a leading attorney at Dover.

James W. Rice attended Lexington University, entered law school at Lebanon, Tennessee in 1871, and graduated the next year. After graduation, he practiced law in Clarksville until 1875, then moved to Dover and became associated with the firm of Brandon and Rice. Colonel Brandon retired in 1880, and Mr. Rice took over. James W. Rice married Ellen D. Quarles, daughter of Judge J. M. Quarles.

Goodspeed's History of Tennessee, Stewart County, 1886, p. 1313.
Manuscripts data file, Rice in Whitley Collection, unpublished.

Richardson

Robert Richardson died in Maryland in 1688. His wife was named Susannah. Charles Richardson died in 1720 in the same colony. Robert Richardson died in 1788, and his son, Robert, left a will in 1793 in which he named his wife, Sarah. Their children were Sarah, Sipporah, and Benjamin. Benjamine was born about 1770 and is listed in the census of 1800 in Boguottonorton Hundred, Worcester County. He married Catharine Bratton on 26 June 1798.

The evidence in hand is not conclusive, but there is strong indication that Benjamine and Catherine were the parents of Benjamin T. Richardson who married Sally Truitt on 21 April 1819. He died in Maryland on 11 December 1835. Sally Truitt was the daughter of John Killam Truitt, whose wife was Mary Teague. Sally was born on 27 March 1800 and died on 22 December 1875. She came to Montgomery County, Tennessee as a widow, bringing her children: Julia A., who married Louis (Lewis) Lowe in May 1856; Mary E., who married Henry C. Wyatt; James, who died unmarried on 24 November 1857; William Bishop, who married Josie Dudley; John T., who married Sarah A. L. Wyatt on 13 May 1845; and Sally Eliza, who married William H. Neblett on 4 December 1845.

These Richardsons came from Snow Hill, Maryland. They came with Mr. Stewart who founded the Southern Cumberland Presbyterian School at Clarksville. Most of the family which came to Montgomery County, Tennessee are buried in the Neblett and Roberts graveyards or in the cemetery at Clarksville.

John Killiam Truitt was the son of William Truitt of Worcester County, Md.

Cemetery Records, Montgomery County, Tennessee
Worcester County, Maryland Misc. records on file in the Court House at Snow Hill, Md. by E. Whitley.
Family records of Neblett, Roberts, Richardson families, Whitley Collection, unpub.

Ryburn

The Ryburns were in the county by 1799, for on 23 July of that year, John Hogan sold some negro slaves to Thomas Rawbourne for $700.00. The name was also spelled Rabourne and Raybourn in the same record.

The will of Thomas Raibourne bears the date 14 August 1799 and was proved soon thereafter. In it, Thomas named his wife, Rebecca, son John, and daughter Candice. He also mentioned the children of Coly (Howel Adams), Thomas Layton, Benjamine Berryman, and the "child wife Rachel is great with." His wife was to have 200 acres of land on which the house stood. In one place he called his wife, Rebecca, but in another place, he referred to her as Rachel. His wife and Howell Adams and John Stewart were named as executors.

There is a bond whereby Nancy Ryburn and William Ryburn, son, are referred to as administrators of Washington Ryburn, deceased. The same returned to court in January 1803. At the 1802/3 court of Montgomery County, 25 April 1803, George Murphy was made guardian of Hiram and Washington Ryburn, orphans of Washington Ryburn, deceased.

In July of the same year, Robert Nelson and Nicholas Conrad were nominated and appointed guardians of Celey, Noah Howell, Benjamine, and William Raybourn, orphans of Thomas Rayburn, deceased.

The Court of April 16, 1816 proved a deed of conveyance from William Ryburn, Sr. to Matthew Ryburn and William Ryburn, Junr. for 13 3/4 acres of land.

On 9 July 1815, William Ryburn, Sr. conveyed a negro to his son William J. Ryburn. At the same time, William Ryburn, Sr. conveyed a negro slave to his daughter Elizabeth P. Wilson and her lawful husband Sanford Wilson.

Green Rayburn was born on 25 June 1794 and died on 10 September 1862. Jennett Rayburn was born on 1 January 1802 and died on 8 March 1868. It seems quite probable that Jennett was the wife of Green Rayburn, as they are buried in adjoining graves in Montgomery County.

There was a relationship between the Raybourns and the Murpheys about the time they came to Red River.

Montgomery County Will Book, 1797-1810, pp. 36, 37, 172, 187, 206; 1811-1818, pp. 268, 269.
Montgomery County Court Minutes 1816-1817, p. 5.

Squires

On 22 October 1810, Thomas Harlbert of Roxberry, Litchfield County, Connecticut; Martha Atwell of Roxberry; Ruth Rand of Southberry, New Haven County, widow and relict of Michael Rand, late of Southberry, deceased; Susannah Canfield of Southberry, widow and relict of Nathaniel Canfield of the same place, deceased; and John Atwell, the husband of Martha, constituted and appointed Squire Harlbert of Roxberry, attorney to settle the estate of Solomon Squire, formerly of Roxberry, but late of Springfield in Robertson County, Tennessee.

On 7 December 1810, Patience Ward of Scipio, Cayuga County, New York, formerly Patience Squires of Roxberry, Litchfield County, Connecticut, widow, appointed Tines Ward of Scipio as attorney to settle the estate in Robertson County, Tennessee of Solomon Squires, deceased.

Solomon Squires, Heber Squires, James Squires, Ann Bill, Rodah Candler, and Hulda Redd were all of the town of Charlotte, Chillender County, Vermont, and Abner Squires was of Arlington, Bennington County, Vermont. Ann, Rhodah, and Hulda were sisters of Heber, James, and Abner Squires. They appointed Solomon Squires, attorney to receive and settle in Robertson County, Tennessee, 29 May 1810.

There is also a power of attorney in which Solomon Squires gives authority to Zenos Ward to settle and receive for the "Heirs of James Squires," brother of Solomon Squires, deceased, 9 July 1810.

A deposition of Gideon and Seth Hunt of Roxberry, Connecticut states that they were acquainted with the family to which Solomon Squires, deceased, formerly of Roxberry, but late of Springfield, belonged. The deponents said that they were well acquainted with James Squires, formerly of Roxberry but afterwards of Vermont, the oldest brother of Solomon. The deponents had heard that James died many years ago leaving children, but they did not know the number. The deponents also knew Olive Harlbert, a sister of Solomon and wife of Gideon Harlbert. They said that Olive had died years since and had left an only child named Thomas Harlbert, who lived in Roxberry. The deponents were well acquainted with them all. They said that they also knew Patience Squires, a sister of Solomon and wife of Tines Ward. The deponents believed that she still lived in Cayuga, New York. The deponents also knew Ruth Squires, another sister of Solomon and the widow of Michael Hand. She was then living in Southberry, New Haven County. The deponents also knew Lamur, another sister of Solomon and wife of John Heines of Southberry. They said that Lamur died, leaving two daughters: Susannah, who was still living, the widow of Nathaniel Canfield, and Elizabeth, who had married Elijah Bucham, who resided in Danbury, Joinfield County. The deponents also knew Martha Squires, a sister of Solomon and wife of John Atwell. Martha and John were both living in Roxberry.

I have found no evidence that descendants of this family are yet to be found in Robertson County, Tennessee.

Robertson County, Tennessee Will Book 1, pp. 352, 355, 356, 360, 361.

Stark - Primm

James Stark came to Virginia from Scotland. His son, Jeremiah Stark, was born and reared in Stafford County, Virginia. John Stark, the son of Jeremiah, was born in Stafford County on 22 November 1748. He died in Sumner County, Tennessee on 16 May 1814. His wife, Sarah English, was born in King George County, Virginia on 4 July 1749 and died in Sumner County, Tennessee on 28 September 1820. They were married in King George County on 4 January 1769 by the Rev. Brook. Their son, John Stark, was born on 8 May 1788 and married Margaret Primm, who was born on 1 October 1787. They were married by the Rev. Mr. Arnet on 6 September 1812. The children of John and Margaret Stark were: James, who was born on 30 January 1814 and died in infancy; Elizabeth, who was born on 30 January 1815 and died on 10 October 1846; Lydia, who was born on 16 April 1816; Joseph Carter; Louisa, who was born on 30 May 1819; Sarah Ann, who was born on 4 September 1820; Mary Magdalene, who was born on 25 December 1821; Evelina, who was born on 8 April 1823; John Primm, who was born on 29 August 1824; Margaret Malvina, who was born on 19 April 1826; and Catherine Hansbrough, who was born on 13 January 1828.

James Stark died on 5 December 1814. Lydia Stark Judd died on 28 July 1848. Evalina Stark died on 23 February 1843. Elizabeth Stark died on 10 October 1846. Louisa Stark Patton died on 12 August 1852. Margaret Malvina Stark died on 28 July

1853. Catherine Stark died on 18 July 1821. Joseph Carter Stark died on 6 November 1890. John Primm Stark died on 1 April 1891. Mary Stark Cartwright died on 19 August 1891. Sarah Ann Stark Cunningham died on 4 December 1908. John Stark died on 28 May 1862. Margaret Primm (consort of John) died on 10 December 1872. John W. Judd, Sr. was born on 8 February 1812 and died on 20 February 1861. Thomas Carter Judd was born on 4 April 1837. John Walters Judd was born on 6 September 1839.

Jeremiah Stark was a Lieutenant in King George's War. John Stark, the son of Jeremiah, was a Captain in the Revolutionary War and saw four years of service.

The will of John Stark, dated 5 April 1814, is recorded in Sumner County, Tennessee. In it, John Stark devised a negro whom "I bought of Mr. Bailey Washington in Virginia" to his son Thornton. He left other property to his son John. Other bequests were made to wife Sarah, daughters Prudence and Charlotte and daughter Elizabeth Shelton. A daughter, Tarver Bryan, was mentioned as well. He also mentioned sons Jeremiah and Alexander. He made a bequest to his grandson John, son of Alexander.

One of the most beloved and outstanding judges of the county was the Honorable Joseph Carter Stark. He was born on 30 December 1817 in Sumner County, the son of John and Margaret (Primm) Stark. Joseph C. Stark studied law under the Honorable John J. White for eighteen months then went to Springfield and entered into practice. In 1848, he married Lamiza A. Baird, a native of Tennessee, born in 1829. Their children were: Charles B., a lawyer of St. Louis, Missouri; Joseph C., Jr. of Texas; John L., a lawyer in Springfield with his father; Robert L.; Felix J.; and Annie L. Stark. In 1844, Judge Stark was appointed Clerk and Master of Chancery Court of Robertson County, an office which he held until 1851 when he was elected to the State Senate, representing Robertson and Montgomery Counties. In 1878, he was elected Judge of the Tenth Judicial Circuit Court. The Starks were mostly Methodist.

The Primm family Bible is in the possession of a descendant at Goodlettsville, Tennessee, near the Robertson-Davidson line. It gives the following information:
John Primm born May 17, 1750.
Elizabeth Hansborough, wife of John Primm, born January 5, 1761, married in 1777.
William Primm born September 1, 1778.
John Primm born July 25, 1780.
Thomas Primm born May 11, 1782.
James Primm born September 10, 1783.
Peter Primm born June 25, 1785.
Daniel Primm born June 23, 1786.
Margaret Primm born October 1, 1787.
Enoch Primm born December 15, 1788.
Elijah Primm born March 8, 1790.
Silar Primm born January 6, 1792.
Betsy Primm born May 26, 1793.
Parmenas Primm born October 26, 1794.
Joseph Primm born September 8, 1795.
Levi Primm born June 11, 1797.
Aram Primm born July 28, 1799.
Lydia Primm born January 31, 1801.
Mary Primm born July 31, 1804.
The Bible states that John Primm and his wife were natives of Stafford County, Virginia and migrated to St. Clair County, Illinois with their family, except the oldest son, William. John Primm was a Captain at Yorktown and served seven years in the Revolution.

At Owens Chapel Methodist Church, in the 10th Civil District of the County, about eight miles from Springfield, is a cemetery containing many tombstones and inscriptions. Space will not permit all of them to be recounted, but the following are of interest:
William Winfield, born 1836 died May 26, 1897.
E. E. Shannon, born April 15, 1862 died January 12, 1929.

Rosa Shannon, December 18, 1879. [Does not say whether birth or death.]
Wm. Crocket, born July 31, 1846 died January 9, 1906.
Wm. Spurlock, born April 4, 1867 died December 1, 1928.
Martha Ellen Covington, born November 2, 1874 died July 2, 1937 and [on the
same stone] Eugene LeRoy Covington, born February 19, 1869.
W. A. Owen, born October 4, 1870 died December 20, 1924 and D. T. Owen, born
September 14, 1881. [a double stone]
    Thomas A. Cook 1866-1923 and Sarah B. Cook 1868-1931. [another double stone]
    D. B. Stark, born December 20, 1849 died November 20, 1919.
    Bonie Owen, wife of W. A. Owen, born October 2, 1866 died May 4, 1915.
    W. B. Owen, born March 25, 1843 died July 4, 1895.
    Albert Polk Owen, born February 18, 1945 died June 12, 1876.
    J. C. Murphey, born September 30, 1843 died June 12, 1876.
    D. A. Murphey, October 20, 1861, February 2, 1892.
    C. J. Owen, November 22, 1836, March 21, 1888.
    Angeline Owen, February 16, 1840, September 6, 1905.
    James Owen, Sr., October 21, 1797, July 29, 1871.
    Sophronia, wife of James Owen, born October 21, 1809 died November 4, 1880.
    Frances Elizabeth Winnifield, born Jan. 27 1835 died Feb. 12, 1881.
    Martha A., wife of W. B. Owen, born August 14, 1847 died May 27, 1871.
    Thomas J. Owen, born April 25, 1841 died 12-11-1867.
    Jesse Ellis Owen, born July 23, 1848 died June 12, 1876.
    Robert L. Choate, born December 29, 1845 died July 23, 1903.
    Mary Jane Choate, born May 24, 1846 died February 26, 1912.
    John Hancock, born August 14, 1814 died August 31, 1891.
    W. T. Stark, 1837 died 1909.
    Angeline, wife of W. T. Stark, 1841-1905.

Thomas Stark left a will in Robertson County, dated 17 July 1800 and proved in
1802. His wife was Rachel. He had a son Walter Stark, a grandson Thomas Stark,
and a grandson Thomas, son of James Stark. His wife and son Walter were named
as executrix and executor of the estate.

Bible Records by Acklen, 1933, pp. 169-170.
Sumner County, Tennessee Will Book 1, p. 181.
Goodspeed's History of Robertson County, 1886, p. 1189.
Primm Bible.
Robertson County, Tennessee Will Book 1, p. 91.

Stewart

    There were at least two different Stewart families in Montgomery County. One
of these arrived during the period that the county was a part of "Old" Tennessee
County. The other branch of the Stewart family were what may be termed "late
comers," as they did not arrive until 1832.

    The Southwestern Presbyterian University had its inception in 1848, in which
year the Masonic Grand Lodge of the State of Tennessee determined to establish a
first-class institution of learning in the town of Clarksville. The Masonic Frater-
nity of Montgomery County united to erect a suitable edifice and obtained donations
from non-Masonic friends to aid in the enterprise. The college was organized on 5
January 1849 and went into operation on January 8, following. The building was
erected in 1849, but before it was fully completed, the Grand Lodge of Tennessee
directed the appropriation, made for the support of this college at its establishment,
into an entirely different channel, thereby crippling the institution in the very beginning.

    The Masonic bodies of Clarksville, in order to prevent further dissention in the
Grand Lodge, asked that the connection between the college and the Grand Lodge be
dissolved. They, themselves, determined to carry out the original design of establishing a Masonic institution and thus keep faith with the donors. The lodges of Montgomery borrowed $6,000.00 to complete the building. The institution, therefore,
was carried on from 1851 to 1855 under the auspices of the Masons of the county and

was known as the Montgomery Masonic College. Its presidents during that time were W. T. Hopkins, T. M. Newell, W. A. Forbes, and W. M. Stewart.

In 1855, it became evident that the institution could not succeed unless its debts were liquidated. On October 12 of that year, the Synod of Nashville (Presbyterian) held a meeting at Florence, Alabama, at which time the transfer of the college to that synod was discussed and finally determined upon. A board of trustees was appointed, consisting of W. M. Stewart, John Stacker, W. B. Munford, Bryce Stewart, J. E. Bailey, A. Robb, W. P. Hume, John McKeage, C. R. Cooper, D. N. Kennedy, T. J. Pritchett, J. T. Hendrick, D. D., R. A. Lapsley, D. D., W. H. Mitchell, D. D., R. B. McMullen, D. D., and Duncan Brown, D. D. They were to receive the deed when executed and to take charge of and manage the college.

The college was named "Stewart College" in honor of William M. Stewart, in consequence of his munificent donations, his long continued and disinterested service, his ardent and untiring devotion to science, and his high moral and Christian character. In the transfer on 5 February 1856, the trustees bound themselves by signing an obligation to pay $7000.00 of the indebtedness of the institution, provided the Synod of Nashville would pay $5000.00. These trustees were John McKeage, D. N. Kennedy, Bryce Stewart, W. P. Hume, A. Robb, W. B. Munford, T. J. Pritchett, and J. E. Bailey. W. M. Stewart's name does not appear on the minutes as one of the obligators, but nevertheless he was one of them in fact. The faculty was reorganized under W. M. Stewart as president, and the institution was conducted by the board of trustees appointed by the Synod of Nashville named above. In 1858, W. M. Stewart was succeeded as president by the Rev. R. B. McMullen, D. D. However, Stewart continued his labors as professor of natural science. The school was progressing in funds, patronage, and appliances for teaching when the civil war came on and caused a cessation of its work. At this time, Dr. McMullen was conducting it under a special arrangement with the board of Trustees. His second session under this arrangement commenced on 20 January 1862 in the Presbyterian Church, the college building being used as a hospital for the Confederate soldiers. Only a few weeks of the session had passed when Fort Donelson capitulated, and Clarksville was occupied by the Federal soldiers. Upon their arrival in the city, the Confederate soldiers were removed from the college, and the building was used by the Union for a similar purpose. They thus occupied it about a month, leaving on 25 March. In April, the Seventy-first Ohio Volunteer Infantry took possession of the building and occupied it as barracks until 18 August 1862.

By then the library apparatus, furniture, and cabinets were completely demolished, and nothing was left of the building itself but the bare walls and floors.

After the war, a private school was taught within the building for about two years, and in 1868-70 the work of putting the building in repair was completed at a cost of $8,000.00. On 15 June 1869, a competent corps of professors was elected as follows: W. M. Stewart, professor of natural history; Rev. D. O. N. Davies, professor of logic, rhetoric, and belles-lettres; and D. M. Quarles, principal of preparatory department. After failures in other directions to elect a president, the Rev. J. B. Shearer, D. D. was at last elected to that position on 25 August 1869. Under this arrangement, the institution prospered until 1873.

In 1873, a meeting was held at Memphis, consisting of members of the Synods from Alabama, Mississippi, Arkansas, Nashville, and Memphis. At this meeting, a plan of union was adopted under which the university, when established, should be conducted. There were numerous competitive locations for the university, besides Clarksville. The principal among them were Jackson, Tennessee and Huntsville, Alabama. It was finally decided, however, to erect the "Stewart Cabinet Building." The faculty of Stewart College was continued provisionally, and the school was conducted on the same scale as before. In June 1879, the board of directors abolished the curriculum and reorganized the institution on the new plan.

Professor Stewart came from Worcester County, Maryland. He was born in Philadelphia, Pennsylvania in March 1803. He came to Tennessee in 1832 and first lived at Lafayette Furnace. Mrs. Sally Truitt Richardson, a widow with several children, came with him from Maryland. It was not until 1852 that Prof. Stewart moved to Glenwood, about two and one half miles from Clarksville.

Bryce Stewart was prominent in the Annals of Clarksville. There was a time when half the coffee pots in use in Clarksville rested on tiles from Bryce Stewart's castle. It was a homely place. The building of Bryce Stewart's castle was probably the biggest architectural news in the nineteenth century in the county. The walls were never completed, but enough of the mansion remained at the end of the century to remind one who saw it as a child of "Balmoral, the residence of the Duke of Argyll, the Petit Trianon... and the Mosque of Saint Sophia."

There are numerous legends as to why work was discontinued. One is that Stewart was broken-hearted at the death of his wife, for whom it was intended. Another is that its construction was halted by the War Between the States and that Union soldiers used the unfinished rooms as a small-pox ward.

Stewart's villa entrance interior, now a business establishment, still contains huge doors once destined for the builder's unfinished castle. Ornaments were used here with a lavish hand. The house, built by a tobacco man who had traveled to New Orleans, dates from about 1858. It faces the Cumberland River, and once had a nine foot observatory on the roof.

I know little of the ancestry of Bryce Stewart. He may have been descended from the Stewarts who were in Montgomery County while it was still "Old" Tennessee County and who were prominent in the development of the county and the surrounding territory.

The name Duncan Stewart may be found in the history of every Middle Tennessee County from long before Tennessee became a state. His activities in the building and development of the Miro District were so great that a county was named for him in 1803. The new county was cut from Montgomery and Davidson, and Yellow Creek, the section of Montgomery where Stewart, White, the Smalls, and others lived at one time. Most of the creek fell in Dickson County.

Charles Stewart, a brother of Duncan Stewart, was also prominent in the section. There is a power of attorney, dated 15 September 1787 (W. B. 1797-1810, p. 197, Montgomery County) in which Thomas Brown of Bladen County, North Carolina, for causes, appointed Col. Duncan Stewart of Tennessee to sell 640 acres of land patented by Jacob Messack on the south side of Cumberland River.

There is a bond in which Charles Stewart was nominated and appointed guardian of Tingnal Jones Stewart, son of Duncan Stewart, and Tignal Jones Stewart, son of Charles Stewart, in October 1810. (W. B. 1797-1810, p. 511, Montgomery County)

One of the Duncan Stewarts of Montgomery County moved to Mississippi, for on p. 505 of Will Book 1797-1810, Montgomery County, the following information is found: "Duncan Stewart now of Mississippi Territory and at the Natchez Landing because of moving, gives power of attorney to my father James Stewart of Montgomery County" to sell and collect certain property in Montgomery County, 5 February 1811.

Both Duncan and Charles Stewart were assigned land on Sulphur Fork of Jones Creek. These two places fell in Stewart and Dickson Counties after the new counties were created. Duncan Stewart was granted 640 acres of land on warrants no. 3863 and 3853 on South Harpeth River. A 1000 acre and a 228 acre tract of land, warrants no. 536 and 557, were on the east side of Wells Creek. This is where Duncan Stewart lived in Montgomery, later Stewart, County (Davidson County, Tennessee Deed Book D, No. 4, p. 27).

Duncan and Charles Stewart were both land dealers, buying and selling large tracts at least as early as 1794.

Henry Small, who located in Clarksville, was associated with Duncan Stewart. Small was there as early as 18 March 1797, for it is recorded that he purchased lot No. 7 in the town from Wm. Capshaw. Henry Small was Sheriff of Montgomery County in 1802, 1804, 1808, and 1810. Mr. Small did a great deal of business with a man named Roe, and their transactions were made in the name of Small and Roe. In addition to his other services, Mr. Small was actively engaged in the progress and erection of the public buildings in the county. After Stewart County was created in

1803, Mr. Small moved from Clarksville to the new county where, with Duncan Stewart, he took part in the formation of that county. Small later moved on westward, and the last I know of him, he was in Tipton County, Tennessee.

William White of Waxhaw, North Carolina married Margaret Williamson of Bladen County. Their daughter, Mary Elizabeth White, married Henry Small as his second wife. Small's first wife, Anna Bailey, was probably the daughter of Charles Bailey, an early settler of Montgomery County, for Bailey and Small are found associated in deeds. The two wives of Mr. Small are thought to have been cousins.

Henry Small had several children. However, a complete record is not available at this time. One daughter, Catherine Weedon Small, was born in 1827 in Tipton County, Tennessee, died in 1915 in Grenada, Mississippi, and was married in 1845 to Samuel H. Young (Mss. data, Whitley Collection).

Henry Small served in many capacities of public office in Montgomery while it was still "Old" Tennessee County. In 1809, Henry Small was overseer of the road from Clarksville to Wine Miller's old place on the Nashville Road.

There was an Andrew Stewart in Montgomery County in 1808, whose wife was named Sarah. There is a deed registered, which states that Sarah Stewart, wife of Andrew Stewart, sold 290 acres to Robert Bigger. The deed was proved in open court (W.B. Montgomery County, 1797-1810, p. 28).

There was evidently a close connection between the Stewarts and the Whites of Montgomery County, for William Stewart White petitioned the court for permission to build a mill on Spring Creek in Montgomery County where William Dickins formerly had a mill on the north side of White's land (W.B. Montgomery County, 1808-1810, p. 84, Sept. 1808).

Tatum

Nathaniel Tatum came over to Virginia in the "George" before 1683 and settled in Charles City County. He was in Prince George County in 1703. His wife was named Ann. Their known children were Samuel, Mary, and Nathaniel who was in Prince George in 1704.

It has been clearly proven in several publications that the second Nathaniel was the father of Nathaniel, Jr., Edward, Chris., and possibly others.

Nathaniel Tatum, Jr. had a wife named Elizabeth. He had died by 1750, leaving children Peter, Rebecca, Jesse, Edward, and Nathaniel.

Edward Tatum, son of the second Nathaniel, died in 1739. His wife was Rebecca Rives. Edward Tatum's will was recorded in Surry County, Virginia 1736-9. They had at least two sons, Nathaniel and Peter. Peter had a wife named Mary, by whom were born: Littleberry (April 10, 1739), Eps, Ruth, and Peter (went to Georgia in 1743 and died in 1791). The second Peter Tatum was the father of Epps, Thomas, Peter, Rebecca, Howell (married H. Ogden), Nancy, and Sally.

Chris. Tatum, son of the second Nathaniel, was born in 1683 and died in 1750 in Surry County, Virginia. He married Bridget Scott, daughter of John Scott of Prince George County. Chris and Bridget (Scott) Tatum were the parents of Joshua, Bethia, John, Frances (married George Rives), and Chris (died in 1769 in Sussex County, Virginia and had a wife, Elizabeth) (W.B. 3 Surry County, Virginia, p. 132).

Joshua Tatum, son of Chris and Bridget, married Amey Chappell, who was born in Virginia, the daughter of James Chappell. Joshua Tatum and his wife Amey were blessed with sons Major Howell Tatum (born in 1753) and James Tatum. James died in Davidson County, Tennessee, leaving a will, dated 1821 (W.B. 8, p. 28 Davidson County, Tennessee). He left no issue, but left his property to "my only brother Howell Tatum."

Howell Tatum was a Revolutionary soldier and advanced to the rank of "Major."
He married Rosannah Wendel in Davidson County, Tennessee on 24 December 1795.
Their children were Edward M. and Eliza, who married Macijah Wade.

Major Tatum divorced his wife in 1812. His pension application (R 2027) was
based upon Revolutionary War service rendered while he was a resident of North
Carolina. On 21 August 1773, he was appointed ensign of the First North Carolina
Regiment. In 1776, he was promoted to Lieutenant, and on 3 April 1777, he was made
a captain of said regiment. He also acted as aid-de-camp and assistant deputy quartermaster. He was captured at the surrender of Charleston, South Carolina, was
held prisoner until August 1781, and continued in service until sometime in 1783. He
also served under General Andrew Jackson and fought against the Indians during the
War of 1812. After this service, he was military storekeeper at Nashville, Tennessee for a year or more. He was Judge of the Circuit Court in Nashville District.
He died at Nashville in October 1822. Rosannah Tatum was living with her son, Edwin M. Tatum, in 1853. Rosannah was married in Bedford County, Tennessee in
September 1828 to Anderson Claxton, who died in September 1849 in Pulaski County,
Arkansas.

On 16 November 1853 while living in Sebastian County, Arkansas, Rosannah Claxton, aged seventy-six years, applied for a pension on the account of the Revolutionary
War service of Howell Tatum. Her claim was not allowed, as she had been divorced
from Howell Tatum.

In 1853, Stephen Cantrell of Jefferson County, Arkansas stated that he became
acquainted with Howell Tatum about 1804 and that afterwards he went to live with the
firm of Dederick and Tatum in the city of Nashville, of which firm said Howell Tatum
was a member, and that in 1809 he married Howell Tatum's wife's sister.

Howell Tatum was assigned a large number of grants in nearly all the Middle
Tennessee counties. From the records in the various court houses, I believe Mr.
Tatum was what might be called a real estate dealer, buying and selling lands.

The Davidson County records (Book P, p. 345) 17 November 1829, the settlement
of Howell Tatum, deceased, shows cash paid to Edwin M. Tatum, one of the heirs of
the said Howell Tatum. Micajah Wade married Eliza Tatum. John P. Wiggins is
also mentioned, but the record does not reveal whether he married a daughter of
Tatum or not. Andrew Erwen, Junior is also mentioned as guardian.

There is a will in Davidson County, dated 26 February 1836, recorded 23 August
1844, and signed by Nathaniel Tatum, in which there is mention of a "sister" Rebecca
Tatum and a "niece" Margaret Edwards (W. B. 13, p. 78).

Peter Tatum married Fanny Jones on 24 September 1811 in Davidson County (M.
B. 1, p. 119).

David Spears, asking that he be issued a military warrant in Davidson County,
Tennessee, stated that Howell Tatum, a captain in the First North Carolina Regiment
in the Revolutionary War, knew him and knew that he, Spears, was a soldier or a
non-commissioned officer in the Second Regiment of that state from the spring of 1776
until after the fall of Charleston in May 1780, at which time Spears and Tatum were
both captured (Tennessee Genealogical Records, Vol. 4, p. 38 by Whitley).

There is an indenture, dated 5 June 1799, between Howell Tatum and Rosannah
Tatum, his wife, on the one part and Anthony Foster, Robert Searcy, and Francis B.
Sappington, carpenters, on the other part for $350.00, etc. (Davidson County, D. B.
E, p. 231).

As I have previously stated, Howell Tatum was a dealer in real estate. He never
actually resided in Montgomery County, that I can find, but did a rather large business in that section of the country.

The Tatum family was well represented in Middle Tennessee prior to 1820. By
that year, Dasney, John C., William, Nathaniel, Howell, Jesse, Edward, Edward,
Jr., Jonathan, Isaiah, Benjamin, James, John, Jr., Peter, Stephen, Dry, and two

William Tatums were living in Davidson County. Most, if not all of them, came to Tennessee from North Carolina.

The Tatums were active in the War of 1812. Howell Tatum was principal engineer under Major General Andrew Jackson in the General's expedition against the Creek Indians. He is recorded as having been sick on 26 February 1814. Ira, Isaiah, Jesse, Jonathan, Nathaniel, and Peter Tatum were all privates in the War of 1812, and James Tatum was a wagon-master.

Major Howell Tatum of Nashville and Middle Tennessee was a distant relative of Howell Tatum of Alabama, who was the son of Peter Tatum of Wilkes County, Ga.

In addition to his own activities, Major Howell Tatum transacted much business in land deals for General Andrew Jackson in Montgomery, Robertson, and Sumner Counties, Tennessee and in several counties in southern Kentucky.

Major Howell Tatum's grave has been marked by the General Francis Nash Chapter, D.A.R. He is buried in Old City Cemetery, Nashville.

Stewart Mss. file, unpub. in Whitley Collection. Includes Maryland data.
Tatum Mss. file, unpub. in Whitley Collection.

Tribble

The court of Montgomery County, 20 June 1809, named William Barton, Joseph Hardeman, Wm. Bearden, Joseph Barton, Abel Man, Absalom Tribble, and Henry Funk to view and lay off "a road leading from Absalom Tribble's ferry to where it intersects Davises old road leading and leaving the old road at the foot of the Bluff thence running up the first hollow so as to intersect the old Road again near the Cross Road leading from Joseph Hardiman's to Jacob Randolph's place."

On 23 March in the same year, only a few months before the above court order, there is mention of a road from Tribble's Ferry to Vaughan's Mill which road "is to be shortened and is to be from said Ferry to the first large branch below William Whiteheads and that Joseph Whitehead be overseer of said road in place of Goodman Traywick and the hands be as follows — Frederick Moody, David Leach, Josiah G. Duke, Richard Whitehead, Abner Harris, Robert Ray, Francis Neblett, John Moore, Peter Hubbard, William Hubbard, John Hubbard and David Hubbard."

A bond was made by James Matlock, Stephen Cocke, and Thomas Smith in April 1810. On 21 December 1809 Mary Tribble, a single woman of said county, had accused James Matlock of being the father of a bastard child which she had. The court ordered Matlock to pay $10 per year for the support of the child until it reached the age of twelve years.

The case of James Wall, executor of Alex. M. Roberts vs. Shadrick, Spilsby, Jensey, Absalom, Andrew, James, and John Tribble, Goodman Traywick and wife Nancy, Richard Cocke and his wife Elizabeth, and Polly Tribble, heirs of Spilsby Tribble, deceased, involved property of the deceased Tribble and would indicate that the parties named were all heirs of the deceased.

Montgomery County Court Minutes, 1808-1810, pp. 171, 225, 329.
Montgomery County Record Book A, p. 64.
Tribble file, Whitley Collection.

Trice

The Trice family lived in both Robertson and Sumner Counties in the Red River section. In the first will book of Sumner, there is the will of one John Trice, dated 20 December 1803. In it, he styled himself as "of Robertson County" and named his wife, Patsey, and Thomas Keefe as Executors. According to the statement of Mr.

Trice, his children were not all of age. He mentioned having money, negroes, and land. The children mentioned by name were: Nancy, who married James Wood; William Anderson Trice; Patsy Derby Trice; Dorothy Anderson Trice; Adagela Trice; Emeyan Trice; John Trice; and the child his wife was probably "pregrant with."

James Trice, Shepherd Trice, and Edward Trice are shown as heads of families in the 1820 census of Montgomery County.

It would appear that practically all the Trices had left Sumner and the border of Robertson County for the western portion of Montgomery County by 1816. They lived between Russellville, Kentucky and Palmyra, Tennessee or in that vicinity in 1816 and 1817, for the court of 17 July 1816 ordered that Hiram Cooper be overseer of a road leading from Russellville to Palmyra between the little West fork of the Red River and the road leading from Clarksville to Hopkinsville. The hands living on that road were to work the same: Lemuel Peters, John Wilson, Mrs. Martin, Drury Bonds, William Jordan, John Starkey, William Elliott, Henry Williams, Roland Peterson, James McCarroll, Taylor Chism, Samuel McNicholas, Washington Lee, Edward Trice, John Chism, Robert Trice, Nace F. Trice, Shepherd Trice, John Dodson, Stephen Mallory, Joshua Pike, John Mallory, Ezekiel Jones, and William Lowther.

On 19 July 1916, the court ordered Bingham Trice to be appointed overseer of the road leading from the mouth of Red River to John Trice's, with hands: James Trice, Lee Trice, Mark Booth, Reuben Chisenhall, Matthew Thomas, Lee Chisenhall, John Riggins, Sterling Ingram, Mary Trice, Abram Brantley, Hugh Brantley, Nace F. Trice, Robert Trice, and Rachel Trice's hands. These two court records clearly indicate the neighborhood in which most of the Trices lived.

Sumner County, Tennessee Will Book 1, p. 116
Sumner County, Tennessee Will Abstracts by E. Whitley.
Montgomery County Court Minutes, 1816-1817, pp. 79 and 83.

Trotter

Isham Trotter was among the early settlers in Montgomery County, Tennessee. He had several land transactions in the county before 1800 (Deed Book A, pp. 221, 241, 247, 451, 474, 485, 507). His wife, Elizabeth, was living when he made his will. In it, Mr. Trotter named his youngest son, Michael, and set out that the "younger" children were Isham, Richard, and Betsy. The other children named were Benjamine W., James, and William. There is a mention of Ambrose Martin and his wife Mary, but the relationship is not stated. The will was made on 31 March 1827 and probated in January 1829 (W. B. E, p. 306, Montgomery County).

In October 1811, a settlement was made by Isham Trotter with the court of Montgomery in regard to his administration of the estate of Robert Trotter, deceased. In the settlement, the exact relationship among those mentioned is not made clear, but there is mention of Willis Jackson, John Harris, William Hightower, James Trotter, John and Isham Trotter. It is indicated that all these received benefits from the estate (Montgomery County Wills, 1811-1818, p. 20). Isham Trotter gave bond as the administrator of Robert Trotter, deceased, on 16 July 1810 (W. B. A, p. 485).

Josiah G. Duke, Isham Trotter, William Good, and Joseph B. Whitehead, all of Montgomery County, were bound to Governor John Sevier on 6 December 1805, the condition being that Duke and Trotter be given an order to erect a cotton gin in the county (W. B. A, p. 241, Montgomery County).

James Trotter was living in the county in 1820. He was one of the hands ordered by the court in 1808 to work a new road "from Mosley's Ferry on Cumberland River to intersect the road from Weakley's Ferry to Col. Richard Napier's Forge on Barton's Creek (Montgomery County Minutes, 1808-1810, p. 41). On 16 April 1816, the court ordered James Trotter to be overseer of the road from Mosley's Ferry to Napier Iron Works (Montgomery County Court Minutes, 1816-17, p. 8).

William Trotter was born in 1804 and died in 1857 in Montgomery County. He was married about 1827 to Martha Dickson, who was born in the same county in the same year as her husband. She died there in 1859. William Trotter and his wife were the parents of Elizabeth Trotter, who was born in 1831 in Montgomery County, died in 1859 in Humphreys County, and was married about 1847 in Humphreys County to Samuel Yarborough, who was born in 1823 in Montgomery County. Samuel and Elizabeth (Trotter) Yarborough had a daughter, Martha Yarborough, who was born in 1850 and became the wife of Robert Alexander, who was born in 1841 in Maury County, Tennessee.

Martha Dickson, the wife of William Trotter, was the child of Joseph Dickson, Jr., who was born between 1770 and 1780 in Duplin County, North Carolina. Joseph Dickson, Jr. died leaving a will, 29 August 1839 in Montgomery County, Tennessee. His wife, Martha, died in 1839 in Tennessee. Joseph Dickson, Jr. was the son of Joseph Dickson, Sr., who was born in 1743 in Duplin County, North Carolina and died in 1803 in Dickson County, Tennessee. Joseph Dickson Sr. was married prior to 1765 in Duplin County to Jane Molton (Moulton). Joseph Dickson, Sr. was the son of John Dickson, who was born in 1704 in Ireland, died on 25 December 1774, and married Anne. Jane Moulton, wife of Joseph Dickson, Sr., was the daughter of Lieut-Colonel Abraham Moulton (Molton) (1732-1791) and his wife, Sarah Norris. Sarah Norris was the daughter of George Norris (died in 1766) and his wife Sarah. (N. C. State and Colonial Records, Vol. 17, p. 383; D. A. R. Magazine, March 1928, p. 160; and D. A. R. Magazine, April 1930, p. 257).

William Trotter was an entry taker for Montgomery County in August 1836 (W. B. G, p. 419, Montgomery County).

It is not clear whether Isham Trotter was a brother or the father of William Trotter, mentioned above, and Robert Trotter, mentioned below, but it is strongly indicated that both William and Robert were sons of Isham Trotter.

Isham Trotter, William Whitehead, Stephen Cocke, and William Hightower, all of the same county, were bound to Morgan Brown, chairman of the county court of Pleas and Quarter Sessions, 3 September 1804. The condition was that Isham Trotter was appointed guardian to Robert Trotter. It is believed that this Robert Trotter was a grandson of Isham and son of Robert Trotter, deceased.

There were probably two William Trotters in the county at the same time. One of them was certainly the son of Isham Trotter, as he named his son, William, in his will.

There is a deed in Davidson County (D. B. G, p. 453), dated 12 March 1808, wherein Edmund Cooper and John Camp, both of Davidson County, Tennessee, sold a tract of land in Davidson County to William Trotter of Brunswick County, Virginia. The land lay on the waters of Dry Creek, adjoining Mrs. Hope's and Jane Allen's line, 199 1/2 acres part of 320 acres which Joseph Walker deeded to Cooper on 10 September 1807.

William Trotter, son of Isham, died in 1827. He was born in Virginia and married Elizabeth Whitehead in 1795 in Brunswick County, Virginia. She was the daughter of Benjamin Whitehead who was aged between eighty and ninety years in 1830 and was living in Montgomery County, Tennessee.

The inventory of Benjamine Whitehead, deceased, indicates that William Trotter married Elizabeth Whitehead. It states, "Grace and her children had been delivered to Elizabeth Trotter several years before the death of Benjamine Whitehead, deceased." The record was rendered in court in June 1837 and was signed by William Trotter, executor of Benjamin Whitehead, deceased (W. B. C, p. 609, Montgomery County).

Another record in Montgomery states that Benjamine Whitehead deeded certain property to the children of Gincy Trotter and George Fort (W. B. B, p. 166).

Benjamine Whitehead, a farmer of Montgomery County, made a deed of gift of a negro girl Delph and a negro boy Jack to "loving sons" Joseph and Richard, both of the state and county aforesaid, farmers, 24 October 1800 (Record Book A, p. 126).

Tyson

Although not one of the first families of Montgomery, the Tysons should not be omitted in the annals of Montgomery County, Tennessee. John Tyson, a miller, was proprietor of the Cumberland Valley Flouring Mills and also operated planing mills. He was born in Liverpool, England on 28 March 1838, the son of William and Frances (Haughton) Tyson. Both of his parents died in England. John Tyson came to America in 1857 and settled in Illinois for a short while. He came to Tennessee in 1861 and settled in Springfield, Robertson County. He remained there until 1870 when he removed to Pleasant View, Cheatham County. It is thought that he lived for a while in Montgomery County, where he carried on extensive business even after he finally settled in Ashland City in the fall of 1884. He purchased the Cumberland Valley Mills in 1884.

He married Joella Orndorff in 1864, and they had two children, William H. and John P. Mrs. Tyson died in January 1881, and Mr. Tyson was united in marriage with Miss Mary E. Wall of Montgomery County, daughter of William Wall. By the second marriage there were two children, Henry W. and Peter R. Tyson. They were devout members of the Methodist Episcopal Church.

Villines

Another Methodist family in Robertson County were the Villines. William Villines was born in Caswell County, North Carolina on 14 November 1814 and came to Tennessee in 1830. His wife, Mary Cothern, was a sister of the noted William Cothern, a merchant of Philadelphia. Upon arriving in Robertson County, Villines built a saw and grist mill on Red River. After about eight years, he began trading in negroes. He was bitterly opposed to the war against slavery and took no part in the hostilities. He visited hospitals and did all he could to alleviate the suffering of his friends. He spent many thousands of dollars in this way. After the war, he built a mill near Cross Plains. He erected many of the best buildings in Springfield. Mr. Villines died on 9 January 1876.

Near Cross Plains there is a Villines Burial Ground which has a number of tombstone inscriptions. Some of them are very difficult to read and are left blank in the following transcript:

William Villines, born in Caswell County, North Carolina, November 14, 1814 died Jan. 9, 1876.

Mary Villines, wife of William, born October 1, — died June 26, 1890.

Robert M., oldest son of William and Mary Villines, born April 20, 1830 died October 2, 1870.

Susan Hollis, daughter of William and Mary Villines, born January 25, 1828 died October 5, 1854.

Elizabeth A. Davis, daughter of William and Mary Villines, born July 21, 1826 died November 17, 1854.

William E., son of W. H. and N. J. Villines, born April 4, 1865 died September 19, 1879.

Nancy J., wife of W. H. Villines, born July 17, 1838 died November 26, 1879.

T. J. Villines, born April 20, 1839 died May 26, 1908.

Sallie, wife of T. J. Villines, born March 24, 1842 died Aug. 3, 1913.

Calista Villines, born March 23, 1854 died August 5, 1879.

Lydia K., wife of James W. Villines and daughter of S. G. and Mary Strother, born December 23, 1837 died October 13, 1862.

J. W. Villines, born November 11, 1833 died October 29, 1877.

A. J. Cole, born Oct. 30, 1816 died September 13, 1868.

Ellen M. Cole, daughter of William and Mary Villines, and wife of A. J. Cole, born January 6, 1832 died January 3, 1860.

M. E. Cole, daughter of A. J. and E. M. Cole, born March 9, 1851 died July 13, 1852.

W. S. Cole, son of A. J. and E. M. Cole, born December 7, 1851 died January 14, 1857.

In this same burial ground, I find Capt. W. S. Winfield, born November 29, 1831 died March 6, 1892, and Elizabeth Bell, born January 15, 1867 died age 73 years. Thomas Kilgore, one of the earliest settlers on the Red River is buried in this graveyard.

Eddie Lee Villines was born on 22 April 1861, died on 30 September 1925, and married Elizabeth Jernigan, who was born on 2 March 1868. They are buried in the Jernigan-Jones Cemetery, thirteen miles from Springfield, in District 15, on the Jernigan and Jones farm in Robertson County.

Wm. H. Villines, son of William and Mary, was born in the Cross Plains community on 22 June 1836. He married Nancy Yates, daughter of Charles and Nancy Yates. Mr. and Mrs. William H. Villines were the parents of eight children, among whom were: Lizzie, Nannie, Mattie, Charley, and John. The mother of these children died on 26 November 1879, and on 4 December 1883, Mr. Villines married his second wife, Bell Bransford, daughter of John Bransford of Massachusetts.

Tombstone Inscriptions by Acklen, 1933, p. 158.
Goodspeed's History of Robertson County, Tennessee, 1886, Biog. section.

Vance - Morgan - Brown

Samuel Vance was present at the court of March 28, 1808 in Montgomery. The next year, he sold Lot No. 3 in Palmyra to Hawkins and Thornton. The deed was proved by the court. The same year, he deeded one half of Lot No. 68 in Palmyra to James G. Wheland, and the same court proved a deed that he made to John H. Hyde for a lot in the same town.

In consideration of the love and affection that he had for Benjamin Morgan, son of Isaac Morgan, Samuel Vance gave and granted property which was then in the possession of his father, the said Isaac Morgan. This was 31 March 1810.

Adam Harman, Jr., for love and affection to Joseph Morgan and good causes, gave to said Joseph Morgan, certain property then in possession of said father Isaac Morgan, April 6, 1818, Montgomery County.

On 21 October 1807, Morgan Brown, for love and affection to daughter Elizabeth and in consideration of a marriage having taken place between her and Capt. Samuel Vance, transferred certain slaves to Elizabeth and Samuel Vance.

It is an established fact that Dr. Morgan Brown came to Montgomery from South Carolina in 1795. He was a distinguished citizen until 1808 when he removed to Kentucky. He returned to Davidson County, Tennessee, where he died in 1840, aged 82 years. He was a Revolutionary soldier.

It is not known whether there is any connection between John Brown and Morgan Brown. John Brown, under 21 years of age and a child of Hannah Brown, was bound to James Lockhart on 26 January 1801 in Montgomery.

Morgan Brown's grave has been marked by the D.A.R., Nashville, Tennessee, distinguished ancestry and distinguished descendants.

Montgomery County Court Minutes, 1808-1810, pp. 1, 154.
Montgomery County Will Book 1797-1810, pp. 45, 137; Will Book A, p. 128.
Mss. Vance Fam. (extensive research), Whitley Collection, unpub.
"Morgan Brown, Ancestry and Descendants" by Whitley, unpublished manuscript.

Walker

Several different families by the name of Walker came into Middle Tennessee during pioneer days. There is hardly a county in the state which does not have some mention of a Walker among its records.

One branch of the family came quite early and located in Robertson County. The earliest record I have of this particular branch concerns John A. and Elizabeth (Bellamy) Walker. J A. Walker learned the cooper's trade, beginning at the age of fifteen. He enlisted in Capt. Bidwell's Company, the Thirteenth Tennessee C.S.A., and served about one year. He was taken prisoner at Fort Donelson and was held at Camp Butler. After forty days, he escaped and returned home. In 1863, he went to Montgomery County and located at New Providence, where he continued in the cooper's trade until 1874, when he began dealing in tobacco.

R. H. Walker, the son of John A. and Elizabeth, was born in Robertson County on 9 March 1840. In 1868, R. H. Walker married Caroline Watts, and they had five children: Herschel, Alfonso, Tracy, Prince, and Hattie. Mr. R. H. Walker and his family were active members of the Methodist Episcopal Church at New Providence.

Another branch of the Walker family which was closely associated with Robertson and Montgomery Counties, was the Enos or Eneas Walker family. On 15 July 1829 in Davidson County, Eneas Walker sold 85 1/4 acres of land on the head waters of White's Creek to Mansker's Creek, on which said Walker then lived, to William Neeley. In September of the same year, Eneas Walker sold 17 acres of land in Davidson County on the head waters of Mansker's Creek to George Campbell. About the same time, Walker went security for Wm. Lytle and John Hinton, endorsers of various notes.

The records of Davidson County, 13 January 1827, show that Eneas Walker of Davidson County sold 55 1/2 acres to William Neely of the same place. The land was located in Davidson County, in Neely's Bend of Cumberland River, adjoining Edmund Lanears and Samuel Neely's corner, and on the north to Overton's east line, and on the south to the road running from the mouth of Stones River to Mathew P. Walker, then north of said road to the beginning. This land was being held in trust by Eneas Walker for the benefit of William Neely's wife and children.

The will of Philip Walker, 3 March 1802, indicates that Enos Walker's wife was also a Walker. In the will, Phillip Walker called his wife, Gennett, and left 150 acres of land he formerly lived on, also 150 acres in Kentucky to his eldest son, John. To his son-in-law, Alexander Campbell, he devised 100 acres of land he bought from Hays. To Matthew McCance, called son-in-law, he left 100 acres on which he (McCance) then lived. He called Enos Walker his son-in-law and left him 100 acres of land claimed in Kentucky. The remainder of his property was left to his son Philip Walker.

Philip Walker owned the land on White's Creek in Davidson County in 1805, for on December 20, he sold an estimated 50 acres on the waters of White's Creek to William Neely (blacksmith) for $500.00.

On 22 January 1816 in Davidson County, Eneas Walker made a covenant with John Anderson, in consideration of $1600.00 to be paid to him "within the present year" and if also a "certain written obligation given by him to Charles Cabiness shall be given up" or cancelled same agreed with Enos Walker, to convey all said Anderson's title and interest in a tract of land in Neeley's Bend of Cumberland River in Davidson County, deeded by William Neeley to said Cabinass, purchased at Sheriff's sale by said Anderson.

In 1938, Mrs. Georgia Walker Marshall of Springfield, Tennessee owned an old Bible which contained the following record of the Enos Walker family:
Enos Walker, born March 1787 died July 21, 1856 in Arkansas.
Elizabeth Walker, born Nov. 29, 1794.
Elizabeth Connell, born 18 October 1829 died 23 March 1901.
Sarah Jane Walker, born 16 October 1847 died 27 February 1852.
Caroline Walker, born September 12, 1849.
Ollevia Ann Walker, born October 16, 1852 died 8 September 1853.
Catherine Walker, born 20 February 1856.
George W. Walker, born 15 August 1812 died 10 March 1901.
Matthew McChance Walker, born 20 March 1815 died September 9, 1855.
Mary Ann Walker, born 3 May 1817.
Wm. Neely Walker, born 18 August 1819.

Eliza Jane Walker, born 9 June 1822.
Jas. O. Walker, born 5 November 1824 died —.
Jno. Bell Walker, born 13 October 1828 died Oct. 29, 1888.
Ephraim Foster Walker, born —.
Jackson L. Walker, born 5 March 1834.
Martha White Walker, born 25 Feb. 1837.
Mary Ann Walker, born July 25, 1858.
William Connell Walker, born 11 Dec. 1860.
Martha Walker, born 10 Aug. 1864 died June 28, 1929.
George Bunn Walker, born 25 August 1867.
Annie Catherine Marshall, born August 11, 1905.
David Hershel Marshall, born May 16, 1906.
Gilbert E. Marshall, died December 19, 1937.
Martha House Walker married Luther B. Marshall, December 25, 1901. He
died February 19, 1909.
Georgia Bunn Walker married Gilbert E. Marshall, July 31, 1902.

There were probably two Enos Walkers in Davidson and Robertson Counties about
1802. They were probably father and son, but they are not referred to as Senior and
Junior.

John Walker lived in Robertson County as early as 1802, for on 18 January, John
Walker of Robertson County appointed Thomas Little of the same place to recover
money due said Walker.

Goodspeed's History of Tennessee, Montgomery County, 1886, p. 1111.
Davidson County, Tennessee Deed Book F, p. 313; Deed Book R, p. 353; Deed Book
S, pp. 198, 347, 805.
Davidson County, Tennessee Will Book 1 and 2, p. 231; Will Book 7, p. 290.
Robertson County, Tennessee Will Book 1, p. 69.
Two volumes unpub. mss. on Walker family in Whitley Collection.

Warfield

James H. Warfield was born in 1750 and married Ann Gassaway, a native of
Maryland. James H. Warfield died on 18 October 1812. After his death, Mrs. Warfield emigrated to Tennessee, where she died on 10 June 1849.

George H. Warfield, the son of James H. Warfield, was born on 9 May 1804. He
attended school in Maryland, and on reaching his majority, he entered into the mercantile business. He had charge of a number of vessels on the Chesapeake Bay. The
vessels belonged to a wealthy relative. At the age of twenty-three, he married Susan
Waters, a native of his home state, born on 23 March 1802. They were the parents
of James H., Ann Elizabeth, Milton, Susan Virginia, Charles H., Margaret, and
George W. Warfield.

About the year 1835, George H. and his family emigrated to Montgomery County,
Tennessee. There his wife Susan died on 28 October 1844. In 1848, Mr. Warfield
married his second wife, Elizabeth Johnson, a native of Tennessee, born on 14 March
1821, the daughter of Joseph and Nancy Johnson of Montgomery County. To this second marriage were born Amanda M., Charles P., Joseph G., Annie M., Pattie H.,
Samuel J., Laban J., Hanson, and Alexander G. Warfield.

After arriving in Montgomery, George H. Warfield purchased a large tract of
land which he cleared and improved. For many years, he was a stockholder and di-
rector in the Planter's Bank at Clarksville, and at one time, he was President of the
Montgomery County Agricultural and Mechanical Association. He amassed a fortune.
He died on 9 December 1870. He was one of the strongest supporters and contribu-
tors of the Methodist Episcopal Church in Clarksville.

George W. Warfield, son of George H. and Susan (White) Warfield, was educated
at Stewart College in Clarksville. In 1861, when he was seventeen years old, he enlisted in Co. E, 15th Tennessee Volunteer C.S.A. He was captured at Fort Donelson

and taken prisoner to Camp Douglas, Chicago, Illinois, where he was detained for seven months. He was wounded at Chickamauga and was on patrol duty at Petersburg, Virginia at the time of the surrender at Appomatox Court House, Virginia. After the war, Mr. Warfield returned home to Montgomery County and engaged in farming his 545 acres of land until September 1885, when he moved to Clarksville. On 20 October 1869, he married Dora Pollard, who was born on 30 April 1850, the daughter of B. F. and Susan A. Pollard. Mr. and Mrs. Geo. W. Warfield were the parents of six children: Walter Wilson, who was born on 30 July 1870; Lulu Bell, who was born on 27 January 1873; Susie Lizzie, who was born on 17 January 1876; Harrison Pollard, who was born on 10 February 1878; Dora Pollard, who was born on 7 January 1881; and Mary Eia, who was born on 7 March 1886.

Charles M. Warfield was born on 15 January 1808. At the time of his marriage, he was living in Robertson County, where he died on 7 September 1879. His wife, Mary Elizabeth Warfield, was a native of Greene County, Kentucky, born on 15 August 1827. Mr. and Mrs. C. M. Warfield had three children. Their third child, William C. Warfield, was born in Robertson County on 14 February 1850. After receiving a common school education, he attended Bryant and Stratton's Commercial College in Louisville, Kentucky. On 17 March 1872, he married Nannie Sadler, daughter of Robert and Rhoda Ann Sadler. Nannie Sadler was born on 24 November 1850. She was the mother of six children: Laban C., Robert S., Lizzie, Laura, George Buford, and Tom Pepper Warfield. They were all members of the Methodist Episcopal Church.

Goodspeed's History of Montgomery County, Tennessee, 1886, p. 1112.
Montgomery Co. Notes, unpub. Mss., Whitley Collection.

West

Dr. J. B. West, a prominent teacher at the Clarksville Female Academy from 1866 to 1872, was a native of Alabama, born in 1825. His wife, Mary Jarrad, was a native of Virginia, born in 1830. For more than thirty years, Dr. West was a leading minister of the Methodist Episcopal Church, and in 1886, he was in charge of the Tulip Street Church in Nashville, Tennessee.

Dr. and Mrs. West were the parents of John J. West, who was born in Todd County, Kentucky on 30 December 1853 and became a prominent attorney-at-law in Clarksville. John J. was educated in the common schools. In 1868, he entered Stewart College at Clarksville and graduated in 1872. He immediately began the study of law under the Honorable John F. House. During 1875, he was deputy Circuit Clerk of Montgomery County, and in the same year, he received his license to practice law. Three years later, he was elected public administrator. In 1882, he was elected City attorney for the town. On 3 October 1878, John J. West married Georgia Beaumont, who was born in Montgomery County in 1858. Their children were Laura B., Mary, and John. The West family were life-long members of the Methodist Church.

Goodspeed's History of Montgomery County, Tennessee, 1886, p. 1114
West family, unpublished mss. data in Whitley Collection, 4 vols.

Whitehead - Gardner

There is a story among the citizens of Robertson and Montgomery Counties, that everyone in the two counties can, in some way, trace a relationship to the Whitehead family. They were one of the earliest pioneer families. They arrived while the territory was still "Old Tennessee County," before Tennessee became a state in 1796.

In 1808, the Whiteheads resided on the road from Tribble Ferry to Vaughan's Mill and in the vicinity of the ferry to the first large branch below William Whitehead, according to the court records. It appears that William, Joseph, and Richard Whitehead all lived in the same community.

A record in Montgomery states that Benjamin Whitehead of Montgomery County, farmer, made a deed of gift to "loving sons Joseph and Richard" both of the state and county aforesaid, farmers. To Joseph, he gave a negro girl named Delph, aged seven years. To Richard, he gave a negro boy named Jack, aged three years. These gifts were made on 24 October 1800.

On 6 February 1815, Benjamine Whitehead "for love and good will and affection which I have and do bear toward my grandchildren the heirs of Gency Trotter of said county" gave and granted to his grandchildren a negro girl, Frances. The above mentioned property was to be divided amongst Gincy (Cinthy) Trotter's heirs on the death of George and Gincey Trotter. Richard Whitehead was appointed trustee in the transaction.

William Whitehead was born in Robertson County on 8 June 1811, the son of Robert Whitehead, a native of North Carolina, an early immigrant to Middle Tennessee. William married Louisa B. Polk. She was born in the same county as her husband in 1812 and died in 1858, the same year as her husband passed away. Their deaths were only a few days apart. Mrs. Louisa B. Polk Whitehead was a cousin of President James K. Polk.

William H. Whitehead, the son of William and Louisa B. (Polk) Whitehead, was born on 18 November 1831. William H. was a farmer. On 5 July 1860, he married Harriett E. Gill, who was born on 29 October 1840, the daughter of Robert R. and Isabel E. (Adkins) Gill. In 1861, William H. Whitehead enlisted in Company F, 49th Regiment of Tennessee. He took an active part in the battles of Fort Donelson, Atlanta, Franklin and numerous minor engagements. At the surrender of Fort Donelson, he was taken to Camp Douglass and detained for seven months but, at last, was exchanged. At the surrender of Franklin, he was again captured and taken to the same prison where he remained five months. He was wounded twice, once in the head and once in the left side, neither seriously. In 1865, he returned home and bought thirty acres of land west of Adams Station, where he settled. Mr. and Mrs. William H. Whitehead had one child, Robert Nicholas Whitehead. They were members of the Methodist Episcopal Church.

Robert Whitehead was born in North Carolina in 1774 and came to Robertson County in his youth. There he married Merilla Martin, purchased property, and died in 1832. Mrs. Merilla Whitehead was born in Tennessee in 1783 and died in 1838.

George H. Whitehead, the son of Robert and Merilla, was a prominent citizen of the county. He was born on 20 March 1820 at the same place he resided most of his life. After his parents' deaths, he resided on the home place for one year and then went to Clarksville and was engaged as clerk in a general store. A year later, he returned to his birthplace. On 24 November 1833, he wedded Adaline Gardner, daughter of Joshua and Mary (Polk) Gardner. Mary Polk was a cousin of President James K. Polk. Mrs. Mary Polk Whitehead was born on 8 February 1830 [?] and became the mother of five children. Only one of them, George H., was living in 1886.

George H. Whitehead changed his place of residence many times. He finally located on a 260 acre farm near Turnersville. His wife died on 1 February 1864, and on 4 January 1870, he married Lou Pickering, who died on 24 November 1884. Mr. Whitehead was married a third time on 10 November 1885 to Sally Murphy, daughter of Elias and Nancy (Williams) Murphy. She was born on 30 October 1854 and was a school teacher in her younger days.

Joshua Gardner was born in Virginia in 1785 and died in 1847. He was the son of Henry Gardner, who came to Robertson County in 1795. Joshua's wife, Mary Polk, was born in 1798 in Robertson County and died in 1858.

T. H. Gardner, the son of Joshua and Mary (Polk) Gardner and a native of Robertson County, was born on 26 January 1820 and lived all his life in the house in which he was born. When he was about twelve years of age, he left home and went to West Tennessee. He obtained a job there as clerk in a dry goods store. In 1840, he returned to his parents' home and began farming. On 16 December 1842, he married Francis M. Whitehead, the daughter of Robert and Marilla Whitehead. Frances M. was born on 14 January 1827 in the same county as her father. Mr. and Mrs.

Gardner were the parents of Charles N., Robert E., Mary S., Thomas L., George N., Almus E., William W., Lizzie D., Hart W., Fannie A., and Edward R. Gardner.

The Polks, Gardners, Whiteheads, Trotters, and numerous others of the earliest families are yet well represented in the Red River Country.

The estate of Martha Polk, deceased, Olivia Polk, deceased, and a plat of land, estate of the late John Polk, deceased, were returned to the Court of Robertson County in 1805.

William Polk was appointed administrator of John Polk, deceased of Robertson County. He was also appointed guardian of Mariah Harris, a minor in the said court, and he made a statement regarding the estate of Edmond Kearney Harris, deceased. Mention was made of the Polks' coming from York District, South Carolina. I do not believe that there was any connection between the Harrises and the Polks.

The inventory, dated 10 November 1814, of Thomas Polk, deceased, is a matter of record in Springfield. The division of the estate in November 1815 shows lots drawn by Abigail Polk, J. J. Polk, S. J. Polk, Mary W. Gardner, L. N. Polk, L. B. Polk, S. A. Polk, Ezekiel Polk, and C. A. Polk.

John Gardner married Priscilla Whitehead in 1796. John and Priscilla were both natives of Virginia. John died in 1845, and his wife survived until the following year. Their son, Col. John A. Gardner, was born in Robertson County in 1809.

Colonel Gardner went to Weakley County in 1826. The following year, he went to Parish, Henry County, Tennessee and established a weekly newspaper, The West Tennessean, and was the editor for one year. He sold out and moved to Dresden where he entered into the study of law. His preceptor was the Hon. William Fitzgerald. In 1829, he was admitted to practice law before the courts of Tennessee and opened a law office in Dresden, where he practiced for fifty years.

In 1838, he was again in the newspaper business as editor of the Jacksonian in Dresden, which position he held only a few months. In 1841, he was elected to the State Senate and served six years. Col. Gardner has long been remembered for a seven hour long speech he delivered before the State Senate on the manner of electing United States senators. He was called one of the "Immortal Thirteen." In 1847, Col. Gardner threw his hat into the ring as a candidate for Congress on the Democratic ticket. His competitor, on the Whig ticket, was William H. Haskell. The Colonel was defeated. In 1848, he was elector for General Cass, and in 1870, he was a member of the Constitutional Convention. He was a member of the lower house of the State Legislature, 1878-1879.

In 1828, Colonel Gardner married Maria Terrell, daughter of Jeptha Terrell. Mrs. Gardner was a native of North Carolina and the mother of four children: Algemon C., Ada B. (wife of the Hon. W. P. Caldwell, ex-member of Congress), Laura (wife of James Gardner), and Lou M. (wife of M. Z. Hankins).

Mrs. Maria Gardner passed away in 1848. In 1850, Mr. Gardner married Agnes H. Cowardin of Nashville. She was born in 1830 and became the mother of five children: Almus H., Ernest M., Percy W., Fannie G., and Josia Lee.

At one time, Colonel Gardner owned 7500 acres of land. The settlement was called Gardner's Station in 1865. In 1852, the Colonel organized the Nashville and Northwestern Railroad Company and served as its president for four years. Colonel Gardner and his family were members of the Methodist Episcopal Church. He was also a Mason.

Joshua Gardner, one of the seven sons and two daughters of John and Priscilla (Whitehead) Gardner and brother of Colonel Gardner, was born in Robertson County on 30 March 1800. Descendants of this branch of the family say that the Tennessee pioneers came from Southampton County, Virginia and that both John and Priscilla were born there in 1775 and came to Tennessee in 1796, first residing in Robertson County and later in Weakley, where John died in 1851 and Priscilla died in 1854.

The tradition does not seem to follow through the other branches of the family.

On 28 February 1829, Joshua Gardner married Sarah C., daughter of James and Esther Donelson. Esther Donelson, a native of Iredell County, North Carolina, was born in 1808 and died in Tennessee in 1873.

In 1875, Joshua Gardner married his second wife, Tempie Delap, daughter of Hugh and Lucy Delap. Mrs. Tempie Delap Gardner was born in Davidson County in 1821.

Mr. Joshua Gardner was a resident of Henry County until 1840, when he moved to Weakley and purchased 228 acres of land. He is said to have owned, at one time, upwards of 1300 acres of land, but at the time of his death, he held title to only 150 acres. He was a magistrate for a number of years in Henry County. He was a Mason, and he and his family were members of the Missionary Baptist Church.

Jephtha Gardner was born in Robertson County on 27 September 1801, moved to Weakley County with his brothers about 1825, and died in 1865. His wife, Mrs. Emily Gardner, was born in North Carolina and died in Tennessee in 1832.

Dr. J. Almus Gardner, one of six children of Jephetha and Emily Gardner, was born at Dresden on 12 January 1827 and was probably the first male child born in the town. Dr. Gardner studied medicine in the office of Drs. Edwards and Gardner, then entered medical college known as the University of Louisville, Kentucky, where he graduated as an M.D. in 1848. Dr. Gardner took up practice in Dresden where he remained until 1866. In 1850, he married Martha, born in 1833, the daughter of Hillary and Unity Bondurant. Dr. and Mrs. Gardner were the parents of Inez, Chaley (died young), and Eunice (wife of Warren Baker).

After leaving Dresden, Dr. Gardner located at Gardner Station, a village near the home of his uncle, Colonel Gardner. Dr. Gardner was a Mason, and his family belonged to the Methodist Episcopal Church.

Montgomery County Record Book A, p. 126.
Montgomery County Will Book B, p. 166.
Goodspeed's History of Tennessee, Robertson County, 1886, p. 1201
Goodspeed's History of Tennessee, Weakley County, pp. 998-999.
Montgomery County Court Minutes, 1808-1810, p. 171.
Robertson County Will Book 1, pp. 158, 209, 210, 255, 328.
Robertson County Court Minutes, 1800-1816.
Mss. material in Whitley Collection, 3 vols. on Polk family, unpublished.

Whitfield

The Whitfields appear to have been among the earliest arrivals along Red River. Bryan Whitfield of Montgomery County, for divers good causes, appointed Needham Whitfield of said county, as attorney to sell and convey two tracts of land in Knox County on Bull Run on Tennessee River and a tract on the south side of Cumberland River in Montgomery County, April 23, 1798. This record would indicate that Bryan Whitfield had moved from the county by the date of the deed.

The will of George Neville, April 22, 1811, names wife Rachel; son Joseph B.; son George W.; son John, to have the 640 acres "I live on;" four daughters, Violette Pollock, Sophia Owens, Rachel Williams, and Marion Whitfield; granddaughter Rachel Whitfield, ; Vilette's daughter, Violette; and other grandchildren, George Pollock, Presley Pollock, John Pollock, Lewarius Travis, and Letty Lynes.

The court of 1816 proved a deed from Bryant Whitfield to Needham Whitefield for 416 acres of land in Ray County in North Carolina. (There is no Ray County in North Carolina.)

Montgomery County Will Book 1797-1810, pp. 11, 56.
Montgomery County Court Minutes, 1816-1818, p. 27.

Wilcox - Wilcocks

The Wilcoxes were among the first families to settle on the Red River. With the Suggs, the Princes, and others, they founded the Red River Baptist Church, the first Baptist Church in the section. Some historians have credited this church with being the first church of any denomination established in Middle Tennessee, but that statement has been proved erroneous. Red River Church was located at Adams when it was organized in 1791 and is still used by the Baptists of that section.

On 5 July 1791, the membership included Isaac Wilcox, Samuel Wilcox and Hannah Wilcox. The July 1803 list of members showed the names of Isaac and Samuel.

The Wilcox lands extended into both Tennessee and Kentucky.

Samuel Wilcox deeded a negro girl slave to Thomas French as a gift for "affection." The Frenches were also members of Red River Church. In 1808, the French house was in Montgomery County, near or on the Great Road leading to Clarksville on Brushy fork.

The court of June 1808 for Montgomery appointed John French overseer of the road from the West fork Road to Brushy Fork of the Piney Fork and Robert Searcy's to the State line.

The first John French who came to Red River appears to have died in 1796-7, as there is mention of the estate of John French, deceased, wherein Keziah and Joseph French had an interest. The exact relationship of Keziah and Joseph is not shown.

On 25 June 1796, James Waddleton and his wife Margaret were received into Red River Church by letter. At the same time, "Brother" Jesse Brooks and his wife, Nancy, and Mary French were received. On 8 April 1798, Moses French, Black London, and Rebeckah French were received at Eddy Grove by letter. The July 1803 membership list of Red River shows the name of Moses French.

William Pennington, Wm. Cohoon, Samuel Wilcox, David C. Penny, and Pray Whipple were ordered to view a road from the Robertson Line by the mouth of Sulphur Fork to the Kentucky line at the "93 mile tree" "do say" the present road with straighting in the few short "RMAS" and the new road cut by the bridge on the south side of Red River to the road, March 1809.

It would appear that Samuel Wilcox died shortly after 19 January 1811, the date of his will, which was presented into court in April of the same year. He was the father of John Earle Wilcox to whom he left $10.00. He had a son John, mentioned in the will. He also mentioned his daughter-in-law, Elizabeth, and grandsons, Chesterfield Lewis Wilcox and Ethelbert Samuel Wilcox. Christopher Owen and William McGowen were named the executors.

Some of the Wilcoxes appear to have been down nearer Nashville, for the name is frequently found among the early records of Davidson County. One Thomas Wilcox married Mary Bryant in Davidson County on 12 September 1792 while the entire Middle District was still a part of North Carolina. Another Thomas Wilcox married Sally Chism on 2 April 1817 in Davidson County, and James Wilcox married Polly Kernell on 10 February 1819.

It is a fact that the Wilcoxes left many records in the border counties of Kentucky where some of the descendants later settled. Descendants of this pioneer family are still found throughout Middle Tennessee and Southern Kentucky.

Benjamin Wilcox, a Revolutionary soldier of Maryland or Virginia, migrated to Adair County, Kentucky, where his daughter Susan Elizabeth, called Betty, married William Barron on 24 November 1814. Mr. Barron died about 1834, leaving five children: Perry Walker Barron, who was born in 1815; James Harker Barron, who was born in 1817; Susan Ann Barron, who was born in 1818; Mary Jane Barron, who was born in 1820; and Silas Barron, who was born in 1822.

Montgomery County Court Minutes 1808-1810, pp. 34, 173.
Montgomery County Wills and Inv. 1797-1813, pp. 13, 380.
Red River Baptist Church Records.
Davidson County, Tennessee Marriage Bonnds Book 1.
National Historical Magazine, May 1940, p. 43.

Williams

E. W. Williams came from Virginia to Montgomery County where he married
Miss A. Davis, daughter of David Davis, a farmer of the same locality. They remained in Montgomery until 1839 then moved to West Tennessee, settling in Lauderdale County. He was a blacksmith and died in 1851. Mrs. Williams, a native of Middle Tennessee, died in 1859.

John T. Williams, their son, became a prominent citizen, a farmer and miller
of Lauderdale County. He operated a Saw Mill Business along with farming. On 15
June 1854 in Lauderdale, he married Martha Whetson, who was born on 23 March
1832, the daughter of James Whetson of Missouri. Mr. and Mrs. J. T. Williams
were the parents of seven children: James E., John T., Mary C., William B., David A. (died young), Oliver D., and George Robert. Mr. Williams and his family
were members of the Methodist Church.

Goodspeed's History of Tennessee, Lauderdale County, p. 883.
Unpublished Williams family data, Whitley Collection, 3 vols.

Wimberly

The Wimberly family are believed to have lived on or near the Kentucky line,
probably in the extreme southern part of Logan County.

Joseph Wimberly died before November 1813, leaving several minor orphans:
Sarah, Sterling George, Joseph, Robert Dogg, Catherine, and William. Their guar-
was Sugg Fort.

The estate was settled and returned to court on 11 February 1814, at which time
seven lots were set out: Lot No 1, Dolly Fort; Lot No. 2, Robert Wimberly; Lot No.
3, William Wimberly; Lot No. 4, Elizabeth Wimberly; Lot No. 5, Sterling G. Wimberly; Lot No. 6, Sally Nevill; and Lot No. 7, Joseph Wimberly.

The Wimberlys were not an outstanding family, but intermarried with the most
prominent people of the county.

It is evident that they were Baptists, for the records of the Red River Baptist
Church, also known as "Fort's Church," show that Sarah Wimberly was received by
experience on 14 May 1803. The church register shows her name several times.

The inventory of Joseph Wimberly appears in record book 1796-1812, p. 433 of
Robertson County.

The wife of Joseph Wimberly may have been a Lawson, for in the will of Apoph-
roditus Lawson (Lasson), dated 8 May 1815 and proved in Robertson County in November 1815, James Norfleet is named as executor. The only bequest set out in the will
reads, "To William Wimberly son of Unity Wimberly, all my estate."

Another clue to the identity of the widow Wimberly is that her given name was
Sarah, for a Sarah Wimberly was given a dower at the August 1815 Court.

Sixteen miles west of Adams, in the 17th Civil District of Robertson County,
there is an old cemetery known by those in the neighborhood as the Mallory-Fort
cemetery. The families who used the place for burials were the Mallorys, Alleys,
Wimberlys, Suggs, Forts, Triggs, and Barneses. There are very few late dated

tombstones in the cemetery. It is evident from the dates on the stones that the ceme-
tery was in use as early as 1827, but most of the inscriptions indicate the place was
used largely between 1827 and 1870. Among those buried there are:
Emma Lou Alley, Dec. 5, 1845, January 28, 1860.
Amanda L. Alley, born September 8, 1819, died April 29, 1853.
Joseph W. Wimberly, born March 21, 1831, died July 19, 1850.
Charlotte A. Wimberly, consort of George S. Wimberly, born June 23, 1809,
died November 19, 1845.
George S. Wimberly, born February 22, 1810, died July 13, 1850.
Laura L. Wimberly, born February 10, 1824, died July 17, 1850.
Margarette A. Wimberly, born August 17, 1833, died August 12, 1850.
Robert H. Wimberly, born December 20, 1830, died March 28, 1857.
Richard H. Wimberly, born May 19, 1842, died September 22, 1842.
Joseph Wimberly, born October 6, 1855, died September 14, 1857.
Eugenia, wife of J.B. Sugg, born January 14, 1838, died August 5, 1858.
R.A. Barnes, born July 11, 1837, died June 15, 1898.
Dorothy, wife of Whitmel Fort, born May 17, 1791, died January 1, 1827.
Whitmel Fort, born October 23, 1788, died January 10, 1866.
Catherine W. Bowrne [?], born April 9, 1800, died December 10, 1862 in Brandon.
Mary Anne Fort, born May 28, 1798, died May 1828.
Sallie B. Wimberly, wife of Joseph, born Sept. 1, 1801.
Arnold C. Trigg, wife of L.C. Trigg, born December 25, 1822, died April 1843.

Robert D. Bellamy, a native of Lexington, Kentucky, was born on 14 December
1818. In 1839, he married Miss Sarah A. Northington of Montgomery County, the
daughter of John and Mary Northington. Mrs. Bellamy died on 17 December 1852.
Her husband continued to reside in Todd County, Kentucky.

Their son, John T. Bellamy, was born in Montgomery County on 13 September
1840. He was educated in the Montgomery Institute. After the death of his mother,
he and his sisters were reared by their grandmother, Mary Northington.

In 1861, John T. Bellamy married Bettie Wimberly, the daughter of George S.
and Charlotte Wimberly. Mr. and Mrs. Bellamy were the parents of five children:
Ella N., Mary, Lizzie, Robert S., and Douglas. Mrs. Bettie (Wimberly) Bellamy died in August 1873, and in October 1874, Mr. Bellamy married his second wife,
Miss Nannie L. Keesee, the daughter of Reuben C. and Judith P. Keesee. To this
union, two children were born: E. Ross, and Reuben K.

Mr. Bellamy owned considerable valuable farming land in the first and sixth
Civil Districts of the county. The family belonged to the Methodist Episcopal Church.
———————
Robertson County, Tennessee Will Book 1812-1818, pp. 78 and 104.
Red River Baptist Church records in Tennessee State Library.
Goodspeed's History of Montgomery County, 1886, p. 1006.
Wimberly family file, mss. data, Whitley Collection.

Woodard - Woodward

The Woodwards or Woodards were of English origin, partly Methodist and partly
Missionary Baptist.

Moses Woodward and wife Mary, of Edgecombe, appear to have been the parents
of at least three children, Noah, Thomas, and Mary.

Noah was born in Edgecombe on 14 January 1758, died in Robertson County, Tennessee on 14 January 1818, and married Delilah Briant, who was born on 16 January
1771 and died on 7 Marcy 1838, the daughter of Thomas and Fathia (Faithe) Briant
(Bryant). Noah Woodard was the father of eleven children.

Thomas Woodard was born in Edgecombe on 15 August 1766, died in Robertson
County on 14 January 1836, and married Elizabeth Pitt, who was born in 1768 and died
in 1836, the daughter of Arthur Pitt. Thomas had seven children.

Mary, the daughter of Moses Woodward, was born on 14 July 1770, married Thomas George, and lived in Robertson County.

Noah and Thomas came from North Carolina to Robertson County, Tennessee. Noah came from Green County, but lived in Edgecombe. There is a deed which styles him as "of Edgecombe County, State of North Carolina." Thomas came from Johnston County.

North Carolina grant No. 561 was issued to Thomas Woodward, as assignee of John McDowell, who was a private in the Continental Line of North Carolina. The tract contained 640 acres on the North Fork of Red River, corner to Noah Woodward. At the time the grant was issued, the land was in Davidson County, but after the organization of Robertson in 1796, it fell in that county.

Noah Woodward was given grant No. 590 by the State of North Carolina, as assignee of Samuel Simpson, a private in the Continental line. This tract contained 640 acres on the North Fork of Red River. It lay in Davidson County at the time of granting but later fell in Robertson. The date shown on the grant is September 15, 1787.

A second grant, No. 415, was issued to Thomas Woodward. It was issued by North Carolina on 27 June 1793. The land was situated in Sumner County on the north side of Cumberland River on a creek known as Lick Creek, about four miles from the mouth.

North Carolina grant No. 416, dated 27 June 1793, issued 640 acres in Sumner County, on the north side of Cumberland River, opposite the Big Salt Lick, to Simon Woodward.

In Davidson County, the will of Micajah Woodward, dated 22 August 1808, mentions his wife Mary, daughter Sally Fly or Frey, son Jeremiah, son Micajah Lewis, daughter Polly Rutherford, and daughter Mary.

The North Carolina Revolutionary Army Claim Accounts in Raleigh, N. C. states, "Paid by the Treasurer to the Comptroller July 1790 — Thos. Woodward —£11. 4. 0," also, "Paid by the Treasurer to the Compt. July 1790 — Thomas Woodward£0. 15. 0 — Interest£0. 17. 10, Philip Raiford, Sheriff of Johnston County," and "List of Certificates paid by Green Hill for Halifax District — 1783 — Noah Woodard —£13. 10. 0 — From North Carolina Revolutionary Army Accounts."

There is a deed in Robertson County which states, "Noah Woodward to Thomas George, who married Mary the sister of Thomas and Noah." Another deed, dated 21 September 1799 in Robertson County, mentions N. Woodard of Edgecombe County State of North Carolina for the consideration of $500, a certain tract or parcel of land in the County of Robertson in Harrington's Fork of Red River, 369 acres being tract of land granted by the State of North Carolina, bearing date 20 May 1793 and No. 2273.

William Woodward, a native of North Carolina, came to Robertson County quite early. One of his sons, James (called Junior), was born in Tennessee on 25 February 1814 and married Amanda Porter on 26 March 1840. James settled near Springfield on a 130 acre tract of land, where he remained until 1858 when he sold it and bought his father's farm. James died on 7 October 1861. Mrs. Amanda (Porter) Woodward was born on 22 July 1822 in the Red River country. When she was about twenty-six years of age, she became an invalid.

Mrs. and Mrs. James Woodward had a son, M. D. Woodward, who was born on 5 February 1846. On 14 February 1865, he married Polk L. Johnson, a native of Robertson, born on 28 November 1845, the daughter of William H. and Charity (Morris) Johnson. M. D. and Polk Woodward had six children: James H., William J., Thomas M., Eunice R., Bessie C., and Harry H. Woodward. Mr. and Mrs. M. D. Woodward owned and occupied the home place of 270 acres, which had been in the family for three generations.

Another branch of the family which came from Edgecombe County in 1792 and settled in the present limits of Robertson, included a man who died near Springfield in 1836. He was one of the first settlers in the county and the grandfather of Daniel Woodward.

The Honorable Wiley Woodward was the son of one of the pioneers. He was born in 1810 and was married in 1829, at the age of nineteen, to Elizabeth Henry. Wiley Woodward became a successful farmer and owned upwards of 2000 acres of land at one time. He was elected to the Legislature in 1849 and again in 1851. He died on 28 October 1877. Elizabeth Henry Woodward was born on 11 December 1811 and was living in 1866.

James H. Woodward, one of the sons of the Hon. and Mrs. Woodward, was born on 28 April 1832 and was married in 1877 to Nannie L. Draughon, the daughter of Dr. George E. and Tabitha (Couts) Draughon. Nannie L. was born in Tennessee on 15 February 1849. Mr. and Mrs. James H. Woodward were the parents of Coutie Warren Woodward, who was born on 13 January 1880, and James Draughon Woodward, who was born on 28 September 1882 and died on 19 January 1886. This branch of the Woodward family belonged to the Methodist Episcopal Church.

Daniel Woodard or Woodward, a brother of James H., was born on 26 June 1836 and was educated at Bethel College at Russellville, Kentucky after attending county schools. On 18 November 1869, he married Julia Young, the daughter of F. G. and Missouri Young. Julia was born in Robertson County in 1846 and became the mother of Wiley, Joseph and Florence (twins), Frank, Mary, Elizabeth, Lula, Daniel, and a daughter who died young. After Daniel Woodard's marriage, he lived in the house with his parents for seven years and then built himself a house on part of the old home place.

Kichen H. Woodward was born in North Carolina in 1792, and when he was four years old, he was brought to Tennessee by his parents. He lived in Robertson County until his death on 26 November 1855. His wife, Martha Pope, was born in North Carolina in 1800 and died in 1877.

Meredith Woodward, the son of Kichen H. and Martha (Pope) Woodward, was born in Robertson County on Christmas Day 1828. He was married in 1848 to Sarah Woodward, the daughter of Thomas and Winnifred Woodward. Sarah was born on 30 December 1830. Mr. and Mrs. Meredith Woodward had the following children: Cephas, Lee, Ellen who married Pinckney Gunn, Thomas R., and Neicy. Most of this family belonged to the Missionary Baptist Church.

There is an old Woodard graveyard in the 13th Civil District of Robertson County in which the following tombstones are found:
Dr. T. M. Woodward, born January 15, 1828, died January 4, 1878. [He married Catherine Woodward on 24 December 1852, and was married a second time to Mrs. M. D. Pepper. He practiced medicine for twenty-six years.]
Catherine Woodward, wife of Dr. T. M. Woodard, born Jan. 12, 1828, died December 17, 1861.
James Woodward, born March 8, 1799, died November 5, 1875. [He was a prominent Baptist.]
Margaret, wife of James Woodard, born June 24, 1803, died June 3, 1883.
Franklin Woodard, son of James and Margaret, born September 1831, died July 4, 1862.
Gustavus A. Woodard, born March 5, 1840, died February 13, 1877.
Marens L. Woodard, born July 16, 1836, died November 30, 1883.
Julia W. Bell, born July 24, 1849, died May 20, 1921.
J. G. Woodard, born July 4, 1833, died August 2, 1918.
Virginia Woodard, born December 22, 1845, died July 13, 1911.
William Woodard, son of James and Margaret, born May 19, 1826, died August 16, 1840.
M. E. Patterson, born October 8, 1830, died June 20, 1896.

There was an Elbert Woodard who married Harriett Moore on 28 November 1840. Willie L. Norfleet married Sarah Woodard on 14 December 1829.

The Woodard family is well represented in the county and surrounding country to this day.

Robertson County, Tennessee Deed Book B, pp. 79, 273; Book 1, p. 466.
North Carolina Grant Book A-1, pp. 282, 297; Grant Book G, pp. 200, 201 in Tennes-
    see State Archives and Land Office, Nashville.
Davidson County, Tennessee Wills, 1808.
North Carolina Army accounts, Vol. VII, p. 85, folio 1 and p. 88, folio 1; Vol. X,
    p. 4, folio 1.
Robertson County Tennessee marriages, Book 1, pp. 8, 17, 28.
Goodspeed's History of Robertson County, Tennessee, 1886, p. 1203.
Tombstone Records by Acklen, 1933, p. 160.
Mss. data in Whitley collection, Woodard and Woodward.

Woodson - West

Daniel Woodson was born in Virginia in 1739 and lived until 1810. He lived and
died in Buckingham County. His wife, Elizabeth Jones, was born in 1755. After the
death of her husband, she moved to Christian County and took up residence among
her children. She died in 1840 in Christian County, Kentucky where she lies buried
in the cemetery at Oak Grove, on the lot of her daughter, Mrs. Patsy Jones Fletcher.

Daniel Woodson never came to Kentucky or Tennessee. He was the son of Obediah Woodson and his wife, Constance Watkins, of Albemarle and Prince Edward
Counties.

Obediah Woodson was born in 1712, the son of Richard and Ann (Smith) Woodson.
Richard was the son of Robert, who was the son of John Woodson of Henrico County,
Virginia.

Bettie Ann Woodson, a remarkable woman, the daughter of Daniel Woodson, was
born on 9 March 1784 in Buckingham County and married three times. Her first husband, John or Joseph Epperson, was a wealthy tobacco plantationer of the James
River and operated a Tobacco Warehouse at "Planter's Town." An old account book,
which was in the possession of Mr. Irvin Davie a number of years ago (1929), contains much information regarding the Buckingham families at Planter's Town, along
the James in Virginia. Mr. Epperson, Bettie Ann's first husband, met his death
shortly after their marriage. He had taken a trip on a stage coach and was killed
enroute. Mrs. Epperson remained a widow only a short time.

Bettie Ann Woodson was married the second time to Claiborne West, also a Virginian and several years her senior, in 1799. He was born on 15 November 1759.
His first wife was a Miss Tindall, the daughter of Washington Tindall of Buckingham
County, Virginia. After Mrs. West's death, he married a Miss Sanders, who also
lived only a short time. Then, he married his third wife, Mrs. Bettie Ann Epperson.

Mr. West and Bettie Ann had a large family. About 1810 or 1812, they moved
from Buckingham County to Christian County, Kentucky, locating on the place where
they spent the remainder of their lives. Mr. West died on 1 March 1822, according
to his tombstone and the records in the Christian County Court House at Hopkinsville.
I visited the old home place, a short distance from the Tennessee-Kentucky line, in
1929 and observed the stately tombs of Claiborne West, called "Colonel" by his asso-
ciates, and of his wife, Bettie Ann.

Claiborne West was a gentleman farmer. On 1 July 1815, he purchased two sur-
veys of land containing 800 acres or more on the waters of the West Fork of Red River from Joshua Cates and Eustatia, his wife. In the deed, West is styled "of Buckingham County, State of Virginia."

From 1815 until his death, Claiborne West had many land transactions in Christian County and some in Montgomery County, Tennessee, where a small portion of
his tract of land reached. After his death, Mrs. West became noted for her business
ability. She was known far and near as the best trader in "the parts."

The will of Claiborne West provided for his children quite well. The children of

Bettie Ann by her West husband were: Hector, who married Virginia Overton and had Lou and Hector; Claiborne, Jr.; William Henry Harrison, who married Susan Long in Christian County; Virginia Louisa, who was married first to Mr. Cocke, second to Mr. Wilkins, and third to Mr. Newman; Elvira Ann, who was born on 12 November 1816, died on 1 August 1896, and was married in 1842 to Erasmus Stribling Crawford, who was born on 16 March 1815 and died in 1865; Bettie Claiborne, who married Patrick Henry and whose descendants are in Mississippi; and John J., who married Susan J. Glass.

William Henry Harrison West and his wife, Susan Long, the daughter of Gabriel Long, had children: John T., Henry Claiborne, Bettie, and Lucy. John T. married Jennie Weathers of Christian County. Their daughter, Jennie West, became a teacher in the schools of Bowling Green; their son, John T., Jr., died in infancy; and their third child, Nolan S. West, married Salena Hill of Christian County but removed to Texas. Henry Claiborne West married Mildred Loving of Kentucky, and they were the parents of Bettie, who married a Mr. Soule, and Alexander Loving West, who was living in Tulsa, Oklahoma in 1929. Bettie West, who was named after her grandmother, married a Mr. Young. Lucy West, the fourth child of Mr. and Mrs. Wm. Henry Harrison West, married a Mr. Bradley.

Elvira Ann West was born on 12 November 1816 and was married in 1842 in Christian County, Kentucky to Erasmus Stribling Crawford. They had six children. Their daughter, Bettie Ann Crawford, was born on 15 May 1849, died on 19 July 1918, and was married in 1872 to Richard Dudley Jordan, who was born on 7 October 1849 and died on 10 November 1907. They resided in Memphis, Shelby County, Tennessee. They were the parents of: Louise Crawford Jordan, who married Wm. Louis Davis of Nashville; Elvin Jordan, who married Dr. E. M. Holder; Richard Dudley Jordan, who married Helen Briggs; and Laura Banks Jordan, who is unmarried and resides in Memphis. Other children of E. S. and Elvira Ann (West) Crawford were: James Crawford, who was married; Ida Crawford; Louisa Crawford, who married Julian Taylor; West J. Crawford, who married Catherine Smith; and Mary Crawford, who married a Captain Biser.

John J. West and his wife, Susan J. Glass, had only one child, Alice, who married Benjamin D. Moore and became the mother of two children, Mary Elizabeth and Harry W. Moore. Mary Elizabeth Moore married F. C. Clardy. Their children were Anne Bacon, John M., and Flem C. Clardy, Jr. Anne Clardy married Will Johnson and had two children, William and Harry C. Johnson. Flem C. Clardy, Jr. married Miss Logan, and they became the parents of Betty Florence and Flem, the third.

After Claiborne West died, Mrs. Bettie Ann West married her third husband, Colonel Ambrose Davie, by whom she had two sons, Winston and Montgomery Davie.

Colonel Davie, knowing the great love she had for her West husband, buried Bettie Ann by the side of Colonel West on 21 July 1839. Shortly thereafter, Colonel Davie married a widow Phillips of Georgia. This information came from Mr. Irvin Davie, who resided at the old West-Davie homestead.

Winston Davie was valedictorian of the class of 1845 at Yale. It is from this family that George M. Davie, once notable lawyer of Louisville, Kentucky, descends. The Honorable and Mrs. Geo. M. Davie were the parents of Preston Davie of New York. Winston Davie was also the father of Iredell Davie.

Montgomery Davie was born on 16 August 1827 and married Cornellia Leavell, a member of one of the most prominent and wealthy families of Kentucky. Their children were: Louis Leavell; Ambrose; Eugene Snead; Maud, who married Robert Owsley; Winston Jones; Eugenia, who married Mr. Giles; Cornellia Frances, who was first married to her cousin Iredell Davie and second to Mr. Bagby; Irvine, who owned the old account book brought from Buckingham County, Virginia to Christian County, Kentucky in 1812 by Mr. and Mrs. West.

The West and Davie families are undoubtedly among the outstanding settlers just above the Tennessee-Kentucky line in Christian County, Kentucky.

Account book of Claiborne West, brought from Va. to Ky. A complete copy is in the

Whitley Collection, courtesy of Irvin Davie, 1929.
Christian County, Kentucky Deed Book E, p. 297; Deed Book G, p. 465.
Christian County, Kentucky Wills
Christian County, Kentucky Marriage Records.
Tombstone records at Old Davie-West home, Christian County, Kentucky.
Papers of Irvine Davie, 1929, Old West home.
Records of Mrs. Louis Davis, Nashville, Tennessee, 1929.
D. A. R. Records, application of Mrs. Louis Davis, prepared by E. R. Whitley, 1929.
Mss. records in Whitley collection, unpublished manuscript.

Yarborough

The Yarborough or Yarboro family in Montgomery County came from South Carolina.

The 1850 census of Montgomery County, Tennessee lists the following families:
Susan Yarborough, aged 60, with Joseph W. Yarborough, aged 22, and Susan Yarborough, aged 16, all born in South Carolina.
Moses Yarborough, aged 27, with Lucy, aged 27, Elizabeth, aged 5, and James, aged 3, all born in South Carolina.
Samuel Yarborough, aged 27, with Elizabeth J., aged 19, and Mary S., aged 2, all born in Tennessee.
John Yarborough, aged 47, with wife Mary, aged 44, and William A., aged 20, all born in North Carolina, plus Milly, aged 15, Frances M., aged 17, Henry, aged 11, Elizabeth, aged 7, Eliza J., aged 6, and Nelson, aged 4, all born in Tennessee.
J. Yarborough, a farmer, aged 49, born in Virginia, with wife Elizabeth, aged 48, and Elizabeth, aged 17, both born in Kentucky, plus Joseph, aged 14, Amy, aged 12, and Eudora, aged 9, all born in Tennessee.
Ellick Yarborough, a farmer, aged 36, with Mary (no doubt his wife), aged 29, George, aged 19, Eliza, aged 7, and Elizabeth, aged 6, all born in Tennessee.
Abner Yarborough, aged 50, born in Virginia, with Susan, aged 38, and Sarah, aged 16, both born in Kentucky, and Wm. E., aged 10, born in Tennessee.

It is said by some of the descendants of the Yarborough family that the Yarboroughs of America are descended from William Yarborough, who was one of the sixty thousand Normans who embarked in vessels with the Duke of Normandy in the year 1046 to conquer England. For his valor, William the Conqueror of England gave him the Earldom of Yorkshire County, England, which Earldom still exists.

Some of the Yarborough gentry came from England in the early settlement of Virginia and located in Amelia County. Between the years 1729 and 1775, seven brothers, Zachariah, Archibald, Monoah, Alexander, Thomas, Henry, and John.

In 1775, Zachariah left Louisburg, Franklin County, North Carolina and moved to that part of Rowan County which is now Davidson County. There he met and married Elizabeth Dowd by whom he had several children. It is believed that some of the Tennessee Yarboroughs descend from the seven brothers who went from Virginia to North Carolina. The Yarboroughs in North Carolina intermarried with such families as the Lightfoots, Deatons, Hicks, Chisholms, Bethunes, and other prominent families of Montgomery, Franklin, and Rowan Counties.

There were other branches of the family in Halifax and Edgecombe Counties in North Carolina. They also came from Virginia. It is believed that the Yarboroughs of Montgomery County, Tennessee represent more than one branch of the descendants from the emigrant ancestor.

Elizabeth Yarborough was born on 22 December 1808 in Montgomery County, Tennessee, was married in 1830 in Illinois to Abraham Coon, and died in Salt Lake City, Utah on 15 January 1894. Elizabeth is thought to have been the daughter of William Yarborough whose wife was Pemelia Parker. William Yarborough was probably the son of George Yarborough whose wife was Elizabeth Norrid.

Yates

John Yates was born about 1720 in Maryland or Virginia. Was he a brother of George Yates, Elijah Yates, Hannah Shelton, Ann Gibson, and Martha Watts, children of John and Elizabeth Yates? Tradition has it that John Yates married a Miss Kilgore and had at least three sons: William, Thomas, and James. John Yates and his three sons are said to have fought in the Revolutionary War and moved from Halifax County, Virginia to Caswell County, North Carolina soon afterwards. They remained in North Carolina only a few years then moved to Cross Plains, Robertson County, Tennessee in the Kilgore party.

William Yates was born in 1744 and married Agnes Price in Virginia. Thomas Yates was born in 1752 in Bedford County, Virginia and was married in 1776 in North Carolina to Rebecca Ragsdale, the daughter of William Ragsdale. James Yates married Lydia Kilgore, said to have been the daughter of Thomas and Phoebe Lee Kilgore.

John Yates, son of either William or Thomas, is said to have married a daughter of George and Mary Isabell. John and his wife were the parents of Sally (married Lewis Ragsdale), Mary, Agatha, and Nancy.

One William Yates, a Lieutenant-Colonel, was muster master general, 11 April 1777. He was married in Virginia to Agnes Price. About 1780, he moved to Caswell County, North Carolina and later to Robertson County, Tennessee where he died. His father was John Yates, who it is believed moved to Virginia from Ann Arundel County, Maryland.

In the Kentucky pension list, there is a John Yates who was born in Virginia in 1750 and died in Kentucky in 1820. He was a Lieutenant in the Virginia State Regiment, 1780-1781.

There was a John Yates of Culpepper County, Virginia, who married Elizabeth Gaines. They were the parents of Major James G. Yates of the 93rd Regiment, 10th Brigade, Adair County, Kentucky, 15 January 1814/1815.

James Gaines Yates was born in Virginia on 5 February 1781 and died on 28 July 1845 near Clarksville, Tennessee. He was married in Virginia on 24 December 1801 to Mary Malinda Browning, who was born in Culpepper County, Virginia. Their twelve children were: Malinda M. S. (probably Malinda Mary Strother), who was born on 11 November 1802 and married Benjamine Childress; Charles Wesley, who was born on 18 December 1804 and died on 19 March 1837; John M., who was born on 3 October 1806 and married Malinda Royce on 14 February 1828; James L., who was born on 9 September 1808 and died on 11 June 1833; Willis Browning, who was born on 10 June 1810 in Gradyville, Adair County, Kentucky, died on 13 January 1848 in Montgomery County, Tennessee, and was married in Logan County, Kentucky on 10 December 1840 to Mary Jane Amanda Ellen Poor, who was born in Christian County, Kentucky circa 1822; Joseph Arthur, who was born on 18 September 1812 and married Margaret Jane Johnson on 30 November 1837; Cassandra A., who was born on 1 November 1814 and was married on 28 March 1834 to George W. Childress, who was born on 25 December 1814; Mary Anne Morrison, who was born on 1 August 1817 and was married on 11 January 1836 to James F. Watwood; Sarah Enfield, who was born on 1 August 1817 and was married on 16 March 1835 to George Watwood, brother of James F.; Caroline S., who was born on 20 January 1820 and died on 5 August 1826; Elizabeth Gaines, who was born on 13 February 1822 and married John Newman; and Almira, who was born on 13 April 1824, died on 8 March 1887, and married Uriah Jack Holland on 13 June 1843.

D. A. R. Magazine, March 1951, p. 243; Nov. 1949, p. 946; Sept. 1935, p. 563 (Bible of James Gaines Yates, owned by Mrs. Henry L. Kinnison).
Yates file, unpub. mss., Whitley Collection.

Yoes - Atkins - Connell

The Yoes, Atkins, and Connell families were related when they came to Red River.

William Atkins, Nathan Yoes, and John Yoes, all of the said state and county, moving, appointed friends and brothers, William Connell and Giles Connell, attorneys to recover and receive all or part of property or estate of "our Father-in-law Giles Connell, deceased" of South Carolina, Spartanburg District, and also empowered the said William and Giles Connell to sell land that may have belonged to the said estate by the said Giles Connell, deceased, 2 June 1804.

The Connells and the Walkers intermarried in Robertson County. I believe these families, especially the earlier ones in the Tennessee settlement, were all Baptist. Sarah Connell's name appears on the Red River Baptist Church records as a member of that congregation under the date July 5, 1791. Giles Connell was a member in 1803. A notation by his name, about that year, says, "excld."

During the first half of 1818, Elias Fort was appointed guardian to the minor orphans of William Connell, deceased, with Enoch P. Connell and Giles Connell as security. About the same time, Sally Connell was appointed guardian to Parrisada Connell.

The will of William Connell is not found on the records, but there is an account of the division of his estate in 1820. In it, the name is spelled Connell and Cornwell. Elizabeth Connell was to have Lot No. 1; Oliver Connell, Lot No. 2; James Gardner, husband of Charlotte Cornwell, Lot No. 3; Wm. H. Connell, husband of Nancy, Lot No. 4; E. P. Connell, Lot No. 5; Parasada Connell, Lot No. 6; Caty E. Connell, Lot No. 7; Thomas Connell, Lot No. 8; William Connell, Lot No. 9; Lou Connell, Lot No. 10.

There is little or nothing in the early records about the Yoes. They have never been a well known family in the neighborhood, and it is thought that they moved from the community shortly after arriving.

Robertson County Will Book 1, p. 132; Will Book 1819-21, p. 87.
Red River Baptist Church Records, Tennessee State Library.

Zech

Jacob Zech may have been the son of John Zech, the Revolutionary soldier who was living in Robertson County in 1840 and drew a pension for his Revolutionary service. The 1832 pension list gives the name of the Revolutionary patriot as Jacob, aged 76 years. It is believed that Jacob and John are one and the same man.

The Zeches came from Pennsylvania. There is very little mention of the name in the deeds and minutes of the county. It is thought that they were not a family of any great means.

In the Cook graveyard, eleven and a half miles from Springfield, there are several tombstones which indicate that a group of Pennsylvanians must have located there. Among them:
J. W. Coleman, died June 8, 1897, age 50 years.
S. Catharine Foreman Cook, born April 26, 1827, died March 1, 1875.
George W. Cook, born August 12, 1823, died March 10, 1911.
Sarah C., wife of G. W. Cook, born April 26, 1827, died March 1, 1875.
Thomas Cook, born January 8, 1834, died September 14, 1854.
John Cook, born March 19, 1796, died August 22, 1886.
Margaret Cook, born February 17, 1795, died January 25, 1874.
Clara, wife of Jacob Zech, born October 24, 1819, died January 11, 1897.
Anjilene H., wife of T. J. Choat, died April 21, 1895.
T. J. Choat, died June 18, 1887, age 85 years.
J. W. Powell, born October 29, 1856, died May 2, 1914.
Margaret A. Powell, born October 29, 1856, died May 2, 1914.

The marriage records of Robertson County from 1829 to 1860 show that a John Zech married E. P. Walton on 8 November 1840.

Although there is little indication that the Zeches were especially prominent, persons of that name have married into the best families of the Red River community.

The Hopewell Cemetery at Hopewell Baptist Church in the Second District of Robertson County, about eight miles from Springfield, was a community burying ground. Among the families represented there are: Dorris, Pitt, Widick, Holman, Murphy, Sawyers, Beasley, Fisher, Randolph, Brakefield, Willis, McMurry, Dozier, Winkler, White, Dean, Tate, Holland, Barrow, Moulton, Clayton, Outlaw, Doran, West, Chapman, Fletcher, Stack, Smelser, Chatman, Ballard, Reid, Zech, Porter, Wilson, Pinson, Barber, Holland, Arnold, Carver, Edens, Traughber, Spencer, Cook, Brooks, Groves, Trenway, Corkan, Setser, Pike, Buch, Hightower, Simmons, Carter, and McIntosh.

LAND GRANTS ISSUED BY NORTH CAROLINA

Land Grants issued by North Carolina — Red River, and Tennessee, Montgomery, and Robertson Counties.

Grant No. 827. no service shown. dated 1, 17, 1789. Assigned to Andrew Armstrong, Warrant No. 3384 for 640 acres. Recorded Book A-1, p. 417. In Davidson County on Red River.

Grant No. 763 to John Acinclash, a private, dated 7, 11, 1788. Assigned to William Bowman, Warrant No. 2496 for 640 acres. Recorded Book A-1, p. 384. Both sides of the North Fork of Red River.

Grant No. 3379 to Howell Adams, no service, dated 12, 1, 1801. No warrant number for 323 acres. Recorded Book D-1, p. 294. Montgomery County on Barton's Creek.

Grant No. 701, Joshua Adcock, a private, dated 7, 11, 1788. Assigned to William McKadow (McAdoo), Warrant No. 438 for 224 acres. Recorded Book C-3, p. 190. Tennessee County, South side Cumberland River.

Grant No. 271 to Thomas Aims, a private, dated 1, 24, 1787. Assigned to Col. James Glasgow, Warrant No. 1154 for 640 acres. Recorded Book A-1, p. 137. South side Red River.

Grant No. 293, Levy Aker, soldier, dated 6, 13, 1787. Assigned to John Rice, Warrant No. 1088 for 640 acres. Recorded Book A-1, p. 148. Cumberland and Red Rivers.

Grant No. 2466 to Henry Albritton, a private, dated 12, 23, 1793. Assigned to Jesse Cobb, Warrant No. 1325 for 640 acres. Recorded Book B-2, p. 192. Guises Creek in Tennessee County.

Grant No. 1161 to John Alford, dated 11, 26, 1789. Assigned to Richard Fenner, Warrant No. 2165 for 640 acres. Recorded Book C-3, p. 44. Tennessee County, north side Cumberland River.

Grant No. 314 to Thomas Allen, a private, dated 5, 28, 1787. Assigned to Richard Fenner, Warrant No. 2163 for 640 acres. Recorded Book A-1, p. 159. Sulphur Fork.

Grant No. 913 to David Ambrose, dated 5, 18, 1789. Warrant No. 890 for 1000 acres. Recorded Book E-5, p. 28. Davidson County, on Sycamore Creek.

Grant No. 868 to Daniel Anderson, no service shown, dated 1, 17, 1789. Warrant No. 2898 for 640 acres. Recorded Book E-5, p. 6. Sumner County on Red River.

Grant No. 1206 to Daniel Anderson, dated 12, 10, 1790. Warrant No. 2909 for 640 acres. Recorded Book C-3, p. 103. On North side of Cumberland River.

Grant No. 1222 to Daniel Anderson, dated 12, 10, 1790. Warrant No. 2935 for 640 acres. Recorded Book C-3, p. 68. In Tennessee County, North side Cumberland River.

Grant No. 1247 to Daniel Anderson, dated 12, 10, 1790. Warrant No. 2888 for 640 acres. Recorded Book C-3, p. 80. In Tennessee County, South side Cumberland River.

Grant No. 1256 to Daniel Anderson, dated 12, 10, 1790. Warrant No. 2854 for 640 acres. Recorded Book C-3, p. 85. Tennessee County, north side Cumberland River.

Grant No. 1301 to Daniel Anderson, dated 12, 10, 1790. Warrant No. 3486 for 640 acres. Recorded Book C-3, p. 105. In Tennessee County, north side of Cumberland River.

Grant No. 1306 to Daniel Anderson, no service shown, dated 12, 10, 1790. Warrant No. 2875 for 1000 acres. Recorded Book C-3, p. 107. Tennessee County, north side of Cumberland River.

Grant No. 1310 to Daniel Anderson, no service stated, dated 12, 10, 1790. Warrant No. 2884 for 640 acres. Recorded Book C-3, p. 109. In Tennessee County, north side of Cumberland River.

Grant No. 1317 to Daniel Anderson, no service shown, dated 12, 10, 1790. Warrant No. 1658 for 640 acres. Recorded Book C-3, p. 113. Tennessee County, south side of Cumberland River.

Grant No. 1238 to David Anderson, dated 12, 10, 1790. Warrant number not shown for 640 acres. Recorded Book C-3, p. 76. Tennessee County, west side of Cumberland River.

Grant No. 1922 to John Anderson, a private, dated 5, 20, 1793. Assigned to Jesse Cobb, Warrant No. 1922 for 640 acres Recorded Book E-5, p. 256. Tennessee County.

Grant No 1490 to Thomas Archer, no service shown, dated 1, 4, 1792. Warrant No. 2344 for 640 acres. Recorded Book C-3, p. 193. Tennessee County, south side of Cumberland River.

Grant No. 866 to Andrew Armstrong, no service shown, dated 1, 17, 1785. Warrant No. 1701 for 640 acres. Recorded Book E-5, p. 5. Davidson County on north side Red River.

Grant No. 1634 to Richard Armstrong, no service, dated 2, 23, 1793. Warrant No. 2808 for 640 acres. Recorded Book C-3, p. 256. Tennessee County on Wells Creek.

Grant No. 25 to William Armstrong, a captain, dated 3, 14, 1786. Warrant No. 52 for 3840 acres. Recorded Book A-1, p. 13. Below Red River.

Grant No. 1408 to James Arnold, no service shown, dated 12, 20, 1791. Warrant No. 2494 for 640 acres. Recorded Book C-3, p. 157. Tennessee County on west side of Pine River.

Grant No. 2513 to Wm. Arron & John Lamb, dated 12, 4, 1795. Warrant No. 3833 for 1000 acres. Recorded Book C-3, p. 337. Tennessee County.

Grant No. 3335 to Charleston Atkinson, no service, dated 12, 6, 1797. Warrant No. 3859 for 640 acres. Recorded Book D-4, p. 246. Tennessee County.

Grant No. 1522 to John Atkinson, a corporal, dated 4, 10, 1792. Assigned to Robert Nelson, Warrant No. 198 for 358 acres. Recorded Book C-3, p. 206. Tennessee County on north side of Sycamore Creek.

Grant No. 1992 to Zadock Badwell, a non-commissioned officer, dated 5, 20, 1793. Assigned to Joseph Dixon, Warrant No. 2593 for 1000 acres. Recorded Book E-5, p. 291. Tennessee County on East Fork of Barton's Creek.

Grant No. 1187 to John Bailey, no service, dated 11, 30, 1790. Assigned to Edward Dickson, Warrant No. 241 for 640 acres. Book C-3, p. 53. Tennessee County on south side of Cumberland River.

Grant No. 2809 to Morriss Bailey, dated 1, 12, 1797. Assigned to Stokley Donelson, Warrant No. 3420 for 640 acres. Recorded Book D-4, p. 38. Tennessee County, south side Cumberland River.

Grant No. 1969 to Elias Baker, a private, dated 5, 20, 1793. Assigned to Benjamin McCulloh (McCulloch), Warrant No. 2079 for 640 acres. Recorded Book E-5, p. 280. Tennessee County, south side of Cumberland River.

Grant No. 1158 to Samuel Baker, dated 11, 26, 1789. Assigned to Richard Fenner, Warrant No. 2167 for 640 acres. Recorded Book C-3, p. 43. Tennessee County on North side of Cumberland River.

Grant No. 694 to James Ballard, a private, dated 7, 11, 1788. Assigned to Nancy Sheppard, Warrant No. 1750 for 640 acres. Recorded Book A-1, p. 348. Sycamore Creek.

Grant No. 290 to John Ballard, a soldier, dated 5, 3, 1787. Assigned to Andrew Beaky, for 640 acres. Recorded Book A-1, p. 146. South side Red River.

Grant No. 1493 to Hezekiah Barnes, dated 1, 4, 1792. Warrant No. 1574 for 357 acres. Recorded Book C-3, p. 195. Tennessee County, south side Cumberland River.

Grant No. 1865 to James Barnet, a private, dated 5, 20, 1793. Assigned to Jesse Benton, Warrant No. 3128 for 274 acres. Recorded Book E-5, p. 227. Tennessee County, south side Cumberland River.

Grant No. 2334 to Simon Barnet, a private, dated 5, 20, 1793. Assigned to John Boren, Warrant No. 1173 for 220 acres. Recorded Book B-2, p. 114. On Crunk's Branch in Tennessee County.

Grant No. 1146 to Jno. Bartholomew, dated 11, 26, 1789. Assigned to James Cole Mountflorence, Warrant No. 599 for 228 acres. Recorded Book C-3, p. 38. Sumner County on Red River.

Grant No. 1153 to David Bartley, dated 11, 26, 1789. Assigned to Josiah Love, Warrant No. 1490 for 640 acres. Recorded Book C-3, p. 41. Sumner County, north side Red River.

Grant No. 3028 to Samuel Barton, dated 4, 10, 1797. Warrant No. 1033 for 640 acres. Recorded Book D-4, p. 119. Tennessee County, north side Cumberland River.

Grant No. 3065 to Samuel Barton, dated 7, 19, 1797. Warrant No. 3298 for 1000 acres. Recorded Book D-4, p. 136. Tennessee County on Red River.

Grant No. 2820 to Robert Beach, dated 1, 12, 1797. Assigned to Stokley Donelson, Warrant No. 3443 for 640 acres. Recorded Book D-4, p. 43. Tennessee County on Red River.

Grant No. 2420 to Robert Bean, a private, dated 1, 7, 1794. Assigned to Conrod Nicholas, Warrant No. 3418 for 226 acres. Recorded Book B-2, p. 166. Miller's Creek, Tennessee County.

Grant No. 1516 to Samuel Beede, dated 4, 10, 1792. Warrant No. 3408 for 640 acres. Recorded Book C-3, p. 204. In Tennessee County, south side Cumberland River.

Grant No. 1190 to William Beek (Becks [?]), an ensign, dated 11, 30, 1790. Warrant No. 1103 for 640 acres. Recorded Book C-3, p. 54. Tennessee County, both sides Barton Creek.

Grant No. 2835 to Stephen Begworth, dated 1, 12, 1797. Assigned to Stokley Donelson, Warrant No. 2559 for 640 acres. Recorded Book D-4, p. 50. Tennessee County, on Red River.

Grant No. 1619 to Joel Bennet, a private, dated 4, 27, 1793. Assigned to George Curtis, Warrant No. 1619 for 357 acres. Recorded Book E-5, p. 108. Tennessee County, on Cumberland River.

Grant No. 1514 to Robert Berry, no service, dated 4, 10, 1792. Assigned to James

Berry, Warrant No. 789 for 640 acres. Tennessee County, south side Cumberland River.

Grant No. 3024 to William Betts, dated 4, 10, 1797. Warrant No. 3930 for 640 acres. Recorded Book D-4, p. 117. Tennessee County, on Barrett's Creek.

Grant No. 2475 to John Bhone, a private, dated 12, 31, 1793. Assigned to Elijah Hamilton, Warrant No. 2004 for 640 acres. Recorded Book B-2, p. 197. Tennessee County, on Red River.

Grant No. 1606 to Nathaniel Bilberry, a private, dated 4, 27, 1795. Assigned to Nathaniel Bilberry, Warrant No. 3747 for 228 acres. Recorded Book B-5, p. 102. Sumner County, on Red River.

Grant No. 2933 to Francis Bird, dated 2, 19, 1797. Assigned to William Johnson, Warrant No. 3072 for 640 acres. Recorded Book D-4, p. 82. Tennessee County.

Grant No. 2124 to Anthony Black, a private, dated 5, 20, 1793. Warrant No. 3088 for 640 acres. Recorded Book B-2, p. 16. Tennessee County, south side Cumberland River.

Grant No. 3005 to William Blackfar, no service, dated 4, 10, 1797. Warrant No. 4397 for 640 acres. Recorded Book D-4, p. 106. Tennessee County, south side Cumberland River.

Grant No. 3001 to William Blackfarr, dated 4, 10, 1797. Warrant No. 4252 for 640 acres. Recorded Book D-4, p. 104. In Tennessee, north side Cumberland River.

Grant No. 589 to Frederick Blount [?], a private, dated 9, 15, 1787. Warrant No. 531 for 640 acres. Recorded Book A-1, p. 295. Sulphur Fork.

Grant No. 1235 to John Gray Blount, dated 12, 10, 1790. Warrant No. 2532 for 640 acres. Recorded Book C-3, p. 74. Tennessee County, north side Cumberland River.

Grant No. 1333 to John Gray Blount, no service, dated 12, 10, 1790. Warrant No. 3502 for 640 acres. Recorded Book C-3, p. 129. Tennessee County, north side Cumberland River.

Grant No. 349 to Elijah Boddie, dated 12, 17, 1794. Warrant No. 1924 for 2500 acres. Recorded Book A, p. 187. Middle District on Elk River.

Grant No. 322 to Elisha Boon, a soldier, dated 7, 12, 1787. Assigned to William Ross, Warrant No. 2634 for 640 acres. Recorded Book A-1, p. 163. On Red River.

Grant No. 542 to John Bowers, a private, dated 9, 15, 1787. Warrant No. 94 for 228 acres. Recorded Book A-1, p. 275. On Sulphur Fork.

Grant No. 1622 to John Boyd, dated 2, 23, 1793. Warrant No. 1833 for 640 acres. Recorded Book C-3, p. 250. Tennessee County, on Red River.

Grant No. 1633 to John Boyd, dated 2, 23, 1793. Warrant No. 518 for 274 acres. Recorded Book C-3, p. 255. Tennessee County.

Grant No. 2122 to James Braby, a private, dated 5, 20, 1793. Warrant No. 1304 for 228 acres. Recorded Book B-2, p. 15. Tennessee County.

Grant No. 1228 to Gloster James Brehon, no service, dated 12, 10, 1790. Warrant No. 2895 for 1000 acres. Recorded Book C-3, p. 71. Tennessee County, south side Cumberland River.

Grant No. 1266 to Gloster James Brehon, dated 12, 10, 1790. Warrant No. 3379 for 640 acres. Recorded Book C-3, p. 98. Tennessee County, south side Cumberland River.

Grant No. 1297 to Gloster James Brehan, no service, dated 12, 10, 1790. Warrant

No. 2889 for 640 acres. Recorded Book C-3, p. 103. Tennessee County, south side Cumberland River.

Grant No. 1001 to James Gloster Brehon, dated 5, 18, 1789. Warrant No. 2899 for 640 acres. Recorded Book E-5, p. 67. Sumner County, on Red River.

Grant No. 3025 to Mitcheon Brenaman, no service, dated 4, 10, 1797. Warrant No. 4358 for 640 acres. Recorded Book D-4, p. 117. Tennessee County, north side Cumberland River.

Grant No. 2331 to Silas Briggs, a private, dated 5, 20, 1793. Assigned to Thos. & Jno. Blount, Warrant No. 2792 for 640 acres. Recorded Book B-2, p. 112. Tennessee County, on Cumberland River.

Grant No. 2128 to James Brister, a private, dated 5, 20, 1793. Warrant No. 348 for 228 acres. Recorded Book B-2, p. 18. Sumner County, on Red River.

Grant No. 319 to Sherrod Britt, a soldier, dated 6, 28, 1787. Assigned to J. C. Mountflorence, Warrant No. 2169 for 640 acres. Recorded Book A-1, p. 161. Sulphur Fork.

Grant No. 1862 to Philip Brittain, a private, dated 5, 20, 1793. Assigned to Thomas Bailey, Warrant No. 972 for 274 acres. Recorded Book E-5, p. 226. Tennessee County, on a small creek on the west side of Pine River, a fork of Duck River.

Grant No. 482 to George Britton, a private, dated 9, 15, 1787. Assigned to Stephen Cantrell, Warrant No. 351 for 640 acres. Recorded Book A-1, p. 243. On Red River.

Grant No. 859 to Joseph Brock, no service, dated 1, 12, 1789. Warrant No. 337 for 640 acres. Recorded Book E-5, p. 1. Sumner County on Red River.

Grant No. 861 to Joseph Brock, dated 7, 11, 1789. Warrant No. 3358 for 640 acres. Recorded Book E-5, p. 2. Sumner County on Red River.

Grant No. 2103 to John Browan, a private, dated May 20, 1793. Assigned to Archibald Allen, Warrant No. 2049 for 640 acres. Recorded Book A-1, p. 6. Tennessee County, Yellow Creek.

Grant No. 2998 to Morgan Brown, dated 4, 10, 1797. Warrant No. 3942 for 640 acres. Recorded Book D-4, p. 102. Tennessee County, south side Cumberland River.

Grant No. 1165 to John Browner, dated 11, 26, 1789. Assigned to Robert Nelson, Warrant No. 3531 for 274 acres. Book C-3, p. 46. Tennessee County on Red River.

Grant No. 1157 to Isum Burns, dated 11, 26, 1789. Assigned to Richard Fenner, Warrant No. 2168 for 640 acres. Recorded Book C-3, p. 42. Tennessee County, north side Cumberland River.

Grant No. 697 to Hardy Bynes, a private, dated 7, 11, 1788. Assigned to Nancy Sheppard, Warrant No. 1760 for 640 acres. Recorded Book A-1, p. 350. On Red River.

Grant No. 1695 to Drury Bynum, a sergeant, dated 5, 20, 1793. Assigned to Elias Fort, Warrant No. 436 for 1000 acres. Recorded Book E-5, p. 194. Tennessee County, south side Cumberland River.

Grant No. 2488 Thomas Byren, dated 9, 26, 1795. Assigned to Robert Nelson, Warrant No. 1995 for 640 acres. Recorded Book D-4, p. 6. Tennessee County, on north sid Red River.

Grant No. 1863 to Lawrence Byrum, a private, dated 5, 20, 1793. Warrant No. 202 for 228 acres. Recorded Book E-5, p. 226. Sumner County on Red River.

Grant No. 1167 to Lewis Cannon, a lieutenant, dated 11, 26, 1789. Assigned to Lewis Cannon, Warrant No. 1217 for 1584 acres. Recorded Book C-3, p. 46. Tennessee County, north side Cumberland River.

Grant No. 1400 to Benjamin Cassellman, no service shown, dated 12, 20, 1791. Warrant No. 181 for 640 acres. Recorded Book C-3, p. 153. Tennessee County, south side Cumberland River.

Grant No. 1466 to Jacob Casteele, no service shown, dated 1, 4, 1792. Warrant No. 3288 for 640 acres. Recorded Book C-3, p. 184. Tennessee County, south side Cumberland River.

Grant No. 1500 to William Caswell, no service shown, dated 1, 4, 1792. Warrant No. 480 for 640 acres. Recorded Book C-3, p. 198. Tennessee County, south side of Cumberland River.

Grant No. 2339 to Philemon Chance, a private, dated 5, 20, 1793. Assigned to Jesse Cobb, Warrant No. 1129 for 274 acres. Recorded Book B-2, p. 117. Tennessee County, Red River.

Grant No. 3368 to John Cheek, no service, dated 12, 16, 1800. Warrant No. 3623 for 640 acres. Recorded Book D-4, p. 288. Robertson County on Red River.

Grant No. 187 to John Christmas, a private, dated 3, 7, 1786. Assigned to Humphrey Hogan, Warrant No. 50 for 640 acres. Recorded Book A-1, p. 96. Sulphur Fork of Red River.

Grant No. 186 to John Chunney, a private, dated 3, 7, 1796. Assigned to William Johnson, Warrant No. 983 for 428 acres. Recorded Book A-1, p. 96. On Red River.

Grant No. 1640 to William Church, dated 4, 27, 1793. Warrant No. 1306 for 228 acres. Recorded Book E-5, p. 118. Tennessee County on Spring Creek.

Grant No. 1877 to James Clark, a private, dated 5, 20, 1793. Assigned to James Clark, Warrant No. 378 for 428 acres. Recorded Book E-5, p. 234. Tennessee County on south side Cumberland River.

Grant No. 1609 to Lardner Clark, dated 2, 23, 1793. Warrant No. 2063 for 640 acres. Recorded Book C-3, p. 245. Tennessee County on Wells Creek.

Grant No. 448 to John Cockrall, no service, dated 6, 27, 1793. Warrant No. 825 for 640 acres. Recorded Book G-7, p. 218. Tennessee County, north side Cumberland River.

Grant No. 2514 to John Cockran, dated 12, 8, 1795. Assigned to James Lee, Warrant No. 792 for 128 acres. Recorded Book C-3, p. 137. Davidson County, Sycamore Creek.

Grant No. 3402 to James M. Cofferty, no service, dated 5, 17, 1803. Warrant No. 1450 for 640 acres. Recorded Book D-4, p. 308. Tennessee County on Red River.

Grant No. 3000 to John Coffery, no service shown, dated 4, 10, 1797. Warrant No. 3844 for 640 acres. Recorded Book D-4, p. 104. Tennessee County on Red River.

Grant No. — to Abraham Collarin, a private, dated 5, 20, 1793. Warrant No. 3070 for 640 acres. Recorded Book E-5, p. 232. Tennessee County, between Kerr's and Nelson's Creeks.

Grant No. 2171 to Charles Collins, a private, dated 5, 20, 1793. Warrant No. 687 for 640 acres. Recorded Book B-2, p. 40. Tennessee County, Cumberland River.

Grant No. 2433 to Nicholas Conrod, dated 2, 22, 1795. Warrant No. 3251 for 274 acres. Recorded Book C-3, p. 288. Davidson County on Red River.

Grant No. 78 to Samuel Cooley, Surgeon, dated 3, 14, 1786. Assigned to James C. Mountflorence, Warrant No. 397 for 1428 acres. Recorded Book A-1, p. 40. Davidson County, Red River, "Renfroe's Station."

Grant No. 2340 to Nathaniel Cooper, a private, dated 5, 20, 1793. Assigned to Jesse

Cobb, Warrant No. 1234 for 228 acres. Recorded Book B-2, p. 117. Tennessee County, Red River.

Grant No. 1596 John Corron, private, dated April 27 1793. Assigned to Sarah Allen, Warrant No. 213 for 640 acres. Recorded Book E-5, p. 98. Tennessee County on Cumberland River.

Grant No. 43 to Thomas Cox, no service, dated 10, 8, 1787. Warrant No. 43 for 320 acres. Recorded Book H-8, p. 26. Davidson County on Red River.

Grant No. 1590 to David Cozart, a private, dated 4, 27, 1793. Assigned to William Whitard, Warrant No. 597 for 274 acres. Recorded Book E-5, p. 95. Tennessee County on Red River.

Grant No. 1392 to Archibald Crack, no service, dated 12, 20, 1791. Warrant No. 1365 for 640 acres. Recorded Book C-3, p. 145. Tennessee County, south side Red River.

Grant No. 343 to John Crawford, a private, dated 9, 4, 1787. Assigned to Robert Weakley, Warrant No. 1753 for 640 acres. Recorded Book A-1, p. 173. Sycamore Creek.

Grant No. 3394 to Thomas Creedy, no service, dated 10, 25, 1802. Warrant No. 5033 for 1000 acres. Recorded Book D-4, p. 304. Montgomery County on Cumberland River.

Grant No. 700 to Abraham Crocker, a private, dated 7, 11, 1788. Assigned to Robert Keapx [?], Warrant No. 3426 for 220 acres. Recorded Book A-1, p. 351. Red River.

Grant No. 394 to John Crocker, a private, dated 9, 15, 1787. Assigned to John Nichols, Warrant No. 2565 for 640 acres. Recorded Book A-1, p. 199. Sulphur Fork.

Grant No. 1257 to Hillery Crook, dated 12, 10, 1790. Assigned to Richard Fenner, Warrant No. 2501 for 640 acres. Recorded Book C-3, p. 85. Tennessee County, south side Cumberland River.

Grant No. 725 to Benjamin Daniel, a private, dated 7, 11, 1788. Assigned to John Nichol, Warrant No. 2567 for 640 acres. Recorded Book A-1, p. 364. Land Sulphur Fork.

Grant No. 3366 to Henry Damal, dated 12, 2, 1800. Warrant No. 1343 for 1325 acres. Recorded Book D-4, p. 287. Montgomery County.

Grant No 3378 to Henry Darnell, no service, dated 12, 1, 1801. Warrant No. 27 for 1849 acres. Recorded Book D-4, p. 294. Montgomery County, south side Cumberland River.

Grant No. 3396 to Henry Darnell, dated 11, 15, 1802. Warrant No. 27 for 503 acres. Recorded Book D-4, p. 305. Montgomery County, north side Red River.

Grant No. 3377, Capt. Henry Darnell, dated 12, 1, 1801. Warrant No. 27 for 163 acres. Recorded Book D-4, p. 293. Montgomery County, south side Cumberland River.

Grant No. 2427 to Isaac Darron, a private, dated 12, 11, 1793. Assigned to Nicholas Conrad. Warrant No. 1983 for 274 acres. Recorded Book B-2, p. 170. Tennessee County, Miller's Creek and Brushy Creek.

Grant No. 195 to Benjamin Darrow, Sergeant, dated 7, 20, 1796. Assigned to Annanias McCoy, Warrant No. — for 480 acres. Recorded Book H-8, p 119. Tennessee County on west of Cumberland Mountains.

Grant No. 2062 to Thomas Davenport, a private, dated 5, 20, 1793. Assigned to Ambrose Maulden, Warrant No. 3459 for 274 acres. Recorded Book E-5, p. 326. Sumner County on Red River.

Grant No. 3361 to Samuel Davis, no service, dated 10, 18, 1800. Warrant No. 5731 for 228 acres. Recorded Book D-4, p. 285. Robertson County on Sulphur Fork.

Grant No. 1502 to William Davis, dated 1, 4, 1792. Warrant No. 248 for 2468 acres. Recorded Book C-3, p. 199. Tennessee County, both sides Yellow Creek.

Grant No. 450 to John Deason, dated 6, 27, 1793. Warrant No. 834 for 640 acres. Recorded Book G-7, p. 219. Tennessee County.

Grant No. 1619 to Joshua Devenshire, no service, dated 2, 23, 1793. Assigned to John Baker, Warrant No. 3403 for 640 acres. Recorded Book C-3, p. 248. Tennessee County on south side of Cumberland River.

Grant No. 1463 to John Dickerson, no service, dated 1, 4, 1792. Warrant No. 3661 for 640 acres. Recorded Book C-3, p. 182. Tennessee County, south side Cumberland River.

Grant No. 2483 to David Dickson, a private, dated 12, 31, 1793. Assigned to Philip Shackler, Warrant No. 1801 for 640 acres. Recorded Book B-2, p. 201. Red River.

Grant No. 1507 to Edward Dickson, no service, dated 1, 4, 1792. Warrant No. 3723 for 640 acres. Recorded Book C-3, p. 201. Tennessee County, south side of Cumberland.

Grant No. 1509 to James Dickson, no service, dated 1, 4, 1792. Warrant No. 1913 for 640 acres. Recorded Book C-3, p. 202. Tennessee County, south side Cumberland River.

Grant No. 1424 to John Dickson, dated 12, 20, 1791. Warrant No. 1909 for 640 acres. Recorded Book C-3, p. 165. Tennessee County, both sides Pine River.

Grant No. 344 to Henry Dison, a private, dated 9, 4, 1787. Assigned to William Cubbins, Warrant No. 1802 for 640 acres. Recorded Book A-1, p. 174. Sulphur Fork of Red River.

Grant No. 2381 to Thomas Dixon, a private, dated 5, 20, 1793. Assigned to Aron Lambert, Warrant No. 1341 for 640 acres. Recorded Book B-2, p. 148. Tennessee County, Sycamore Creek.

Grant No. 559 to Spencer Donaldson, a private, dated 9, 15, 1787. Warrant No. 1081 for 128 acres. Recorded Book A-1, p. 281. On Red River.

Grant No. 2822 to Stockley Donelson, dated 1, 12, 1797. Assigned to Thomas Wimpie, Warrant No. 3044 for 640 acres. Recorded Book D-4, p. 44. On Red River

Grant No. 2576 to Stockley Donelson, dated 3, 7, 1796. Warrant No. 2939 for 640 acres. Recorded Book C-3, p. 357. Tennessee County on Red River.

Grant No. 2836 to Stocley Donelson, dated 1, 12, 1797. Warrant No. ── for 640 acres. Recorded Book D-4, p. 50. Tennessee County on Red River.

Grant No. 2809 to Stokley Donelson, dated 1, 12, 1797. Assigned to Morris Bailey, Warrant No. 3420 for 640 acres. Recorded Book D-4, p. 38. Tennessee County on south side Cumberland River.

Grant No. 2817 to Stokley Donelson, dated 1, 12, 1797. Assigned to James McBride, Warrant No. 3281 for 640 acres. Recorded Book D-4, p. 42. Tennessee County, south side Cumberland River.

Grant No. 2818 to Stokley Donelson, dated 1, 12, 1797. Assigned to John Nichory, Warrant No. 521 for 640 acres. Recorded Book D-4, p. 42. On Red River.

Grant No. 2820 to Stokley Donelson, no service shown, dated 1, 12, 1797. Assigned to Robert Beach, Warrant No. 3443 for 640 acres. Recorded Book D-4, p. 43. On Red River.

Grant No. 2823 to Stokley Donelson, dated 1, 12, 1797. Assigned to Josiah Todd, Warrant No. 1590 for 640 acres. Recorded Book D-4, p. 44. On Red River.

Grant No. 2824 to Stokley Donelson, no date. Assigned to Jonathan Henry, Warrant No. 3262 for 640 acres. Recorded Book D-4, p. 45. Red River.

Grant No. 2829 to Stokley Donelson, dated 1, 12, 1797. Assigned to Peter Sanders, Warrant No. 3158 for 640 acres. Recorded Book D-4, p. 47. On Red River.

Grant No. 2832 to Stokley Donelson, dated 1, 11, 1797. Assigned to Jeremiah Thomas, Warrant No. 1589 for 640 acres. Recorded Book D-4, p. 48. On Red River.

Grant No. 2833 to Stokley Donelson, dated 1, 12, 1797. Assigned to Charles James, Warrant No. 3469 for 640 acres. Recorded Book D-4, p. 49. On Red River.

Grant No. 2835 to Stokley Donelson, dated 1, 12, 1797. Assigned to Stephen Begworth, Warrant No. 2550 for 640 acres. Recorded Book D-4, p. 50. On Red River.

Grant No. 3222 to Griffith Douge, a sergt., dated 9, 14, 1797. Assigned to Griffith Dogue [Douge ?] and Duncan Stewart, Warrant No. 407 for 1000 acres. Recorded Book D-4, p. 217. Tennessee County, south side Cumberland River.

Grant No. 1083 to Wm. Dove, no service, dated 11, 6, 1789. Assigned to John Craddock, Warrant No. 3202 for 264 acres. Recorded Book C-3, p. 15. Davidson County, west fork of Red River.

Grant No. 1451 to Morgan Drury, dated 1, 4, 1792. Warrant No. 866 for 640 acres. Recorded Book C-3, p. 194. Tennessee County, both sides Yellow Creek.

Grant No. 3056 to Martin Duncan, dated 7, 19, 1797. Warrant No. 1664 for 640 acres. Recorded Book D-4, p. 132. Tennessee County.

Grant No. 2283 to Thomas Dunn, a private, dated 5, 20, 1793. Assigned to Benjamin McCulloch, Warrant No. 2002 for 640 acres. Recorded Book B-2, p. 89. Red River.

Grant No. 783 to James Dunster, a private, dated 7, 11, 1788. Assigned to James Bowman, Warrant No. 2506 for 640 acres. Sumner County, between North and Middle Forks of Red River.

Grant No. 1856 to Joseph Dupont, dated 5, 20, 1793. Assigned to John Gray and Thomas Blount, Warrant No. 2503 for 640 acres. Recorded Book E-5, p. 223. Tennessee County on Johnson's Creek.

Grant No. 1638 to James Earl [or East], dated 4, 27, 1793. Assigned to heirs of James East, Warrant No. 1420 for 640 acres. Recorded Book E-5, p. 118. Tennessee County on Spring Creek.

Grant No. 2168 to Moses Easter, a private, dated 5, 20, 1793. Assigned to William Wickoff, Warrant No. 2046 for 640 acres. Recorded Book B-2, p. 38. Tennessee County, Red River.

Grant No. 27 to Forkner Elliott and Isaac Peterson, dated 8, 18, 1787. Warrant No. 337 for 480 acres. Recorded Book H-8, p. 16. Davidson County, north side Red River.

Grant No. 157 to John Elliott, a corporal, dated 3, 26, 1795. Assigned to Stephen Boren, Warrant No. — for 480 acres. Recorded Book H-8, p. 102. Tennessee County on Wartrace Creek.

Grant No. 158 to John Elliott, a corporal, dated 3, 26, 1795. Assigned to Jacob McCarthy, Warrant No. — for 480 acres. Recorded Book H-8, p. 102. Tennessee County on Sulphur Fork of Red River.

Grant No. 172 to Levi Ellis, private, dated 8, 27, 1795. Warrant No. — for 400 acres. Recorded Book H-8, p. 108. Sumner County on ridge that divides Red River from Cumberland River.

Grant No. 1844 to Robert Ellis, a private, dated 5, 20, 1793. Warrant No. 2028 for 274 acres. Recorded Book E-5, p. 217. Tennessee County on south side Cumberland River.

Grant No. —— to Underhill Ellis, private, dated 8, 27, 1795. Warrant No. —— for —— acres. Recorded Book H-8, p. 108. On ridge that divides Red River from Cumberland River.

Grant No. 717 to John Emory, a private, dated 7, 11, 1788. Assigned to William Holderness, Warrant No. 309 for 640 acres. Recorded Book A-1, p. 360. Kerr's & Nelson's Creek.

Grant No. 685 to Joseph Fardin, a private, dated 12, 8, 1787. Assigned to Phillip Trammel, Warrant No. 2513 for 640 acres. Recorded Book A-1, p. 344. On Red River.

Grant No. 274 to Richard Fenner, a lieutenant, dated 3, 22, 1787. Warrant No. 399 for 2560 acres. Recorded Book A-1, p. 138. North side Cumberland River.

Grant No. 21 to William Fenner, a major, dated 3, 14, 1786. Warrant No. 332 for 2057 acres. Recorded Book A-1, p. 11. Davidson County, Red River.

Grant No. 3 to Daniel Flanery, dated 8, 18, 1787. Warrant No. 419 for 320 acres. Recorded Book H-8, p. 1. Davidson County on Red River.

Grant No. 1168 to Joseph Fletcher, dated 11, 26, 1789. Assigned to Theodore Myllet, Warrant No. 3342 for 640 acres. Recorded Book C-3, p. 47. Tennessee County, north side Cumberland River.

Grant No. 2012 to Francis Floyd, a private, dated 5, 20, 1793. Assigned to Benjamin McCulloch, Warrant No. 2010 for 640 acres. Recorded Book E-5, p. 300. Tennessee County on south side Cumberland River.

Grant No. 122 to Josiah Fort, dated 4, 27, 1793. Warrant No. 933 for 320 acres. Recorded Book H-8, p. 67. Tennessee County.

Grant No. 120 to William Fort, dated 11, 27, 1793. Warrant No. 496 for 320 acres. Recorded Book H-8, p. 66. Tennessee County, north side Red River.

Grant No. 1607 to William Fort & Howell Tatum, dated 2, 23, 1793, Warrant No. 302 for 640 acres. Recorded Book C-3, p. 244. Sumner County on Red River.

Grant No. 1578 to Anthony Foster, dated 2, 23, 1793. Warrant No. 3526 for 228 acres. Recorded Book C-3, p. 230. Tennessee County, south side Cumberland River.

Grant No. 428 to Alexander Fountaine, a private, dated 9, 15, 1787. Assigned to John Wilson, Warrant No. 843 for 640 acres. Recorded Book A-1, p. 216. Sulphur Fork.

Grant No. 393 to James Fulcher, a private, dated 9, 15, 1787. Assigned to Robert Nelson, Warrant No. 2121 for 640 acres. Recorded Book A-1, p. 198. Grove Creek.

Grant No. 1995 to Wailliam Fuller, a private, dated 5, 20, 1793. Assigned to John Hogan, Warrant No. 3345 for 640 acres. Recorded Book E-5, p. 293. Tennessee County on Red River.

Grant No. 3342 to Henry Funk, dated 12, 6, 1797. Warrant No. 3268 for 274 acres. Recorded Book D-4, p. 250. Tennessee County on McAdorr's Creek.

Grant No. 1452 to Edmond Gamble, a subbatten, dated 12, 20, 1791. Assigned to Flaurance McCarthy, Warrant No. 1172 for 822 acres. Recorded Book C-3, p. 177. South side of Red River.

Grant No. 1457 to Edmond Gamble, dated 12, 20, 1791. Warrant No. 600 for 1150 acres. Recorded Book C-3, p. 180. Tennessee County on Parson's Creek.

Grant No. 173 to James Gambling, a private, dated 3, 7, 1786. Assigned to George Neville, Warrant No. 832 for 350 acres. Recorded Book A-1, p. 89. Davidson County, Red River.

Grant No. 2816 to Wm. Garret, no service, dated 1, 12, 1797. Assigned to Stokley Donelson, Warrant No. 1645 for 640 acres. Recorded Book D-4, p. 41. Tennessee County on Red River.

Grant No. 1307 to Charles Gerrard, dated 12, 10, 1790. Warrant No. 3049 for 640 acres. Recorded Book C-3, p. 108. Tennessee County, north side Cumberland River.

Grant No. 2825 to David Gewin, dated 1, 12, 1797. Assigned to Stokley Donelson, Warrant No. 2609 for 1000 acres. Recorded Book D-1, p. 45. Tennessee County on Kerr's Creek.

Grant No. 2810 to Richard Gideon, no service, dated 1, 12, 1797. Assigned to Stokley Donelson, Warrant No. 2608 for 1000 acres. Recorded Book D-4, p. 39. Tennessee County, Sycamore Creek.

Grant No. 511 to James Gifford, a private, dated 9, 15, 1787. Assigned to William Tate, Warrant No. 3081 for 428 acres. Recorded Book A-1, p. 257. Red River.

Grant No. 481 to Isaac Gillape, a private, dated 8, 15, 1787. Assigned to John Mc-Coy Alston, Warrant No. 1066 for 640 acres. Recorded Book A-1, p. 242. On Red River.

Grant No. 2993 to James Gillingham, dated 4, 10, 1797. Warrant No. 3984 for 640 acres. Recorded Book D-4, p. 100. Tennessee County, north side Cumberland River.

Grant No. 1303 to Thomas Gloster, dated 12, 10, 1790. Warrant No. 3099 for 640 acres. Recorded Book C-3, p. 106. Tennessee County on Red River.

Grant No. 2474 to Anthony Godfrey, a private, dated 12, 31, 1793. Assigned to James Godfrey, Warrant No. 1709 for 1000 acres. Recorded Book B-2, p. 197. Sumner County, Red River.

Grant No. 358 to Enos Gooden, a private, dated 9, 15, 1787. Assigned to Benjamin Sheppard, Warrant No. 2328 for 640 acres. Recorded Book A-1, p. 181. On Red River.

Grant No. 1650 to Wm. Goodman [Gooman], a captain, dated 4, 27, 1793. Assigned to William Goodman, Warrant No. 297 for 3800 acres. Recorded Book E-5, p. 124. Tennessee County, south side Cumberland River.

Grant No. 3148 to James C. Gorham, dated 9, 14, 1797. Warrant No. 4348 for 640 acres. Recorded Book D-4, p. 179. Tennessee County, north side Cumberland River.

Grant No. 3149 to James C. Gorham, dated 9, 14, 1797. Warrant No. 4201 for 640 acres. Recorded Book D-4, p. 179. Tennessee County on Red River.

Grant No. 3151 to James C. Gorham, dated 5, 14, 1797. Warrant No. 4064 for 640 acres. Recorded Book D-4, p. 180. Tennessee County on Red River.

Grant No. 3150 to James G. Gorham, dated 9, 14, 1797. Warrant No. 4065 for 640 acres. Recorded Book D-4, p. 180. Tennessee County, Red River.

Grant No. 3152 to John C. Gorham, dated 5, 14, 1797. Warrant No. 4529 for 274 acres. Recorded Book D-4, p. 181. Tennessee County on Red River.

Grant No. 2013 to John Granadale [Granade], a private, dated 5, 20, 1793. Assigned to Benjamin McCulloch, Warrant No. 2007 for 640 acres. Recorded Book E-5, p. 301. Tennessee County on south side Cumberland River.

Grant No. 1321 to John Granberry, dated 12, 10, 1790. Warrant No. 112 for 792 acres. Recorded Book C-3, p. 115. Tennessee County, south side Cumberland River.

Grant No. 2076 to William Graves, a private, dated May 20, 1793. Assigned to William Allen, Warrant No. 2126 for 640 acres. Recorded Book E-5, p. 333. Tennessee County on the first large fork on the west side of Yellow Creek.

Grant No. 1169 to John Gray, a captain, dated 11, 26, 1789. Assigned to Joseph & James Gray, Warrant No. 3122 for 3840 acres. Recorded Book C-3, p. 47. Tennessee County, north side Cumberland River.

Grant No. 387 to Dempsey Green, a private, dated 9, 15, 1787. Assigned to Robert Nelson, Warrant No. 488 for 640 acres. Recorded Book A-1, p. 195. Red River.

Grant No. 1681 to Samuel Green, a private, dated 5, 20, 1793. Assigned to Joshua Hadley, Warrant No. 3748 for 228 acres. Recorded Book E-5, p. 138. Tennessee County on Parsons Creek.

Grant No. 1164 to William Green, dated 11, 26, 1789. Warrant No. 431 for 640 acres. Recorded Book C-3, p. 45. Tennessee County on Sulphur Fork.

Grant No. 3409 to William Green, dated 2, 10, 1804. Warrant No. 3046 for 228 acres. Recorded Book D-4, p. 311. Robertson County.

Grant No. 1621 to James Griffin, a private, dated 4, 27, 1793. Warrant No. 1163 for 274 acres. Recorded Book A-5, p. 109. Tennessee County on south side of Cumberland River.

Grant No. 2455 to Benjamin Grimes, a private, dated 12, 31, 1793. Warrant No. 1942 for 274 acres. Recorded Book B-2, p. 186. Tennessee County, Montgomery Fork.

Grant No. 1583 to William Gugles [Duglas ?], a non-commissioned officer, dated 11, 27, 1793. Assigned to Gardner Clark, Warrant No. 72 for 1000 acres. Recorded Book E-5, p. 92. Tennessee County on fork of ... between Red River and Sulphur Fork.

Grant No. 1461 to Edward Gwen, dated 1, 4, 1792. Warrant No. 2518 for 640 acres. Recorded Book C-3, p. 181. Tennessee County, south side Cumberland River.

Grant No. 3084 to Thomas Hall, a lieutenant, dated 8, 12, 1797. Assigned to Frederick Barget & James Carney, Warrant No. 1072 for 2560 acres. Recorded Book B-4, p. 36. Tennessee County on Miller's Creek.

Grant No. 2456 to Thomas Hamilton, a private, dated 12, 31, 1793. Assigned to Robert Wilson, Warrant No. 853 for 357 acres. Recorded Book B-2, p. 186. Sumner County, Red River.

Grant No. 12 to Adam Hampton, dated 8, 18, 1787. Warrant No. —— for 320 acres. Recorded Book H-8, p. 7. Davidson County on Red River.

Grant No. 1454 to John Haregrove, dated 12, 20, 1791. Warrant No. 315 for —— acres. Recorded Book C-3, p. 178. Tennessee County on north side Red River.

Grant No. 225 to Abraham Harges, a private, dated 3, 7, 1786. Warrant No. 439 for 228 acres. Recorded Book A-1, p. 114. On Red River

Grant No. 1368 to Frederick Harget, dated 11, 30, 1790. Warrant No. 1254 for 640 acres. Recorded Book C-3, p. 137. Tennessee County, north side Cumberland River.

Grant No. 2463 to Peter Harrell, a private, dated 12, 31, 1793. Warrant No. 1344 for 535 acres. Recorded Book B-2, p. 191. Tennessee County, Red River.

Grant No. 3381 to Edward Harris, dated 12, 10, 1801. Warrant No. 500 for 640 acres. Recorded Book D-4, p. 295. Sumner County on Red River.

Grant No. 3410 to Edward Harris, no service, dated 2, 10, 1804. Warrant No. 3598 for 274 acres. Recorded Book D-4, p. 312. Montgomery County on McAdoo Creek.

Grant No. 321 to Jonathan Harris, a non-commissioned officer, dated May 28, 1787. Assigned to Andrew Armstrong, No warrant number shown for 1800 acres. Recorded Book A-1, p. 182. On Sulphur Fork.

Grant No. 689 to Francis Harrison, a private, dated 12, 8, 1787. Assigned to James Glasgow, Warrant No. 1368 for 640 acres. Recorded Book A-1, p. 346. On Red River.

Grant No. 2495 to Anthony Hart, dated 9, 26, 1795. Warrant No. 2801 for 640 acres. Recorded Book D-4, p. 10. Tennessee County on Miller's Creek.

Grant No. 1968 to Hardy Hart, a private, dated 5, 20, 1793. Assigned to Benjamin McCulloh, Warrant No. 2655 for 640 acres. Recorded Book E-5, p. 279. Tennessee County, north side Cumberland River.

Grant No. 1647 to J. Hawkins, P. Phillips & Michael Campbell, dated 2, 23, 1793. Warrant No. 3125 for 428 acres. Recorded Book C-3, p. 261. Tennessee County, west side Red River.

Grant No. 1275 to John Hays, dated 12, 10, 1790. Warrant No. 2385 for 640 acres. Recorded Book C-3, p. 93. Tennessee County, south side Cumberland River.

Grant No. 1547 to Robert Hays, dated 1, 14, 1793. Warrant No. 1757 for 1000 acres. Recorded Book C-3, p. 218. Tennessee County on Red River.

Grant No. 1301 to Sarah Hays, dated 12, 20, 1791. Warrant No. 1262 for 640 acres. Recorded Book C-3, p. 148. Tennessee County, north side Tennessee River.

Grant No. 1337 to Thomas Hays, dated 12, 10, 1790. Warrant No. 2342 for 640 acres. Recorded Book C-3, p. 120. Tennessee County, south side Cumberland River.

Grant No. 42 to Robert Heaton, dated 10, 8, 1787. Warrant No. 343 for 320 acres. Recorded Book H-8, p. 26. Davidson County on Red River.

Grant No. 3186 to William Hendry, dated 9, 14, 1797. Warrant No. 4070 for 374 acres. Recorded Book D-4, p. 197. Tennessee County on north side of Cumberland River.

Grant No. 1506 to John Henley, dated 1, 4, 1792. Warrant No. 3465 for 640 acres. Recorded Book C-3, p. 201. Tennessee County, south side Red River.

Grant No. 2824 to Jonathan Henry, no service, dated 1, 12, 1797. Assigned to Stokley Donelson, Warrant No. 3262 for 640 acres. Recorded Book D-4, p. 45. Tennessee County on Red River.

Grant No. 746 to Charles Hickman, a private, dated 7, 11, 1788. Assigned to Richard Tenner, Warrant No. 2191 for 640 acres. Recorded Book A-1, p. 375. On Sycamore Creek.

Grant No. 1484 to David Hicks, dated 1, 4, 1792. Warrant No. 239 for 428 acres. Recorded Book C-3, p. 151. Tennessee County, south side Cumberland River.

Grant No. 2443 to Henry Hinnis, a private, dated 3, 18, 1794. Assigned to Robert Nelson, Warrant No. 2453 for 640 acres. Recorded Book B-2, p. 180. Tennessee County, Red River.

Grant No. 1620 to Daniel Hitton [Hutton?], dated 2, 23, 1793. Warrant No. 16 for 2560 acres. Recorded Book C-3, p. 249. Tennessee County on Guinn's Creek.

Grant No. 2693 to John Hogan, dated 6, 6, 1796. Warrant No. 3828 for 274 acres. Recorded Book C-3, p. 405. Tennessee County.

Grant No. 1271 to Thomas Hogg, dated 12, 10, 1790. Warrant No. 2428 for 640 acres. Recorded Book C-3, p. 51. Tennessee County, south side Cumberland River.

Grant No. 1323 to Thomas Hogg, dated 12, 10, 1790. Warrant No. 2429 for 640 acres. Recorded Book C-3, p. 115. Tennessee County, south side Cumberland River.

Grant No. 3331 to Daniel Holland, dated 12, 6, 1797. Warrant No. 4057 for 640 acres. Recorded Book D-4, p. 244. Tennessee County, Spring Creek.

Grant No. 1860 to Reason Hollans, a private, dated 5, 20, 1793. Assigned to George Gillaspie, Warrant No. 252 for 274 acres. Recorded Book E-5, p. 225. Tennessee County on north side of Cumberland River.

Grant No. 1866 to John Hollbrook, a private, dated 5, 20, 1793. Assigned to Joseph Graham, Warrant No. 1883 for 640 acres. Recorded Book E-5, p. 228. Tennessee County on south sid Cumberland River.

Grant No. 330 to Adron Holoman, a soldier, dated 7, 28, 1787. Assigned to William Ross, Warrant No. 2663 for 640 acres. Recorded Book A-1, p. 167. Red River.

Grant No. 2085 to George Hook, a private, dated 5, 20, 1793. Warrant No. 1879 for 274 acres. Recorded Book E-5, p. 337. Tennessee County, east fork of Barton's Creek.

Grant No. 3029 to Abraham Hoover, dated 4, 10, 1797. Warrant No. 1033 for 640 acres. Recorded Book D-4, p. 119. Tennessee County on north side Cumberland River.

Grant No. 2468 to Jonathan Hopkins, a non-commissioned officer, dated 12, 31, 1793. Assigned to Jesse Cobb, Warrant No. 1564 for 1000 acres. Recorded Book B-2, p. 194. Tennessee County on Guises Creek.

Grant No. 178 to Joseph Hopkins, a private, dated 3, 7, 1796. Assigned to Charles Wheaton, Warrant No. —— for 400 acres. Recorded Book H-8, p. 110. Tennessee County on Sulphur Fork of Red River.

Grant No. 1348 to Joseph Hopkins, dated 12, 10, 1790. Warrant No. 949 for 640 acres. Recorded Book C-3, p. 126. Tennessee County, north side Cumberland River.

Grant No. 2102 to John Horley, a private, dated 5, 20, 1793. Warrant No. 243 for 640 acres. Recorded Book B-2, p. 6. Tennessee County, south side Cumberland River.

Grant No. 941 to William Houghlett, dated 5, 18, 1789. Warrant No. 2831 for 640 acres. Recorded Book E-5, p. 42. Davidson County on Red River.

Grant No. 483 to Solomon Howard, a private, dated 9, 15, 1787. Assigned to Thomas Barker, Warrant No. 714 for 220 acres. Recorded Book A-1, p. 243. On Red River.

Grant No. 620 to John Hudler, a private, dated 9, 15, 1787. Assigned to Richard William Caswell, Warrant No. 483 for 640 acres. Recorded Book A-1, p. 311. On Red River.

Grant No. 1450 to David Hughes, dated 12, 20, 1791. Warrant No. 3438 for 274 acres. Recorded Book C-3, p. 177. Sumner County, north side Red River.

Grant No. 3142 to John Hunds [Hinds ?], dated 9, 14, 1797. Warrant No. —— for 920 acres. Recorded Book D-4, p. 176. Sumner County on Red River.

Grant No. 3060 to James Hunt. Warrant No. 3753 for 640 acres. Recorded Book D-4, p. 133. Tennessee County on Spring Creek.

Grant No. 2629 to Thomas Hutchings, dated 12, 8, 1795. Warrant No. 1520 for 274 acres. Recorded Book C-3, p. 354. Tennessee County on Red River.

Grant No. 1403 Claborn Ivey, dated 12, 20, 1791. Warrant No. 3148 for 640 acres. Recorded Book C-3, p. 154. Tennessee County, south side Cumberland River.

Grant No. 751 to Jeremiah Jackson, a private, dated 7, 11, 1788. Assigned to Martin G. Sheppard, Warrant No. 1498 for 640 acres. Recorded Book A-1, p. 378. Sulphur Fork of Red River.

Grant No. 4 to Banejmin Jacobs, a private, dated Feb. 1786. Assigned to Mathew McCawley, Warrant No. 290 for 640 acres. Recorded Book A-1, p. 3. Davidson County, Red River.

Grant No. 2833 to Charles James, dated 1, 12, 1797. Assigned to Stokley Donelson, Warrant No. 3469 for 640 acres. Recorded Book D-4, p. 49. Tennessee County on Red River.

Grant No. 3380 to William Jogan, dated 12, 10, 1801. Warrant No. 3831 for 640 acres. Recorded Book D-4, p. 295. Sumner County on Red River.

Grant No. 693 to Hardy Johnson, private, dated 7, 11, 1788. Assigned to Nancy Sheppard, Warrant No. 1769 for 640 acres. Recorded Book A-1, p. 348. Red River.

Grant No. 693 to Henry Johnson, private, dated 7, 11, 1788. Assigned to Nancy Shappard, Warrant No. 769 for 640 acres. Recorded Book A-1, p. 348. On Red River.

Grant No. 2928 to Henry Johnson, dated 2, 19, 1797. Warrant No. 2646 for 640 acres. Recorded Book D-4, p. 81. Tennessee County on Sulphur Fork.

Grant No. 2933 to William Johnson, no service, dated 2, 19, 1797. Assigned to Frances Bird, Warrant No. 3072 for 640 acres. Book and page not shown. Tennessee County.

Grant No. 1903 to Henry Johnston, a private, dated 5, 20, 1793. Warrant No. 8 for 640 acres. Recorded Book E-5, p. 246. Tennessee County, south side of Cumberland River.

Grant No. 2845 to James Johnston, dated 1, 31, 1797. Assigned to William Tyrrell. Warrant No. 1063 for 1000 acres. Recorded Book D-4, p. 55. Tennessee County on Red River.

Grant No. 1397 to John Johnston, dated 12, 20, 1791. Warrant No. 1789 for 640 acres. Recorded Book C-3, p. 151. Tennessee County on Pine River.

Grant No. 2263 to Rice Johnston, a private, dated 5, 20, 1793. Assigned to Ambrose Jones, Warrant No. 3720 for 274 acres. Recorded Book B-2, p. 80. On Red River.

Grant No. 749 to David Jones, a corporal, dated 7, 11, 1788. Warrant No. 385 for 1000 acres. Recorded Book A-1, p. 376. West Fork of Red River.

Grant No. 1200 to David Jones, a lieutenant, dated 11, 30, 1790. Warrant No. 1297 for 1096 acres. Recorded Book C-3, p. 58. Davidson County, south side Red River.

Grant No. 2927 to David Jones, dated 2, 19, 1797. Warrant No. 3909 for 640 acres. Recorded Book D-4, p. 80. Tennessee County on Red River.

Grant No. 1431 to Henry Jones, dated 12, 20, 1791. Warrant No. 2050 for 640 acres. Recorded Book C-3, p. 169. Tennessee County, Garner's Creek.

Grant No. 508 to John Jones, a private, dated Sept. 15, 1787. Assigned to Samuel Allen, Warrant No. 2132 for 640 acres. Recorded Book A-1, p. 256. Sulphur Fork.

Grant No. 1918 to Leburn [Seburn ?] Jones, dated 3, 10, 1790. Warrant No. 856 for 640 acres. Recorded Book C-3, p. 67. Tennessee County, north side Cumberland River.

Grant No. 1304 to Seburn Jones, dated 12, 10, 1790. Warrant No. 3353 for 1000 acres. Recorded Book C-3, p. 107. Tennessee County, north side Cumberland River.

Grant No. 1972 to Thomas Jordan, a private, dated 5, 20, 1793. Assigned to Benjamin McCulloh, Warrant No. 2081 for 640 acres. Recorded Book E-5, p. 281. Tennessee County, south side Cumberland River.

Grant No. 424 to John Jordon, a private, dated 9, 15, 1787. Assigned to Willoughby Williams, Warrant No. 1167 for 640 acres. Recorded Book A-1, p. 214. On Red River.

Grant No. 1194 to Pilate Jordon, no service, dated 11, 30, 1790. Assigned to William Cockron. Warrant No. 2736 for 640 acres. Recorded Book C-3, p. 56. Tennessee County, south side Cumberland River.

Grant No. 1632 to Lewis Joyner, dated 2, 23, 1793. Assigned to Joshua Hadley, Warrant No. 2666 for 640 acres. Recorded Book C-3, p. 255. Tennessee County, south side Cumberland River.

Grant No. 35 to Kasper Kamsker, dated 10, 8, 1787. Warrant No. 393 for 320 acres. Recorded Book H-8, p. 21. Davidson County on Red River.

Grant No. 3009 to John Keagy, dated 4, 10, 1797. Warrant No. 3931 for 640 acres. Recorded Book D-4, p. 109. Tennessee County, north side Cumberland River.

Grant No. 3172 to Joseph Kemp, dated 9, 14, 1797. Warrant No. 4033 for 274 acres. Recorded Book D-4, p. 190. Tennessee County, south side Cumberland River.

Grant No. 600 to William Kenkins [or Jenkins], a private, dated 9, 15, 1787. Warrant No. 1943 for 273 acres. Recorded Book A-1, p. 302. On Red River.

Grant No. 2511 to Thomas Kilgore, dated 8, 27, 1795. Warrant No. 978 for 640 acres. Recorded Book D-4, p. 12. Davidson County on Red River.

Grant No. 1155 to Michael King, dated 11, 26, 1789. Assigned to James Cole Mountflorence, Warrant No. 2120 for 640 acres. Recorded Book C-3, p. 42. Location not clear.

Grant No. 119 to John Kirk, a private, dated 3, 7, 1786. Assigned to John Kirk, Warrant No. 795 for 1000 acres. Recorded Book A-1, p. 61. Davidson County, South Red River on Parsons Creek.

Grant No. 1426 to Mathew Kirkendale [Kurkendale, also spelled Suykendale in records], dated 12, 20, 1791. Warrant No. 3455 for 428 acres. Recorded Book C-3, p. 166. Sumner County on Red River.

Grant No. 1991 to Hopkins Lacey, a private, dated 5, 20, 1793. Warrant No. 2133 for 640 acres. Recorded Book E-5, p. 291. Tennessee County, south side Cumberland River.

Grant No. 329 to John Lacky, a soldier, dated 7, 28, 1787. Assigned to William Ross, Warrant No. 2745 for 640 acres. Recorded Book A-1, p. 166. On Red River.

Grant No. 2601 to Aaron Lambert, dated 3, 7, 1796. Warrant No. 1399 for 274 acres. Recorded Book C-3, p. 369. Tennessee County on Pine River.

Grant No. 292 to Jesse Lane, soldier, dated 6, 13, 1787. Assigned to John Rice, Warrant No. 865 for 640 acres. Recorded Book A-1, p. 167. Miller's Creek.

Grant No. 855 to Peter Langford, no service shown, dated 1, 17, 1789. Assigned to Andrew Armstring, Warrant No. 2206 for 640 acres. Recorded Book A-1, p. 430. Davidson County, Red River.

Grant No. 1029 to James Lanier, dated 5, 18, 1789. Warrant No. 2538 for 640 acres. Recorded Book E-5, p. 79. Davidson County on Red River.

Grant No. 1910 to Thomas Latham, a non-commissioned officer, dated 5, 20, 1793. Warrant No. 683 for 1000 acres. Recorded Book E-5, p. 250. Tennessee County on south side Cumberland River.

Grant No. 485 to Matthew Lawless, private, dated Sept. 15, 1787. Assigned to Peggy Allen. Warrant No. 2059 for 640 acres. Recorded Book A-1, p. 244. On Red River.

Grant No. 1170 to Andrew Lector, no service, dated 11, 26, 1789. Assigned to John Eaton. Warrant No. 3520 for 640 acres. Recorded Book C-3, p. 48. Tennessee County, north side Cumberland River.

Grant No. 3387 to Robert W. Lemer [Lemar], dated 12, 12, 1801. Warrant No. 5265 for 640 acres. Recorded Book D-4, p. 298. Robertson County on Red River.

Grant No. 1458 to Andrew Letchworth, dated 12, 20, 1791. Assigned to Andrew Irwin, Warrant No. 2521 for 640 acres. Recorded Book C-3, p. 180. Tennessee County on Red River.

Grant No. 1637 to Joel Lewis, dated 2, 23, 1793. Warrant No. 56 for 1463 acres. Recorded Book C-3, p. 257. Tennessee County.

Grant No. 22 to William Linton [or Leeton], a captain, dated 3, 14, 1786. Warrant No. 625 for 1470 acres. Recorded Book A-1, p. 12. Parson's Creek.

Grant No. 2851 to Jonathan Locklear, dated 1, 21, 1797. Assigned to William T. Lewis & William Tyrrell, Warrant No. 3521 for 640 acres. Recorded Book D-4, p. 57. Tennessee County on north side Cumberland River.

Grant No. 2419 to David Love, a doctor, dated 1, 7, 1794. Assigned to Daniel Young, Warrant No. 339 for 2057 acres. Recorded Book B-2, p. 165. Davidson County, Cumberland River and Sycamore Creek.

Grant No. 716 to Moses Madry, a private, dated 7, 11, 1788. Assigned to Anthony Hart, Warrant No. 3087 for 640 acres. Recorded Book A-1, p. 359. Kerr's Creek and Nelson's Creek.

Grant No. 396 to John Man [or Mann], a private, dated 9, 16, 1787. Assigned to Robert Nelson, Warrant No. 730 for 640 acres. Recorded Book A-1, p. 200. Cumberland River.

Grant No. 3257 to John Mann, dated 12, 6, 1797. Warrant No. 2913 for 640 acres. Recorded Book D-4, p. 252. Tennessee County on Barrett's Creek.

Grant No. 1039 to George Marshall, dated 11, 26, 1789. Assigned to Jacob McCartey, Warrant No. 870 for 228 acres. Recorded Book C-3, p. 5. Tennessee County on Sulphur Fork.

Grant No. 740 to John Marshall, a private, dated 7, 11, 1788. Assigned to Andrew Hampton. Warrant No. — for 640 acres. Recorded Book A-1, p. 371. On Red River.

Grant No. 270 to Henry Martin, a private, dated 1, 24, 1787. Assigned to Willoughby Williams, Warrant No. 394 for 640 acres. Recorded Book A-1, p. 136. South side Red River.

Grant No. 640 to Azariah Massey, a private, dated 9, 15, 1787. Assigned to Thomas Berry, Warrant No. 1112 for 640 acres. Recorded Book A-1, p. 321. On a small creek that runs into the Tennessee River.

Grant No. 1483 to John Matchett [or Hatchett], dated 1, 4, 1792. Warrant No. 937 for 640 acres. Recorded Book C-3, p. 191. Tennessee County, south side Cumberland River.

Grant No. 1788 to Joseph Matthews, dated 5, 20, 1793. Assigned to Charles Gerard, Warrant No. 1593 for 640 acres. Recorded Book E-5, p. 190. Tennessee County, south side Cumberland River.

Grant No. 1193 to John Mayo, no service, dated 11, 30, 1790. Assigned to William Cockron, Warrant No. 2749 for 640 acres. Recorded Book C-3, p. 55. Tennessee County, south side Cumberland River.

Grant No. 3180 to John McAuslin, dated 5, 14, 1797. Warrant No. 238 for 1000 acres. Recorded Book D-4, p. 194. Tennessee County, south side Cumberland River.

Grant No. 2817 to James McBride, no service, dated 1, 12, 1797. Assigned to Stokley Donelson, Warrant No. 3281 for 640 acres. Recorded Book D-4, p. 42. Tennessee County, south side Cumberland River.

Grant No. 1452 to Flaurebce McCarthy [McCathry], a subbattand, dated 5, 20, 1793. Assigned to Edmond Gamble, Warrant No. 1172 for 822 acres. Recorded Book C-3, p. 177. Tennessee County, south side Red River.

Grant No. — to Jacob McCarthy, a corporal, dated 3, 26, 1795. Assigned to John Elliot, Warrant No. — for — acres. Recorded Book H-8, p. 102. Sulphur Fork of Red River.

Grant No. 3202 to Robert McConnel, dated 9, 14, 1797. Warrant No. 4689 for 640 acres. Recorded Book D-4, p. 206. Tennessee County, south side Cumberland River.

Grant No. 3203 to Robert McConnel, dated 9, 14, 1797. Assigned to Robert McConnell, Warrant No. 4449 for 1000 acres. Recorded Book D-4, p. 206. Tennessee County, south side Cumberland River.

Grant No. 4178 to Dugal McCoy, dated 1, 4, 1792. Assigned to heirs of Dugal McCoy, Warrant No. 1367 for 1000 acres. Recorded Book C-3, p. 188. Tennessee County, south side Cumberland River.

Grant No. 2426 to Joseph McDillon, a private, dated 12, 31, 1793. Assigned to John Boyd, Jr., Warrant No. — for 230 acres. Recorded Book B-2, p. 169. Tennessee County, Maccadoo Creek.

Grant No. 781 to Archi McDongald, a private, dated 7, 11, 1788. Assigned to William Bowman, Warrant No. 2530 for 640 acres. Recorded Book A-1, p. 393. Sumner County on the north Fork of Red River.

Grant No. 561 to John McDowell, a private, dated 9, 18, 1787. Assigned to Thomas Woodward, Warrant No. 561 for 640 acres. Recorded Book A-1, p. 282. On Red River.

Grant No. 69 to James McFadden, dated 10, 8, 1787. Warrant No. 403 for 320 acres. Recorded Book H-8, p. 44. Davidson County on Red River.

Grant No. 1394 to Daniel McFalter, dated 12, 20, 1791. Warrant No. 933 for 640 acres. Recorded Book C-3, p. 150. Tennessee County, south side Red River.

Grant No. 1482 to heirs of Peter McGee, dated 1, 4, 1792. Warrant No. 1382 for 1000 acres. Recorded Book C-3, p. 190. Tennessee County, south side Cumberland River.

Grant No. 2273 to Joshua McMullins, a private, dated 5, 20, 1793. Assigned to Noah Woodard, Warrant No. 1233 for 369 acres. Recorded Book B-2, p. 85.

Grant No. 3252 to John McNary [McNairy], dated 12, 6, 1797. Warrant No. 4695 for

640 acres. Recorded Book D-4, p. 231. Tennessee County, Red River.

Grant No. 3253 to John McNary, dated 12, 6, 1797. Warrant No. 4741 for 274 acres. Recorded Book D-4, p. 232. Tennessee County on Red River.

Grant No. 3255 to John McNary [or McNairy], dated 12, 6, 1797. Warrant No. 4092 for 640 acres. Recorded Book D-4, p. 233. Tennessee County on Red River.

Grant No. 3226 to Charles McRee, dated 11, 17, 1797. Assigned to John Harden, Warrant No. 2753 for 640 acres. Recorded Book D-4, p. 219. Sumner County on Red River.

Grant No. 2094 to Miles McSkekee, a lieutenant, dated 5, 20, 1793. Assigned to John Russell & heirs of McShekee, Warrant No. 1087 for 3560 acres. Recorded Book B-2, p. 2. Tennessee County on Sulphur Fork.

Grant No. 2462 to Abraham Meadows, a private, dated 12, 31, 1793. Assigned to Phillip Shackler, Warrant No. 1536 for 274 acres. Recorded Book B-2, p. 191. Tennessee County, Sulphur Fork of Red River.

Grant No. 2436 to Mills Medlin, a private, dated 3, 18, 1794. Assigned to John Haywood, Warrant No. 3117 for 640 acres. Recorded Book B-2, p. 177. Tennessee County. This grant also mentions Miles Maudlin.

Grant No. 405 to John Melner, dated 6, 27, 1793. Warrant No. 561 for 640 acres. Recorded Book G-7, p. 194. Tennessee County on head of Milner's [or Miller's] Creek.

Grant No. 2424 to Jno. Miers, a private, dated 12, 31, 1793. Assigned to Wm. J. Brown, Dan'l & Geo. Brown, heirs of James Brown, decd., Warrant No. 823 for 274 acres. Recorded Book B-2, p. 168. Tennessee County on Pine River.

Grant No. 845 to John Mills, dated 1, 17, 1789. Assigned to Anthony Hart, Warrant No. 2812 for 640 acres. Recorded Book A-1, p. 425. Brown's Creek, Sulphur Fork of Red River.

Grant No. 695 to Willis Mills, a private, dated 7, 11, 1788. Assigned to Nancy Sheppard, Warrant No. 2093 for 640 acres. Recorded Book A-1, p. 249. On Red River.

Grant No. 380 to Jacob Mitchell, a private, dated 9, 16, 1787. Assigned to Robert Nelson, Warrant No. 2578 for 640 acres. Recorded Book A-1, p. 192. On Red River.

Grant No. 1415 to Elisha Modlin, no service, dated 12, 20, 1791. Assigned to Thomas Bailey, Warrant No. 1437 for 640 acres. Recorded Book C-3, p. 161. Tennessee County, both sides Pine River.

Grant No. 2973 to Thomas Molloy, dated 4, 5, 1797. Warrant No. 4251 for 640 acres. Recorded Book D-4, p. 89. Tennessee County, south side Cumberland River.

Grant No. 622 to Jacob Moore, a private, dated Sept. 15, 1787. Assigned to Alexander Allen, Warrant No. 2136 for 640 acres. Recorded Book A-1, p. 312. On Red River.

Grant No. 2794 to James Morehead, dated 12, 20, 1796. Warrant No. 1187 for 944 acres. Recorded Book D-4, p. 28. Tennessee County, north side Cumberland River.

Grant No. 124 to William Morris, a private, dated 3, 14, 1786. Assigned to James Brown, Warrant No. 1065 for 640 acres. Recorded Book A-1, p. 64. Davidson County on Red River.

Grant No. 3317 to John Morrow, dated 12, 6, 1797. Warrant No. 1177 for 640 acres. Recorded Book D-4, p. 237. Sumner County on Red River.

Grant No. 3322 to John & James Morrow, dated 12, 6, 1757. Warrant No. 1331 for 640 acres. Recorded Book D-4, p. 239. Sumner County on Red River.

Grant No. 734 to Samuel Morrow, a private, dated 7, 11, 1788. Assigned to William Bowman, Warrant No. 2531 for 640 acres. Recorded Book A-1, p. 369. On Red River.

Grant No. 1195 to Alen Murdock, no service, dated 11, 30, 1790. Assigned to William Cockron, Warrant No. 2528 for 640 acres. Recorded Book C-3, p. 56. Tennessee County, south side Cumberland River.

Grant No. 491 to Hardy Murfree, dated 9, 15, 1787. Assigned to Matthew Wiggins, Warrant No. 731 for 274 acres. Recorded Book A-1, p. 247. Sulphur Fork.

Grant No. 3030 to Hardy Murfree, dated 4, 10, 1797. Warrant No. 3567 for 640 acres. Recorded Book D-4, p. 120. Tennessee County on Red River.

Grant No. 3175 to Hugh Murphy, dated 9, 14, 1797. Warrant No. 3837 for 640 acres. Recorded Book D-4, p. 192. Tennessee County, south side Cumberland River.

Grant No. 1612 to Joshua Murray, dated 2, 23, 1793. Assigned to Thomas Hays, Warrant No. 2351 for 640 acres. Recorded Book C-3, p. 246. Tennessee County, south side Cumberland River.

Grant No. 1449 to Alexander Nelson, dated 12, 20, 1791. Warrant No. 182 for 274 acres. Recorded Book C-3, p. 176. Tennessee County, south side Red River.

Grant No. — to Robert Nelson, no service shown, dated 9, 26, 1795. Assigned to Thomas Byhen, Warrant No. — for 640 acres. Recorded Book D-4, p. 6. Tennessee County, north side Red River.

Grant No. 3233 to Robert Nelson, dated 11, 17, 1797. Warrant No. — for 1280 acres. Recorded Book D-4, p. 223. Tennessee County on the River.

Grant No. 1192 to James Nichleson, no service, dated 11, 30, 1790. Assigned to William Cockron, Warrant No. 2753 for 640 acres. Recorded Book C-3, p. 55. Tennessee County, south side Cumberland River.

Grant No. 2818 to John Nickory, no service shown, dated 1, 12, 1797. Assigned to Stokley Donelson, Warrant No. 521 for 640 acres. Recorded Book D-4, p. 42. Tennessee County on Red River.

Grant No. 1414 to William Nobland, no service, dated 12, 30, 1791. Assigned to Anthony Hart, Warrant No. 3516 for 640 acres. Recorded Book C-3, p. 160. Tennessee County on Beaver Creek.

Grant No. 3385 to Mark Noble, dated 12, 12, 1801. Warrant No. 4188 for 274 acres. Recorded Book D-4, p. 297. Robertson County on Red River.

Grant No. 1655 to Charles Oneal, a lieutenant, dated 5, 20, 1793. Assigned to Joshua Gist, Warrant No. 680 for 853 acres. Recorded Book E-5, p. 126. Tennessee County, north side of the River.

Grant No. 1996 to Isham O'Niel, a private, dated 5, 20, 1793. Assigned to John Mc-Nary & Robt Nelson, Warrant No. 2680 for 640 acres. Recorded Book E-5, p. 293. Tennessee County on south side Cumberland River.

Grant No. 2410 to John Overton, a private, dated 1, 7, 1794. Assigned to John Mc-Keese, Warrant No. 3156 for 274 acres. Recorded Book B-2, p. 160. Tennessee County, Sycamore Creek.

Grant No. 2167 to Thomas Padden, a private, dated 5, 20, 1793. Assigned to Lancelot Johnston, Warrant No. 1853 for 640 acres. Recorded Book B-2, p. 38. On Red River.

Grant No. 2849 to Isaiah Parr, dated 1, 21, 1797. Assigned to Wm. T. Lewis & W. Tyrrell, Warrant No. 410 for 274 acres. Recorded Book D-4, p. 56. Tennessee County on Spring Creek.

Grant No. 709 to Nehemiah Pearcy, a private, dated 7, 11, 1788. Warrant No. 934 for 640 acres. Recorded Book A-1, p. 353. Location not shown.

Grant No. 698 to Stephen Pelter, a private, dated 7, 11, 1788. Assigned to Thomas Love, Warrant No. 1508 for 640 acres. Recorded Book A-1, p. 12. Sycamore Creek.

Grant No. 236 to Isaac Pennington, a private, dated 3, 7, 1786. Warrant No. 707 for 266 acres. Recorded Book A-1, p. 120. Davidson County, Red River.

Grant No. 1432 to Caonstant Perkins, dated 12, 20, 1791. Warrant No. 3071 for 640 acres. Recorded Book C-3, p. 129. Tennessee County on Red River.

Grant No. 1313 to Mann Phillips, dated 12, 10, 1790. Warrant No. 1866 for 274 acres. Recorded Book C-3, p. 110. Tennessee County on Red River.

Grant No. 651 to Mark Phillips, a private, dated 12, 8, 1787. Assigned to William Clark, Warrant No. 1785 for 640 acres. Recorded Book A-1, p. 327. Red River.

Grant No. 1916 to William Price, a private, dated 5, 20, 1793. Assigned to Edward Wgin [?], Warrant No. 3297 for 640 acres. Recorded Book E-5, p. 253. Tennessee County on Barton's Creek.

Grant No. 3408 to Gabriel Rawls, dated 2, 10, 1804. Warrant No. 185 for 228 acres. Recorded Book D-4, p. 311. Robertson County, north side Cumberland River.

Grant No. 3235 to Joel Raybourn, no service, dated 11, 24, 1797. Assigned to Richard Cooke [or Cocke ?], Warrant No. 925 for 640 acres. Recorded Book D-4, p. 224. Tennessee County on Wells Creek.

Grant No. 2448 to John Rayford, private, dated 12, 31, 1793. Assigned to Jesse Cobb, Warrant No. 1236 for 640 acres. Recorded Book B-2, p. 183. Tennessee County, Cumberland River above Clarksville.

Grant No. 444 to Jesse Renfroe, dated 6, 27, 1793. Warrant No. 623 for 640 acres. Recorded Book G-7, p. 216. Tennessee County on south side Cumberland River.

Grant No. 446 to Jesse Renfroe, dated 6, 27, 1793. Warrant No. 503 for 640 acres. Recorded Book G-7, p. 217. Tennessee County, north side Red River.

Grant No. 275 to James Richardson, a private, dated 3, 22, 1787. Assigned to Richard Fenner, Warrant No. 2542 for 640 acres. Recorded Book A-1, p. 139. On Red River.

Grant No. 1895 to William Richardson, a private, dated 5, 20, 1793. Assigned to Nicholas Long, Warrant No. 1895 for 640 acres. Recorded Book E-5, p. 242. Tennessee County on south side Cumberland River.

Grant No. 490 to John Ripley, dated 9, 15, 1787. Assigned to Richard Tenner [or Tanner], Warrant No. 2540 for 640 acres. Recorded Book A-1, p. 247. On Red River.

Grant No. 1684 to Cornelius Robertson, a private, dated 5, 20, 1793. Assigned to Thomas Hickman, Warrant No. 3557 for 274 acres. Recorded Book E-5, p. 139. Tennessee County, north side Cumberland River.

Grant No. 2177 to Edward Robinson, a private, dated 5, 20, 1793. Assigned to James Clark & William Clark, Warrant No. 3687 for 640 acres. Recorded Book B-2, p. 44. On Red River.

Grant No. 226 to Jonah Rochel, a private, dated 3, 7, 1786. Assigned to Job Rochel, Warrant No. 727 for 640 acres. Recorded Book A-1, p. 115. Red River & Sulphur Fork.

Grant No. 1946 to Joshua Rogers, a private, dated 5, 20, 1793. Assigned to Jesse Cobb, Warrant No. 1175 for 640 acres. Recorded Book E-5, p. 268. Tennessee

County on Tennessee River.

Grant No. 1742 to Samuel Roland, a private, dated 5, 20, 1793. Assigned to James Burns, Warrant No. 3250 for 640 acres. Recorded Book E-5, p. 167. Tennessee County.

Grant No. 2011 to John Rulford [could be Burford], a private, dated 5, 20, 1793. Assigned to Benjamin McCulloch, Warrant No. — for 640 acres. Recorded Book E-5, p. 300. Tennessee County on south side Red River.

Grant No. 2208 to John Rus, a private, dated 5, 20, 1783. Assigned to David Shelton, Warrant No. 235 for 274 acres. Recorded Book B-2, p. 54. On Red and Cumberland Rivers.

Grant No. 2051 to James Russel, a private, dated 5, 20, 1793. Assigned to Thomas Hamilton, Warrant No. 1206 for 640 acres. Recorded Book E-5, p. 321. Sumner County on Red River.

Grant No. 1973 to Peter Russell, a private, dated 5, 20, 1793. Assigned to Benjamin McCulloh, Warrant No. 2012 for 640 acres. Recorded Book E-5, p. 282. Tennessee County on Red River.

Grant No. 2467 to John Ryans, a private, dated 12, 31, 1793. Assigned to Jesse Cobb, Warrant No. 1279 for 640 acres. Recorded Book B-2, p. 193. Tennessee County, Guises Creek.

Grant No. 3014 to Edward Sanders, dated 4, 10, 1797. Warrant No. 1506 for 640 acres. Recorded Book D-4, p. 111. Tennessee County on Red River.

Grant No. 2829 to Peters Sanders, dated 1, 12, 1797. Assigned to Stokley Donelson, Warrant No. 3158 for 640 acres. Recorded Book D-4, p. 47. Tennessee County.

Grant No. 3061 to Abraham Savaggerty, dated 7, 19, 1797. Warrant No. 140 for 640 acres. Recorded Book D-4, p. 135. Davidson County on Red River.

Grant No. 1717 to Mathew Scarborough, a private, dated 5, 20, 1793. Assigned to Hopkins Lacey & Thomas Malloy, Warrant No. 3638 for 640 acres. Recorded Book E-5, p. 154. Tennessee County on the first creek north side Cumberland River above Cross Creek.

Grant No. 2079 to John Seanson, a private, dated 5, 20, 1793. Assigned to Nicholas Long. Warrant No. 3060 for 640 acres. Recorded Book E-5, p. 334. Tennessee County on south side Cumberland River.

Grant No. 2780 to Matthew Sellers, dated 10, 17, 1796. Warrant No. 3769 for 640 acres. Recorded Book D-4, p. 21. Tennessee County on Red River.

Grant No. 1971 to James Shanks, a private, dated 5, 20, 1793. Assigned to Benjamin McCulloh, Warrant No. 2237 for 640 acres. Recorded Book E-5, p. 281. Tennessee County, south side Cumberland River.

Grant No. 2446 to Robert Shaw, dated 2, 22, 1795. Warrant No. 1526 for 243 acres. Recorded Book C-3, p. 294. Sumner County on Red River.

Grant No. 2469 to Lewis Shilkes, a private, dated 12, 31, 1793. Assigned to Jesse Cobb, Warrant No. 1174 for 640 acres. Recorded Book B-2, p. 194. Tennessee County, Guises Creek.

Grant No. 2837 to Allen Shockley, dated 1, 12, 1797. Assigned to Stokley Donelson, Warrant No. 3425 for 640 acres. Recorded Book D-4, p. 51. Tennessee County, both sides Cumberland River.

Grant No. 602 to Benjamin Simmons, a private, dated 9, 15, 1787. Assigned to George Wills, Warrant No. 472 for 428 acres. Recorded Book A-1, p. 303. Sulphur Fork of Red River.

Grant No. 782 to Dewey Simms, a private, dated 7, 11, 1788. Assigned to William Bowman, Warrant No. 2818 for 640 acres. Recorded Book A-1, p. 394. Sumner County on North Fork of Red River.

Grant No. 590 to Samuel Simpson, a private, dated 9, 15, 1787. Assigned to Noah Woodward, Warrant No. 901 for 640 acres. Recorded Book A-1, p. 297. On Red River.

Grant No. 771 to Nathaniel Slade, a private, dated 7, 11, 1788. Assigned to William Bowman, Warrant No. 2544 for 640 acres. Recorded Book A-1, p. 388. North side of the North branch of Red River.

Grant No. 1629 to Clement Smith, a private, dated 4, 24, 1793. Assigned to Thomas Smith, Warrant No. 589 for 640 acres. Recorded Book E-5, p. 113. Tennessee County on Red River.

Grant No. 288 to John Smith, a private, no date shown. Assigned to Andrew Breakey [Bleakey] for 640 acres. Recorded Book A-1, p. 145. Waters of Sulphur Fork.

Grant No. 1604 to John Smith, dated 11, 27, 1792. Assigned to Benjamin Hardon, Warrant No. 1230 for 388 acres. Recorded Book E-5, p. 101. Davidson County on Red River.

Grant No. 2186 to Owen Smith, a private, dated 5, 20, 1793. Assigned to Thomas Johnston, Warrant No. 1847 for 640 acres. Recorded Book B-2, p. 48. Sulphur Fork.

Grant No. —— to William Smith and John Davis, dated 4, 27, 1793. Assigned to George Glass, Warrant No. —— for 320 acres. Recorded Book H-8, p. 70. Tennessee County, south side Cumberland River.

Grant No. 1767 to James Southerland, a private, dated 5, 20, 1793. Assigned to Charles Gerald, Warrant No. —— for 274 acres. Recorded Book E-5, p. 179. Tennessee County on the south side of Cumberland River.

Grant No. 1921 to Josiah Stafford, a private, dated 5, 20, 1793. Assigned to Jesse Cobb, Warrant No. 1483 for 274 acres. Recorded Book E-5, p. 255. Tennessee County.

Grant No. 373 to Isaiah Stedham, a private, dated 9, 15, 1787. Assigned to Robert Nelson, Warrant No. 2543 for 640 acres. Recorded Book A-1, p. 188. Sulphur Fork.

Grant No. 3234 to Duncan Stewart, dated 11, 20, 1797. Warrant No. 557 for 228 acres. Recorded Book D-4, p. 223. Tennessee County on Red River.

Grant No. 49 to John Stewart, dated 10, 8, 1787. Warrant No. 137 for 640 acres. Recorded Book H-8, p. 31. Davidson County, south side Red River.

Grant No. 2158 to L. Stone, a private, dated 5, 20, 1793. Assigned to Nathaniel Holley, Warrant No. 2158 for 640 acres. Recorded Book B-2, p. 33. Tennessee County, Cumberland River.

Grant No. 2403 to Samuel Stringer, a private, dated 12, 20, 1793. Assigned to James Glasgow, Warrant No. 1107 for 571 acres. Recorded Book B-2, p. 171. Tennessee County on Cumberland River.

Grant No. 2844 to John Sugg, dated 1, 21, 1797. Assigned to William T. Lewis and William Tyrrell, Warrant No. 425 for 274 acres. Recorded Book D-4, p. 54. Tennessee County on Red River.

Grant No. 193 to James Summers, a sergeant, dated 3, 7, 1786. Warrant No. 310 for 857 acres. Recorded Book A-1, p. 99. Davidson County, Red River.

Grant No. 1605 to Howell Tatum, dated 2, 23, 1793. Warrant No. 2679 for 640 acres. Recorded Book C-3, p. 243. Tennessee County on Sulphur Fork.

Grant No. 1578 to John Tatum, a private, dated 4, 27, 1795. Assigned to William Whitard, Warrant No. 595 for 274 acres. Recorded Book E-5, p. 90. Tennessee County on Red River.

Grant No. 1976 to Henry Taylor, no service, dated 5, 20, 1793. Assigned to Benjamin McCulloh, Warrant No. 2243 for 640 acres. Recorded Book E-5, p. 285. Tennessee County on Blooming Grove Creek.

Grant No. 1641 to James Taylor, dated 11, 27, 1793. Warrant No. 810 for 640 acres. Recorded Book E-5, p. 199. Sumner County on Red River.

Grant No. 1982 to John Taylor, a private, dated 5, 20, 1793. Assigned to Leon Perry, Warrant No. 3664 for 640 acres. Recorded Book E-5, p. 286. Sumner County on Red River.

Grant No. 2485 to Thomas Templeton, a private, dated 12, 31, 1793. Assigned to John Moore, Warrant No. 1644 for 640 acres. Recorded Book B-2, p. 202. On Red River.

Grant No. 2832 to Jeremiah Thomas, no service, dated 1, 12, 1797. Assigned to Stokley Donelson, Warrant No. 1589 for 640 acres. Recorded Book D-4, p. 48. Tennessee County on Red River.

Grant No. 1897 to Lemuel Thomas, a private, dated 5, 20, 1793. Assigned to Nicholas Long, Warrant No. 463 for 640 acres. Recorded Book E-5, p. 243. Tennessee County on south side Cumberland River.

Grant No. 133 to Richard Thomas, a private, dated 3, 14, 1786. Warrant No. 133 for 228 acres. Recorded Book A-1, p. 89. Davidson County on Parson's Creek.

Grant No. 149 to Zach Thomas, dated 4, 27, 1793. Assigned to Robert Nelson, Warrant No. 827 for 320 acres. Recorded Book H-8, p. 81. Tennessee County on Kerr's Creek.

Grant No. 346 to John Thompson, a private, dated 9, 15, 1787. Warrant No. 645 for 640 acres. Recorded Book A-1, p. 175. Red River.

Grant No. 2010 to Joshua Thompson, a private, dated 5, 20, 1793. Assigned to Benjamin McCulloch, Warrant No. 2240 for 640 acres. Recorded Book E-5, p. 299. Tennessee County.

Grant No. 2823 to Josiah Todd, dated 1, 12, 1797. Assigned to Stokley Donelson, Warrant No. 1590 for 640 acres. Recorded Book D-4, p. 44. Tennessee County on Red River.

Grant No. 176 to Christopher Tow, a private, dated 9, 15, 1787. Assigned to Robert Nelson, Warrant No. 3114 for 640 acres. Recorded Book A-1, p. 190. Red River.

Grant No. 322 to Gray Tucker, a soldier, dated 7, 28, 1787. Assigned to William Ross, Warrant No. 2694 for 640 acres. Recorded Book A-1, p. 165. On Red River.

Grant No. 406 to Solomon Turpin, dated 6, 27, 1793. Warrant No. 588 for 640 acres. Recorded Book G-7, p. 195. Tennessee County on Red River.

Grant No. 458 to Solomon Turpin, dated 3, 1, 1797. Warrant No. 588 for 640 acres. Recorded Book G-7, p. 226. Davidson County on both sides Red River.

Grant No. 882 to William Tutom [Tuton, could be Tatom], dated 1, 17, 1789. Warrant No. 3493 for 640 acres. Recorded Book E-5, p. 13. Sumner County, north side Red River.

Grant No. 2744 to William Tyrrell, dated 7, 20, 1796. Warrant No. 1532 for 228 acres. Recorded Book C-3, p. 420. Tennessee County on Kilgore's Station.

Grant No. 2845 to William Tyrrell, dated 1, 21, 1797. Assigned to James Johnston,

Warrant No. 1063 for 1000 acres. Recorded Book D-4, p. 55. On Red River.

Grant No. 2844 to Wm. Tyrrell, dated 1, 21, 1797. Assigned to John Sugg & William Lewis, Warrant No. 425 for 274 acres. Recorded Book D-4, p. 54. Red River.

Grant No. 2555 to John Vance, a lieutenant, dated 3, 7, 1796. Assigned to Stokley Donelson and William Tyreell, Warrant No. 330 for 2560 acres. Recorded Book C-3, p. 352. Tennessee County on Red River.

Grant No. 762 to William Vanderfield, a private, dated 7, 11, 1788. Assigned to William Bowman, Warrant No. 2822 for 640 acres. Recorded Book A-1, p. 383. Sumner County on Red River.

Grant No. 3374 to William Verrell [or Ferrell], dated 9, 29, 1801. Warrant No. 4530 for 357 acres. Recorded Book D-4, p. 293. Robertson County on Sycamore Creek.

Grant No. 1842 to Andrew Wade, a private, dated 5, 20, 1793. Warrant No. 347 for 228 acres. Recorded Book E-5, p. 216. Sumner County on North Fork of Red River.

Grant No. 1450 to Allen Walker, dated 12, 20, 1791. Warrant No. 3438 for 1000 acres. Recorded Book C-3, p. 177. Sumner County, north side of Red River.

Grant No. 615 to William Walker, a sergeant, dated 9, 15, 1787. Warrant No. 1878 for 1000 acres. Recorded Book A-1, p. 309. Sulphur Fork of Red River.

Grant No. 2314 to Jonathan Wallard, a private, dated 5, 20, 1793. Warrant No. 3031 for 640 acres. Recorded Book B-2, p. 104. Tennessee County, Philip's Pond.

Grant No. 2068 to John Ward, a private, dated 5, 20, 1793. Assigned to William Hill, Warrant No. 206 for 640 acres. Recorded Book E-5, p. 329. Tennessee County on north side of Cumberland River.

Grant No. 1994 to William Warren, a private, dated 5, 20, 1793. Assigned to Jesse Cobb, Warrant No. 1161 for 228 acres. Recorded Book E-5, p. 292. Tennessee County on both sides of Red River.

Grant No. 198 to Etheldred Washington, a fifer, dated 3, 7, 1786. Assigned to William Washington, Warrant No. 582 for 1000 acres. Recorded Book A-1, p. 102. Parson's Creek.

Grant No. 3073 to Samuel Weakley, dated 7, 19, 1797. Warrant No. 4396 for 640 acres. Recorded Book D-4, p. 142. Tennessee County, Sycamore Creek.

Grant No. 3008 to Daniel Welburn, dated 4, 10, 1797. Warrant No. 3430 for 274 acres. Recorded Book D-4, p. 108. Tennessee County, south side Red River.

Grant No. 178 to Charles Wheaton, a private, dated 3, 7, 1796. Assigned to Joseph Hopkins, Warrant No. — for 400 acres. Recorded Book H-8, p. 110. On Sulphur Fork of Red River.

Grant No. 171 to Robert White, a private, dated 9, 26, 1795. Assigned to Robert Nelson, Warrant No. — for 400 acres. Recorded Book H-8, p. 121. Tennessee County.

Grant No. 491 to Matthew Wiggins, a private, dated 9, 17, 1787. Assigned to Hardy Murfree, Warrant No. 731 for 274 acres. Recorded Book A-1, p. 247. Sulphur Fork.

Grant No. 1091 to Thomas Wiggins, no service, dated 11, 26, 1789. Assigned to John Craddock, Warrant No. 1448 for 640 acres. Recorded Book C-3, p. 18. Davidson County, north side Red River.

Grant No. 3006 to Daniel Wilburn, dated 4, 10, 1797. Warrant No. 2210 for 1000 acres. Recorded Book D-4, p. 107. Tennessee County, north of Red River.

Grant No. 1918 to John Wilkinson, a private, dated 5, 20, 1793. Assigned to Nicholas Long, Warrant No. 1918 for 640 acres. Recorded Book E-5, p. 254. Tennessee County, south side Cumberland River.

Grant No. 619 to David Willcock, no service shown, dated 9, 15, 1787. Assigned to Richard William Caswell, Warrant No. 479 for 640 acres. Recorded Book A-1, p. 311. On Red River.

Grant No. 1868 to Willoughby Williams, a private, dated 5, 20, 1793. Assigned to Andrew Olliver, Warrant No. 603 for 640 acres. Recorded Book E-5, p. 229. Tennessee County on both sides of Sulphur Fork Creek.

Grant No. 2822 to Thomas Wimpie [or Wimple ?], no service shown, dated 1, 12, 1797. Assigned to Stokley Donelson, Warrant No. 3044 for 640 acres. Recorded Book D-4, p. 44. Tennessee County, Red River.

Grant No. 1189 to Abraham Wise, dated 11, 16, 1790. Assigned to Robert Nelson, Warrant No. 1867 for 274 acres. Recorded Book C-3, p. 54. Tennessee County on Blooming Grove Creek.

Grant No. 2150 to John Yates, a private, dated 5, 20, 1793. Assigned to John M. Alston, Warrant No. 220 for 640 acres. Recorded Book B-2, p. 29. Tennessee County, on Red River.

MISCELLANEOUS RECORDS

Before Tennessee became a state, the early militia organizations, as well as those of the South West Territory, were based on the Militia laws of the State of North Carolina. Under these laws, each county had a separate regiment of militia, divided into Captains' Companies. Each regiment was designated by the name of its county. In 1797, the General Assembly ordered that there be a regiment of militia on the south side of the Cumberland River to be designated as the First Regiment of Davidson County, and one on the north side of the Cumberland River to be designated as the Second Regiment of Davidson County. In each of the other counties, the regiment was designated as the "First Regiment of the County."

Under the Militia Law of 1803, the General Assembly adopted a numerical system of identification, assigning a number to each regiment in each county. Again, these regiments were known locally as the First Regiment of the County.

It was not until 1810 that the increase in population made it necessary, under the law, to organize an additional regiment in some of the counties. These were known as the "Second Regiment" of the county and were assigned a Regimental number in the order in which they were organized by the General Assembly of 1811.

The officers commissioned for Montgomery County Regiments were:

John Beaty, Ensign, September 29, 1797
John Beaty, Lieutenant, December 22, 1798
Samuel Beaty, Ensign, June 16, 1801
William Beeasun, Lieutenant, cavalry Regiment, Mero District, June 6, 1799
William Bell, First Major, May 14, 1800
Charles Brantley, Lieutenant, September 29, 1797
Darden Brown, Ensign, September 29, 1797
James Campbell, Captain, September 29, 1797
Alexander Carns, Captain, June 16, 1801
Aaron Choat, Lieutenant, September 29, 1797
Joseph Choat, Ensign, September 29, 1797
John Cocke, Ensign, December 22, 1798
Richard Cocke, Lieutenant, December 22, 1798
John Edmonston, Captain, cavalry regiment, Mero District, October 4, 1796
John Elliott, Lieutenant, November 18, 1800
James Ford, Lieutenant-Colonel, Commandant, October 4, 1796
Wiston Gibson, Captain, September 29, 1797
William Greson, Ensign, September 29, 1797
Alexander Hambleton, Cornet in cavalry regiment, Mero District, October 4, 1796
John Harris, Lieutenant, September 29, 1797
Thompson Harriss, Captain, December 22 1798
James Hollis, Captain, September 29, 1797
Thomas Hutcheson, Lieutenant, June 16, 1801
Hugh McCollum, Second Major in cavalry regiment, Mero District, October 28, 1797
Richard Miles, First Major, October 4, 1796
William Mitcheson, Second Major, October 4, 1796
Isaac Peterson, Captain, September 29, 1797
Larkin Rogers, Lieutenant, September 29, 1797
William Teas, Cornet in cavalry regiment, Mero District, June 6, 1799
Thomas Tenen, Captain, November 18, 1800
Benjamin Thomas, Captain, September 29, 1797
Alexander Trousdale, Lieutenant, September 29, 1797
Archelas Wells, Lieutenant, cavalry regiment, Mero District, October 4, 1796
Archelus Wells, Second Major, October 20, 1800
Archibald Wells, Captain, December 22, 1796

Henry William, Ensign, September 29, 1797
Andrew Batie, Captain, 24th regiment, June 26, 1807
James Baxter, Captain, Light Infantry, 24th regiment, June 24, 1807
Peter Black, Lieutenant, 24th regiment, June 26, 1807
Barney Duff, Lieutenant, 24th regiment, June 26, 1807
Stephen Ogwin, Ensign, 24th regiment, June 26, 1807
Lewis Pucket, Captain, regiment of cavalry, 6th brigade, December 3, 1807
Grant Thomas [?], Lieutenant, 24th regiment, June 26, 1807
Alexander Tinnen, Lieutenant, regiment of cavalry, 6th brigade, December 3, 1807
Samuel Vance, Captain, 24th regiment, June 26, 1807
Henry H. Bryan, Captain, 24th regiment, May 21, 1808
Henry H. Bryan, First Major, 24th regiment, December 29, 1808
William Bryant, Lieutenant, 24th regiment, May 21, 1808
John Cocke, Lieutenant Colonel Commandant, 24th regiment, December 29, 1808
William Cocke, Ensign, Volunteer Rifle Company, 24th regiment, June 4, 1808
Barney Duff, Ensign, 24th regiment, May 21, 1808
Coilmore Duvall, Captain, Volunteer Rifle Company, 24th regiment, June 4, 1808
Ebenezer Frost, Captain, 24th regiment, December 26, 1808
Adam Harman, Jr., Captain, 24th regiment, February 27, 1808
Samuel C. Hawkins, Lieutenant, 24th regiment, June 4, 1808
Simon Holms, Lieutenant, 24th regiment, December 26, 1808
Brice Jackson, Ensign, 24th regiment, December 26, 1808
James McGowan, Ensign, 24th regiment, June 18, 1808
William McGowan, Ensign, 24th regiment, May 21, 1808
William Newel, Ensign, 24th regiment, June 18, 1808
Edward Niblet, Lieutenant, Volunteer Rifle Company, 24th regiment, June 4, 1808
William Porter, Captain, 24th regiment, December 26, 1808
Amos Rochel, Lieutenant, 24th regiment, February 27, 1808
John Rushing, Ensign, 24th regiment, February 27, 1808
Thomas Ryborne, Ensign, 24th regiment, June 4, 1808
Isaac Shelby, Second Major, 24th regiment, February 27, 1808
Robert Smith, Lieutenant, 24th regiment, December 26, 1808
John Trotter, Ensign, 24th regiment, December 26, 1808
John Weakley, Captain, 24th regiment, June 4, 1808
Needham Whitfield, Captain, 24th regiment, December 26, 1808
Philman [Philmeon] Whitworth, Lieutenant, 24th regiment, June 4, 1808
Francis Baker, Lieutenant, 24th regiment, May 19, 1809
James H. Brigham, Captain, regiment of cavalry, 6th brigade, August 15, 1809
Robert Brownson, Lieutenant, regiment of cavalry, 6th brigade, August 15, 1809
James A. Burtin, Captain, 24th regiment, August 15, 1809
Nathan Dickson, Ensign, 24th regiment, May 25, 1809
John P. Ford, Captain, 24th regiment, August 1, 1809
William Ford, Lieutenant, Light Infantry Company, 24th regiment, August 15, 1809
William Goodwin, Captain, 24th regiment, May 19, 1809
John Hampton, Lieutenant, 24th regiment, May 25, 1809
William Haynes, Ensign, 24th regiment, May 19, 1809
James Lister, Ensign, Light Infantry Company, 24th regiment, August 16, 1809
Willie Outlaw, Cornet, regiment of cavalry, 6th brigade, August 15, 1809
William Penny, Captain, 24th regiment, May 19, 1809
John Poston, Captain, Light Infantry Company, 24th regiment, August 15, 1809
John Robinson, Lieutenant, 24th regiment, August 1, 1809
John Rook, Ensign, 24th regiment, August 15, 1809
Robert Temple, Lieutenant, 24th regiment, August 15, 1809
William Trigg, Captain, 24th regiment, May 25, 1809
Abraham Allen, Junr., Captain, 24th regiment, November 14, 1810
Richard Anderson, Lieutenant, 24th regiment, November 14, 1810
Beand Blodgett, Captain, 24th regiment, March 16, 1810
John Boyd, Captain, 24th regiment, November 14, 1810
Christopher N. Carney, Ensign, Light Infantry Company, 24th regiment, November 14, 1810
William Gord, Lieutenant, Rifle Company, 24th regiment, November 14, 1810
Zachariah Grant, Lieutenant, 24th regiment, November 14, 1810
James Hamilton, Captain, Light Infantry Company, 24th regiment, November 14, 1810
William Handlin, Ensign, 24th regiment, March 16, 1810
William Haynes, Lieutenant, Light Infantry, 24th regiment, November 24, 1810

John Lindsey, Lieutenant, 24th regiment, March 14, 1810
William Logans, Captain, 24th regiment, November 14, 1810
Robert Love, Ensign, 24th regiment, November 14, 1810
Edward Noblett [Niblett], Captain, Volunteer Rifle Company, 24th regiment, November 14, 1810
Elisha Rainey, Ensign, 24th regiment, November 14, 1810
Collin Roberts Ensign, 24th regiment, November 14, 1810
Robert Sommerville, Captain, 24th regiment, November 14, 1810
John B. Tompkins, Lieutenant, 24th regiment, March 16, 1810
Ross Webb, Lieutenant, 24th regiment, November 14, 1810
James Williams, Lieutenant, regiment cavalry, 6th brigade, April 12, 1810
Charles L. Campbell, Lieutenant, 24th regiment, November 19, 1811
Christopher N. Carney, Captain, 24th regiment, April 3, 1811
Zachariah Edgar, Ensign, 24th regiment, November 19, 1811
James Gillespie, Cornet, regiment of cavalry, 6th brigade, September 13, 1811
David Gold, Second Major, 24th regiment, June 3, 1811
William Haynes, Captain, 24th regiment, April 3, 1811
Andrew Holland, Lieutenant, 24th regiment, November 19, 1811
William Holloway, Ensign, 24th regiment, November 14, 1811
John Hutcheson, Ensign, 24th regiment, November 19, 1811
Henry McCall, Ensign, 24th regiment, November 19, 1811
Samuel McGall [McCall], Lieutenant, 24th regiment, November 19, 1811
Right [Wright] Outlaw, Captain, 24th regiment, November 19, 1811
Israel Robinson, Lieutenant, regiment of cavalry 6th brigade, February 21, 1811
Hugh Stanford, Lieutenant, 24th regiment, November 19, 1811
James Trice, Lieutenant, 24th regiment, November 19, 1811
Bray Whipple, Captain, 24th regiment, November 19, 1811
James Williams, Captain, regiment of cavalry, 6th brigade, February 21, 1811
Newton Williams, Ensign, 24th regiment, November 19, 1811
William C. Williams, Captain, 24th regiment, November 19, 1811

The commissioned Officers in the Tennessee Militia, 1796-1811, for Robertson County were:

James Blackwell, Captain, October 18, 1800
Thomas Bounds Captain January 9, 1800
John Briscoe, Ensign, August 15, 1797
John Bryant, Captain, February 23, 1801
Lawrence Carr, Lieutenant, August 10, 1799
John Caughran, Captain, October 10, 1796
Edward Cheatham, Captain, December 17, 1798
Adam Clap, Ensign, October 10, 1796
Charles Colgan, Lieutenant, August 15, 1797
Dawsey Crombwell, Lieutenant, October 1 1798
Robert B. Curry, Lieutenant in cavalry regiment, Mero District, October 1, 1800
Nathaniel Dikerson, Ensign, October 10, 1796
Jonathan Dardin, Captain, November 12 1800
John Dorris, Ensign, October 10, 1796
Isaac Dortch, Captain, August 10, 1799
Martin Duncan, Captain, October 10, 1796
Josiah Fort, Lieutenant, August 10, 1799
William Grimes, Ensign, August 10, 1799
Valentine Groom, Ensign, May 21, 1800
William Haggard, Captain in cavalry regiment, Mero District, October 4, 1796
Isaiah Hamilton, Captain, May 21, 1800
David Hampleton, Lieutenant, September 22, 1797
James Haynes, Lieutenant, October 10, 1796
Hugh Henry, Second Major, vice James Norfleet, resigned, July 30, 1800
Thomas Henry, Lieutenant in cavalry regiment, Mero District, October 4, 1796
Thomas Hutchison, Captain, August 15, 1797
John James, Lieutenant, vice Charles Colgan, July 23, 1798
John Johnson, Ensign, September 22, 1797
Thomas Johnson, Lieutenant-Colonel, Commandant, October 4, 1796
William Johnson, Ensign, October 10, 1796

William Johnson, Captain, February 14, 1798
Eli Jones, Ensign, February 14, 1798
Jesse Jones, Captain, June 16, 1801
Charles Killgore, Ensign, August 22, 1800
Thomas Killgore, Lieutenant, August 22, 1800
John Krisel, Ensign, February 18, 1800
John Krisel, Lieutenant, February 23, 1801
Robert Lancaster, Lieutenant, October 10, 1796
Epephoditus Lawson, Lieutenant, November 12, 1800
James Lockhart, Captain, October 10, 1796
Sampson Mathew, Captain in cavalry regiment, Mero District, October 1, 1800
Sampson Matthews, Cornet in cavalry regiment, Mero District, October 4, 1796
Benjamin Menees, Jr., Ensign, May 31, 1798
Isaac Menees, Lieutenant, October 10, 1796
John Messer, Captain, September 22, 1797
William Miles, First Major in cavalry regiment, Mero District, October 28, 1797
James Norfleet, Second Major, October 4, 1796
Icabud Osborn, Lieutenant, May 31, 1798
Benjamin Owens, Ensign, May 21, 1800
Jonathan Oyler, Cornet in cavalry regiment, Mero District, October 1, 1800
David Patterson, Lieutenant, October 10, 1796
Robert Perry, Ensign, February 23, 1801
Isaac Phillips, Captain, October 1, 1798
Shadrack Rawls, Lieutenant, December 17, 1798
Charles Simmons, Ensign, January 9, 1800
Meredith Walton, Lieutenant, February 14, 1798
Benjamin Weakley, Captain, May 21, 1800
David Weakley, Lieutenant, May 21, 1800
Pierce Williams, Lieutenant, May 21, 1800
Abraham Young, Captain, October 10, 1796
John Young, First Major, October 4, 1796
James Atkins, Ensign, 23rd regiment, July 13, 1807
James Blackwell, Captain, 23rd regiment, July 13, 1807
Peter Cheatham, Cornet, regiment cavalry, 6th brigade, December 3, 1807
Thomas Cheatham, Lieutenant, regiment cavalry, 6th brigade, September 25, 1807
Henry Darr, Ensign, 23rd regiment, July 13, 1807
Nathan Fikes, Ensign, 23rd regiment, September 25, 1807
Jesse Gardner, Lieutenant, 23rd regiment, September 25, 1807
Joshua Gardner, Lieutenant, 23rd regiment, October 9, 1807
Whitmill Harrington, Captain, 23rd regiment, July 13, 1807
Eppaphroditus Lawson, Captain, 23rd regiment, September 25, 1807
Abel Rawles, Lieutenant, 23rd regiment, July 13, 1807
Thomas Swan, Captain, regiment cavalry, 6th brigade, September 25, 1807
Henry Ayers, Lieutenant, 23rd regiment, April 25, 1809
John Brooks, Captain, 23rd regiment, July 20, 1809
William Flewallen, junr., Ensign, 23rd regiment, April 25, 1809
Peter Frye, Lieutenant, 23rd regiment, July 20, 1809
Joshua Gardner, Lieutenant, 23rd regiment, July 21, 1809
William Houston, Captain, 23rd regiment, April 25, 1809
Gabriel Mastin, Ensign, 23rd regiment, August 1, 1809
Henry Stoly, Ensign, 23rd regiment, July 20, 1809
Meredith Walton, Captain, 23rd regiment, April 18, 1809
Abrim Young, Ensign, 23rd regiment, July 21, 1809
John Ball, Junr., Ensign, 23rd regiment, December 11, 1810
Richard Benson, Captain, 23rd regiment, December 11, 1810
Robert Braden, Captain, 23rd regiment, May 29, 1810
Edmund Brewer, Ensign, 23rd regiment, May 29, 1810
John Brewer, Lieutenant, 23rd regiment, May 29, 1810
George Chapman, Captain, 23rd regiment, December 11, 1810
John B. Cheatham, Captain, regiment of cavalry, 6th brigade, June 12, 1810
Avery Clark, Captain, 23rd regiment, January 4, 1810
Richard Crunk, Lieutenant, 23rd regiment, January 4, 1810
Benjamin Elliot, Captain, 23rd regiment, April 24, 1810
William Faunt, Captain, 23rd regiment, May 2, 1810
Zenas Fox, Captain, 23rd regiment, December 11, 1810

Jacob Fyne, Lieutenant, 23rd regiment, May 29, 1810
Richard M. Harwell, Captain, 23rd regiment, May 29, 1810
Josiah D. Huddleston Lieutenant, 23rd regiment, January 4, 1810
James Johnson, Lieutenant, 23rd regiment, December 11 1810
Gabriel Martin, Captain, 23rd regiment, December 11, 1810
Benjamin W. Menees, Ensign, 23rd regiment, May 29, 1810
Hezekiah Morris, Captain, 23rd regiment, December 11, 1810
Gideon Pace, Lieutenant, 23rd regiment, December 11 1810
Robert Perry, Ensign, 23rd regiment, April 24, 1810
Richard Plummer, Cornet, regiment of cavalry, 6th brigade, June 12, 1810
Isaac Redferren, Ensign, 23rd regiment, December 11 1810
Daniel Sanders, Ensign, 23rd regiment, December 11, 1810
Robert Sanders, Lieutenant, 23rd regiment, December 11, 1810
William Smart, Ensign, 23rd regiment, January 4, 1810
Samuel Spearman, Lieutenant, 23rd regiment, December 11, 1810
Thomas Spence, Ensign, 23rd regiment, December 11, 1810
Gray Stringer, Ensign, 23rd regiment, December 11, 1810
John Strother, Captain, 23rd regiment, December 11, 1810
Garland William, Lieutenant, 23rd regiment, December 11, 1810
James Wynne, Lieutenant, 23rd regiment, April 24, 1810
Richard Crunk, Captain, 23rd regiment, May 25, 1811
Joseph Dorris, Ensign, 23rd regiment, April 9, 1811
Henry Elmore, Ensign, 23rd regiment, April 9, 1811
Seth Flood, Ensign, 23rd regiment, June 22, 1811
John Huddleston, Ensign, 23rd regiment, June 22, 1811
Andrew Krisell, Lieutenant, 23rd regiment, June 22, 1811
Daniel Lovell, Ensign, 23rd regiment, October 4, 1811
Wilson Madox [Maddox], Lieutenant, 23rd regiment, April 9, 1811
Sampson Matthews, Lieutenant, 23rd regiment, May 25, 1811
Daniel Pinkley, Captain, 23rd regiment, May 25, 1811
Burwell Pitts, First Major, 23rd regiment, November 23, 1811
William Smart, Lieutenant, 23rd regiment, May 25 1811
William Southerin [Southerlin], Lieutenant, 23rd regiment, June 22, 1811
Henry Steelee, Lieutenant, 23rd regiment, May 25, 1811
William Wilson, Ensign, 23rd regiment, May 24, 1811

The Revolutionary and War of 1812 Soldiers who drew pensions, while living in Montgomery and Robertson Counties and whose pension applications are on file in the pension office in Washington, D.C.:

Henry Ayers; served in Virginia; died Sept. 22, 1833; aged 80 years, list of 1832 pensioners.

David Jones; aged 79, on the list of 1832; also on the census of pensioners 1840; served in the Virginia Militia; drew pension Robertson County.

James Jones; aged 82 years; served in the Virginia service; drew pension, Robertson County.

John Roach; in the list of 1832, aged 74 years; service in the Virginia line; drew pension, Montgomery County.

Archelaus Rosson; aged 84 years; served in the Virginia service; drew pension in Robertson County.

Thomas Shepherd; on list of 1832, aged 79 years; served in the Virginia militia; drew pension in Robertson County.

Abner Dickson; served as private in the Tennessee Volunteers; pensioned May 10, 1818; transferred from Montgomery County, Tennessee to Franklin County, Alabama.

John Adams; list of 1832, aged 75 years; served in the Virginia line; drew pension in Montgomery County, Tennessee.

Baggel [Baggett]; list of 1818, aged 78; served in South Carolina Troops; pensioned in Montgomery County.

Thomas Bell; list of 1832, aged 73 years; served in the North Carolina line; drew pension in Montgomery County.

William Bell; list of 1832, aged 86 years; also in list of 1840; served in North Carolina; drew pension in Montgomery County.

Robert Biggers; list of 1832, aged 73 years; served in North Carolina line; pensioned in Montgomery County, Tennessee.

John Carney, Senr.; list of 1818, aged 86 years; also in list of 1840, aged 106 years; served in North Carolina troops; drew pension in 1818 in Smith County, Tennessee; in 1840, drew in Sumner County, Tennessee.

Stephen Cole; list of 1832, aged 78 years; served in South Carolina line; drew pension in Robertson County.

Conrod Coon; list of 1832, aged 78 years; served in South Carolina line; drew pension in Robertson County.

William Edwards; list of 1832, aged 82 years; served in Virginia line; drew pension in Robertson County.

William Edwards; list of 1832, aged 76 years; served in North Carolina line; drew pension in Robertson County.

Lot Egmond; list of 1832, aged 74 years; served in the New Jersey line; drew pension in Robertson County.

William Evans; list of 1828; served in Tennessee Volunteers; drew pension, Robertson County; War of 1812.

Rowland Felts; list of 1832, aged 79 years; served in North Carolina line; drew pension, Robertson County.

James Fentress; list of 1832, aged 70 years; also in list of 1840; served in North Carolina line; drew pension in Montgomery County.

Elisha Fikes; list of 1832; served in Second Regiment Tennessee Militia (War of 1812); drew pension, Robertson County.

Thomas Fisher; list of 1832, aged 74 years; served in the Virginia line; drew pension in Robertson County.

William Fortune; list of 1832, aged 88 years; also in list of 1840; served in Maryland line; drew pension, Sumner County, Tennessee; lived with Joseph Smith in 1840.

Alexander Frazier; list of 1832, aged 74 years; also list of 1840; served in the Pennsylvania line; drew pension in Montgomery County.

Charles Gent; list of 1832, aged 80 years; also in list of 1840; served in the Georgia line; drew pension in Robertson County, where he lived with James W. Gent.

William Graham; list of 1818, aged 85 years; served in the Virginia troops; drew pension in Montgomery County.

Stephen Handlin; list of 1818, aged 67 years; served in the Pennsylvania troops; drew pension in Montgomery County.

John Hardison; list of 1832, aged 70 years; served in North Carolina militia; drew pension in Robertson County.

Edwin Harris; list of 1832, aged 76 years; served in North Carolina; drew pension in Robertson County.

Hugh Henry; list of 1832, aged 84 years; served in the Virginia line; drew pension in Robertson County.

Charles Hounsler; list of 1832, aged 89 years; served in the Virginia line; drew pension in Montgomery County.

Samuel Hudgens; list of 1832, aged 78 years; served in the Virginia line; drew pension in Robertson County.

Thomas Hunter; list of 1832, aged 71 years; served in the South Carolina line; died Feb. 27, 1834; drew pension, Robertson County.

James Johnson; list of 1832, aged 74 years; served in the North Carolina line; drew pension in Montgomery County.

Thomas McGee, (1st); list of 1832, aged 72 years; served in the North Carolina line; drew pension in Montgomery County.

Charles McIntosh; list of 1832, aged 74 years; served in the North Carolina Militia; drew pension in Robertson County.

Jacob Miles; list of 1832, aged 78 years; served in North Carolina; drew pension in Robertson County.

James Moore; list of 1832; aged 84 years; served in the North Carolina line; drew pension in Montgomery County.

James Owens; list of 1832, aged 72 years; served in South Carolina militia; drew pension in Robertson County.

Benjamin P. Persons; served in Tennessee Militia; in list of 1840, aged 58 years; War of 1812; drew pension in Montgomery County.

Ephraim Pool; list of 1832, aged 78 years; served in South Carolina line; pensioned in Montgomery County. His widow, Lucinda, drew pension; list of 1840, aged 75 years; lived with John Pool in 1840.

Josiah Puckett; list of 1818, aged 82 years; also list of 1840; served in Virginia Troops; drew pension, 1818, Montgomery County; was transferred from Kentucky;

in 1840, drew pension in Humphreys County, Tennessee.

Jesse Robertson; list of 1818, aged 75 years; served with North Carolina Troops; drew pension, Montgomery County.

James Sawyers; list of 1832, aged 68 years; served Virginia line; drew pension in Robertson County.

Jesse Simmons; list of 1832, aged 73 years; served in South Carolina line; drew pension in Robertson County.

Robert Singleton; list of 1818, aged 80 years; served in the North Carolina line; drew pension, Montgomery County.

William Smith; list of 1832, aged 71 years; served in the Virginia line; drew pension, Robertson County.

Stephen Thomas; list of 1828; served in Armstrong's regiment; drew pension, Montgomery County; was transferred from North Carolina; died May 10, 1825; pension commenced in 1798.

William Turbeyfield; list of 1832, aged 84 years; served in the North Carolina line; drew pension, Robertson County.

John Vick; list of 1832, aged 77 years; also in list of 1840; served in the North Carolina militia; drew pension in Montgomery County.

William W. Walker; list of 1840, aged 25 years; War of 1812; drew pension in Robertson County.

Drury Warren; list of 1832, aged 78 years; served in Virginia line; drew pension in Robertson County.

Martin Walton; list of 1832, aged 72 years; also list of 1840; served in the Virginia line; drew pension, Robertson County.

Joseph Weeks; list of 1832, aged 74 years; served in the North Carolina Militia; drew pension in Montgomery County, Tennessee.

William West; list of 1832, aged 81 years; served in the North Carolina line; drew pension in Robertson County.

Gavan White; list of 1832, aged 68 years; served in Virginia line; drew pension in Robertson County. His widow, Ann White, drew pension; in list of 1840, aged 81 years.

William Wiggins; list of 1832, aged 74 years; served in North Carolina line; drew pension, Montgomery County.

Thomas Yeates; list of 1832, aged 76 years; served in the Pennsylvania line; drew pension, Robertson County.

Jacob Zeck; list of 1832, aged 76 years; also list of 1840; served in the Pennsylvania line; drew pension in Robertson County.

Francis Willis, born in Frederick County, Virginia on January 5, 1745; died in Montgomery County, Tennessee on April 25, 1829; enlisted in the Revolutionary War in Berkeley County, Virginia. (D. A. R. National No. 267546.)

Hugh Ferguson Bell; drew pension in Montgomery County.

Stephen Conger; an Adjutant; drew pension in Montgomery County.

Thomas Fletcher; drew pension in Montgomery County.

Elias Fort, Sr.; a Corporal; drew pension in Robertson County.

Peter Hubbard; applied for Revolutionary pension while living in Montgomery County, Tennessee; was born in South Carolina and served in South Carolina line under Capt. Samuel Wise and Capt. John Carraway Smith and Colonel William Thompson; was in the Battle of Sullivan's Island; moved to Tennessee after the Revolution and lived several years in Montgomery County; moved to Bond County, Illinois where he died.

David Henry; applied for Revolutionary pension while residing in Robertson County, Tennessee; in list of 1832; was born in 1753 in Pittsylvania County, Virginia; enlisted, 1777, in Capt. John Donelson's Company, Col. Evan Shelby's Regiment and was in an expedition against the Indians; enlisted again, 1778, in Capt. Thomas Dillard's Company in Col. George Rogers Clark's expedition to Illinois; was discharged August 29, 1778; his children, as shown in the pension application, were Isaac, Lemuel, Elizabeth, and Catherine.

Robert Witt; of Kentucky; applied for Revolutionary pension while living in Logan County, Kentucky; was born in Bedford County, Virginia on April 24, 1765; enlisted in that county on April 24, 1780 and served until 1783 under Capt. John Baley (Bailey) and Col. George Rogers Clark in the Virginia Troops; married Nancy Reese. Note: He died March 31, 1849. His children were William, Martha, Sarah, Rhoda, and Rebecca.

Samuel Young; born May 7, 1762, Cumberland County, Pennsylvania; enlisted in Northumberland County, Pennsylvania, May 7, 1779; after the war, moved to Rowan

County, North Carolina, then to Rutherford County, then to Spartanburg County in South Carolina, then to Franklin County, Georgia, then to Sumner County, Tennessee, then to Logan County, Kentucky, then to Indiana, and finally to Gallatin County, Illinois and later to Marion County, Illinois where he died in 1846; buried in the Young graveyard, Marion County, Illinois; late in life was Captain; drew pension, Marion County, Illinois.

Caleb Williams; applied for Revolutionary pension while living in Stewart County, Tennessee, 1832; was born September 20, 1760 in Dorchester County, Maryland; was living in Orange County, North Carolina when he enlisted for service in May or June 1780; served three months in Capt. David Scobey's Company in Col. Taylor's North Carolina Regiment; volunteered again in January or February 1781 and served three months in Capt. Harris North Carolina Company; several years after the Revolution, moved to Crab Orchard, Kentucky, one year later moved to Montgomery County, Tennessee, and after living there a year moved to Stewart County, Tennessee.

Dudley Brooke; applied for Revolutionary Pension while living in Robertson County, Tennessee in 1833; was born July 3, 1762 in Chesterfield County, Virginia; enlisted, 1777, in Captain White's Company and in 1778, again enlisted; in 1779 enlisted under Lt. Henry Johnson and Col. Anthony New; enlisted again in Capt. Richard Phillips Company; in 1781 served seven months in Capt. Robert Carey's Company, Col. Combe's Virginia Regiment; in 1802 left Louisa County, Virginia where he was then living and moved to Robertson County, Tennessee. Note: The children of Dudley Brooke were Elizabeth, Sarah, Mary, Harry, John and Francis (or John Francis), and Dudley, Junior.

According to the Court Minutes of Montgomery County, 1808-1810, p. 161, the Justices to receive the list of taxable property in the county for 1809 were:

John Blair, esqr. for Capt. Frost's Company
Samuel Vance, esqr. for Capt. Penrice's Company
John H. Poston, esqr. for The Town of Clarksville
Joseph Woolfolk, esqr. for Capt. Bryant's Company
James Moore, esqr. for Capt. Harman's Company
Abner Harris, esqr. for Capt. Callen's Company or Capt. Allen's Company
Samuel Smith, esqr. for Capt. Porter's Company
Samuel Gattis, esqr. for Capt. Whitfield's Company
James Lockhart, esqr. for Capt. Enlow's Company
Wm. McDaniel, esqr. for Capt. Weakley's Company

In the Montgomery County Court Minutes, 1808-1810, p. 202, it was reported that taxes for various landholders were unpaid for the year 1808. The list which was presented to the court shows the following:

James Perkins, 100 acres
Dixon Loggans, 200 acres on Barren fork of Barton Creek
Alexander Tate, 1280 acres part of Adam Tate on Bud's Creek
Heirs of Adam Tate, 250 acres South side Cumberland River
John Benham, 550 acres Barren fork of Barton's Creek
Martin Goss, 55 acres on Barton's Creek
Daniel Anderson, 640 acres on Yellow Creek waters
Heirs of John Davis, 3840 acres at mouth of Barton's Creek
John Meares, 1280 acres on Fletcher's fork of Red River
James McRoberts, 320 acres at mouth of West fork
Bennett Searcy, 150 1/2 acres joining Clarksville and in Clarksville, lots No. 22, 23, 24, 25, 36, 37, 38, 64, 35, and half of 74
Thomas Wendson, 640 acres in the Barrons
Heirs of Seven Powell, 3200 acres on East fork of Yellow Creek
Amos Rochel, 345 acres on East fork of Yellow Creek
Thomas Waters, 150 acres near Palmyra
John Weakley, 150 acres on Cumberland River, obtained by deed
Spencer Griffin, 640 acres at mouth of West fork
Peter Moseley, 190 acres (location not stated)
John Odeneal, 500 acres on West fork

The March court of 1809 (Montgomery County Court Minutes 1808-1810, p. 205) ordered that John Cocke, sheriff, have a credit with the District Treasurer and the County Trustee and Commission of the Public Buildings for the year 1807 on the following persons as being insolvent: William Hogan, Charles Smith, Joseph Moss, Willie Holland, John Henderson, James Burnes, John Dean, Eli Smith, George Thomas, Evan Gaskell, Allen Morgan, Nathaniel Blackwell, Joseph Baker, John Fletcher, Edwin Gore, Robert Norman, Job Wallace, Ezekiel Black, Thomas Wallace, William Baker, Pleasant Casher, Nathan Blackwell, Vinson Ennis, Shadrick Gardner, William McClure, John McClure, Jonathan Stephenson, Herring Taylor, Thomas Flack, and John Whitledge.

At the same time, the list for the year 1808 was presented to the court (p. 206) and included: Isiah Gattis, Reuben Chisenhall, William Woods, Isaac Gattis, Nicholas Green, John Keathley, Jr., James McKee, Saunders Moore, Andrew Murphy, John Ross, Thomas Watkins, James Graves, Robert Saunderson, John Whitledge, Andrew Walker, Ashel Duncan, Philip Duff, William Jones, William Moore, John Mitchell, David Morris, James Nicholas, Roland Vick, William Justice, Joseph Montgomery, Philip Henderson, John Minn, Robert Rushing, William Trice, Thomas Dean, Daniel Tucker, Joseph Hall, Peter Hubbard, Jr., William Knight, John Lockener, Sli Sonny, Lewis Thomas, John D.F. Campbell, George Murphy, Richard Acuff, Henry Bevel, John McLandon, Asa Briggs, and George Robertson.

Overseers of Roads

The court ordered John Chisham to be overseer of the road in place of Stephen Malley; Joseph Ray became overseer in the place of James King. The court entertained a motion to view and lay off a road from Clarksville to Smith's Ferry and thence to intersect Humphreys Road.

In June 1808, the court appointed a jury to clear a road out from near the state line at James Watkin's Blacksmith Shop to intersect the Clarksville Road: to begin at a point on the state line near the shop at a Black Jack in the Barrons running by Robert Searcy's leaving said Searcy's plantation to the left, then crossing the Brushy Fork between Clanton's and Shelby's (Bogard plantation), then direct to John Frenche's leaving said Frenche's house to the right hand, then to the "Great Road" leading to Clarksville, a small distance from Fletcher's Fork. John French was appointed overseer of the road from West Fork Road to Brushy Fork of the Piney Fork and Robert Searcy to the State line. John Lockart, esqr. was to name the hands to work the same.

The same month, Robert Tygert was appointed overseer of the road from Palmyra to Conrad's Creek instead of David Standley, and William Corbin was named overseer from Benjamine Organs to Charnel Corbins instead of Alexander Faith.

At the same time, Benjamin Organ was named to oversee the road from George Humphrey's ferry to William Carlews. The hands to work under him were to be: Mrs. Cocke's, Abraham Cocke's hands, Stephen Cocke's hands, Mrs. Sanderson's hands, Andrew Ingram's hands, Samuel Robert's hands, Thomas Smith's hands, Benjamin Organ's hands, Andrew Tribble's hands, Edward Neblett's hands, Joseph Price's hands, James Downey, John Coffee's hands, William Good's hands, Ambrose Martin's hands, and Spelsbee Tribble's hands.

A road was viewed and marked leading from Mosley's ferry on the Cumberland River, the nearest and best, to intersect with the road leading from Weakley's ferry to Col. Richard Napier's forge on Barton Creek, and William Hightower, Martin Goss, Simeon Miers, James Trotter, Hallow Morris, Frederick Goss were appointed to view the same and make report to the court. William Hightower was named as overseer of the same that Samuel Smith, esqr. had previously.

Charles Stewart, Sr. was appointed overseer of the road in place of Laurence Tennin. This road was from Hambleton's ferry to Stewart's Mill.

On 28 June 1808, the court approved the laying out and viewing of a road from the

Stewart County line leading by or near Capt. West's up the Cave House Bottom so to join the road to Nashville on the Ridge to the west of Benjamin Adams plantation. James Fentress, William Clements, George West, Elijah Parker, and Samuel Mc-Aeleyea were to be appointed to view the same. James Fentress was to be overseer.

The same court named Ambrose Martin overseer of the road from Smith's Ferry to Humphrey's road and ordered that Thomas Smith, Esqr. name the hands to work.

It was ordered that William Pennington, William D. Penny, Samuel Wilcox, Pray Whipple and Wm. Cohoon be appointed to view the road from the Robertson line where the Nashville Road to Port Royal intersects the same thence the nearest and best way by the mouth of Sulphur Fork to the Kentucky line at 93 Mile-Tree where the Christian Road intersects.

The September 1808 court ordered that a road be viewed from the Dickson County line below the Leatherwood Fork to Yellow Creek, to meet and fall into the road leading to Palmyra near Adam Harmon's on the East Fork and that Francis Tompkins, Adam Harman, Benjamin Adams, James Fentress, and William Clements be appointed to view and lay off the said road.

Benjamine Orgain was named overseer of the road from George Humphreys to David Pritchard's Spring. David Pritchard was to oversee the road from his spring to Barren fork of Barton's Creek. Sterling Neblett, Esqr. was to assist with the hands. At the same time, John Neville was to be overseer of that part of the road which had previously been handled by Benjamine Seat.

On September 26, 1808, Vincent Cooper was named overseer of the road leading from John Blair's ferry at the mouth of Yellow Creek. Cooper was to work from Blooming Grove Creek to the state line with all hands on the north side of Blooming Grove Creek not yet appointed on any other road.

The court on the same day appointed David Brigham as overseer of the "GREAT ROAD' from the Palmyra road to Shelly's Mill. Robert Smith were to be the overseer from the mill to the Stewart County line.

Michael Northington was appointed overseer of the road from Edmiston's on the ford of Parson's Creek to the Robbertson line on the Nashville Road, on 21 December 1808.

In March 1809, William Farrior was licensed to keep a ferry across Red River at a place formerly kept by James Bunting.

In 1809, Jesse Martin was given permission to extend his road as far as Benjamin Whitehead's spring. John Lee was appointed overseer of the road from Palmyra to the Dickson County line. David Pritchard was named overseer from Benjamine Whitehead's to the Barron Fork.

William Barton, Sr., William Morrow, Joseph Hardekin, William Bearden, John Barton, Henry Funk, Able Mann, and Absalom Tribble were ordered to view a road leading from Absalom Tribble's ferry to where it intersected the Davises' Old Road. Joseph Hardekins was named overseer of the road from Tribble's Ferry to Davises' Old Road in place of Hayden Wells.

The June 1809 court ordered that a road be cut leading from the Nashville road on the south side of Red River near where MaCade's road turns off, thence the most direct way to Hornberger's old ford crossing Red River, thence up Jedediah Hall's lane with Watkins and Nelson line to the Port Royal road, thence down said road fronting Watkin's house, thence the best and most direct way to White's Mill on Spring Creek. Bright Berring, Wm. White, John Dicas, Thomas Dunbar, Moses Oldham, Daniel Taylor, Isaac Peterson, James Bailey, John Henderson, Jedediah Hall, and James Lester were to be a jury to view the road.

Jedediah Hall was appointed overseer of the road leading from the Nashville road to White's Mill on Spring Creek. The hands were to be John Dicas, William S. White, Charles Cherry, Bright Herring, Watkins, Widow Nelson's hands; Daniel Taylor;

Thomas McCall; James Hambleton and all the hands on the south side of Red River were required to work the road.

The road from Clarksville to Wine Miller's old place on the Nashville Road was to be placed under the overseeing of Henry Small. Moses Oldham, Sr. was named overseer for the road from Clarksville to the first fork on the Road beyond Farrier's ferry.

On 22 March 1809, Robert Nowland was named overseer of the road from the place of George Ury leading from the East Fork of Deason's Creek to the Elizabeth Furnace on Yellow Creek. The same day, John Edmiston was named to oversee the road from Parson's Creek to the Robertson County line toward Nashville by the way of Colonel Ford's old plantation.

The following day, 23 March, it was agreed that the road from Tribble's Ferry to Vaughan's Mill be shortened. It ran from the ferry to the first large branch below William Whitehead's. Joseph Whitehead was to be overseer in the place of Goodman Traywick. The hands to work the road were to be Frederick Moody, David Leach, Josiah G. Duke, Richard Whitehead, John Allen, William Whitehead, Abner Harris, Robert Ray, Francis Neblett, John Moore, Peter Hubbard, and William, John and David Hubbard.

The court received a report from William Pennington, Wm. Cohoon, Samuel Wilcox, David C. Penny, and Pray Whipple regarding their viewing the road from the Robertson line by the mouth of Sulphur Fork to the Kentucky line at the 93 Mile-Tree. The new road was cut by the bridge on the south side of Red River, March 1809.

It is interesting to note the above mention of a bridge. It would indicate that the bridge was already there, not just being placed. I have not been able to determine when the bridge was erected.

The court which met in June 1809 took up considerable time in the naming of road overseers and planning new roads. William Cohoon was placed over the road leading from the Robertson County line through Port Royal and to the Kentucky line in the place of William Pennington and Joseph Woolfolk. Isham Trotter was named overseer of the road from the forks of the road leading to Nelson's ferry to the ferry. Isral Robinson's hands, Prestly Pollock, and George Pollock were to work under him.

William Barton, Joseph Hardeman, William Bearden, Joseph Barton, Abel Man, Absalom Tribble, and Henry Funk made their report regarding the viewing and laying of a road leading from Absalom Tribble's Ferry to where it intersected Davises' old road, leaving the old road at the foot of the Bluff, thence running up the first holler so as to intersect the old road again near the cross road leading from Joseph Hardican's to Jacob Rudolph's. This was the same committee and road which was ordered to be laid out in the previous court.

George West (West fork) was appointed overseer of that strip of road from Smith's Old Cabbin to Noah's Spring at the state line. He was to work all hands within five miles.

On 22 June 1809, the court placed John Watkins in charge of the road which had been in the hands of Alexander Trousdale. It named the hands: David Lamb, Oswell Potts, Thomas Potts, Peter Matheny, John Lamb, James Lamb, John Darnald, Wright Tyre, Samuel Phillingham, Mr. Robertson, and Alexander Trousdale and son.

The court minutes from 1816 through 1817 are full of information pertaining to road improvements.

John Bailey was appointed overseer of the road from Parson's Creek to Hardin Crouch's place. John Wilson was named to oversee the road from Clarksville to Dover. Thomas Cherry, Jr. was overseer of the road leading from Clarksville to Russellville, commencing at the fork of the road about one half mile easterly from Samuel Smith's Ferry and to continue to William S. Whitfield's. The hands to work it were: William S. White, Charles Cherry, Andrew Dicus, James Dicus, and James Ryan.

James Trotter was named as overseer of the road from Mosley's Ferry to Napier's Iron Works.

Christopher Owens, Bright Herring, Amos Hatcher, James Gray, Daniel Taylor, Jedediah Hill, William S. White, William Nelson, Samuel Smith, and others were appointed to view and examine the old road leading from Samuel Smith's Ferry on the north side of Red River to the Robertson line.

At the same time, Nathan Morris, Uriah Tyson, Jesse Morris, Burrell Bayliss, James Bowers, John Blair, John Trousdale, John Mitchell, Vison Cooper, and John Watkins were named to amend and straighten the road leading from John Blair's ferry to the Kentucky line, Christian County.

James Hambleton, Abraham Brantley, Edward Trice, John Hurt (or Hurst), Sterling Ingram, James Trice, and John Trice were ordered to lay off and mark out a road the nearest and best way from old Mrs. Lee's to the mouth of Red River.

An order of the court on 16 April made Jesse Morris overseer of the road in the place of Daniel Mitchell. William Killebrew was appointed overseer of that part of the road leading from Russellville to Clarksville between William S. White's field and the lower end of John Johnson's plantation. Thomas Frazier and his hands, William McElrath, Mary Francier's hands, John Edwards, Daniel Williams, Elisha Redd, Solomon Grace, William Watwood, and William Tull were to work under Killebrew.

Eli Lockhart was to be in charge of the road from Poplar Sink to Capt. Jones. The hands to assist him were: Thomas Blakeney's hands, John Shelby's hands, Samuel Walker, Thomas Walker, and William Walker.

On 17 April 1816, Richard Kelly was named overseer of the road in place of Tandy Walker. The hands under him were to be: William Justice and hands, Thomas Weakley and hands, Adam Stack, John Stack, Thomas Weakley, Jr., Joseph McCully, Larkin Pinson, Duke Pinson, John Hambleton, James Rook, Fielding Smith, and Tandy Walker.

William Milam took over the road from Benjamine Orgains to Charnel Corbin's in place of Isham Trotter. The hands within bounds of the road were to be under Milam.

On 16 July 1816, Thomas Watson was ordered by the court to have lien to build a dam across the big West fork of Red River about two miles below the South Waters present dam across and the mill on the said creek being formerly Barker's Mill.

On 18 July 1816, John Marshall, John Creswell, John Steele, James Adams, and Samuel Young were appointed commissioners to lay off a road the best and nearest way from the mouth of Red River to the Palmyra road on the south side of Cumberland River.

Hiram Cooper took charge of the road leading from Russellville to Palmyra between the little west fork of Red River and the road leading from Clarksville to Hopkinsville. The work hands were: Lemuel Peters, Drury Bonds, William Elliott, James McCarroll, Samuel McNichols, Edward Trice, Nace F. Trice, John Dodson, John Malloy, John Wilson, William Jordan, Henry Williams, Mr. Martin, John Starkey, Roland Peterson, Taylor Chism, Washington Lee, John Chism, Robert Trice, Shepherd Trice, Stephen Mallory, Joshua Pike, Ezekiel Jones, and William Lowther. The road was specified to be sixteen feet wide.

The court of July 19 appointed Bingham Trice overseer of that portion of road leading from the mouth of Red River to John Trice's with the following hands: James Trice, Lee Trice, Mark Booth, Reuben Chisenhall, Mathew Thomas, Lee Chisenhall, John Riggans, Sterling Ingram, Mary Trice, Abram Brantley, Hugh Brantley, Nace F. Trice, Robert Trice, and the hands of Rachel Trice.

In October of the same year, the court made Philemon Whitworth overseer of the road from the Nashville road to Moseley's Ferry. The hands to work under him were to be: Nathaniel King, Willis Morgan, Dudley Councell, James Burton (or Barton), Hillary Burton (or Barton), Charles Perkins, William King, John Whitworth, Joseph Whitworth, John Major, James Major, William Stewart, Darnel Campbell, William McAdams, Samuel Weakley, Howell Adkins, William Barton, Jr., Lemuel Barton, Robert Barton, and William Barton, Sr.

In January 1817, road building and improving was still a big factor in the court. James Elliott was made overseer of the road leading from Fletcher's ford to the state line in place of Cadwaller Lucy. The hands named to assist him were: William Mann, Glidwell Killebrew, Priscilla Jeffer's hands, Bayliss E. Prince, James Lockhart, John Falkner, Cadwaller Lucy, Joe Marr, and Jarrett McCarty.

Thomas Collier took over the road leading from the mouth of Blooming Grove Creek to the Hopkinsville road with hands, Burrell Baylis, Burrell Lanier, and James McGehee.

The court of January 21, 1817 passed a petition that Sarah Penrice and Hayden Wells be permitted to turn the road leading from Clarksville to Charlotte so that it would go around rather than through their plantation.

The same day, the court appointed commissioners to view and lay off a road commencing at James Cocke's landing to the two mile post on the Nashville Road and on the south side of Cumberland River, to run as Cocke's Old Road till it gets to the barrons near Hayden E. Wells, thence on with the Meeting-house road, on by the Meeting-house so as to intersect the road at William Corlew's Spring.

On 22 April 1817, Willie Seagraves became overseer of the road from Clarksville to Port Royal in place of Amos Hatcher.

The court of April 23, 1817 allowed Nancy Speed a permit to keep a ferry across Red River at the mouth of the West for.

Randolph Ramey was made overseer of the road in place of Jesse Davidson. This road led from Alexander Hambleton's ferry.

Montgomery County Court Minutes 1808-1810, pp. 27, 34, 35, 38, 41, 89, 90, 92, 93, 134, 135, 142, 151, 160, 161, 162, 167, 171, 173, 220, 225, 231, 232; Court Minutes 1816-1817, pp. 8, 15, 16, 30, 31, 33, 64, 66, 73, 79, 83, 96, 130, 145, 157, 160, 183, 201, 225.

The Trustees of Logan County, appointed in 1803, were: William Wallace, Walter Jones, William Reading, Maxwell Sharp, Wm. S. Dallam, Ninian Edwards, Reuben Ewing, Jno. Porter, Robert Ewing, Heazen Davige, Moses Steele, James McMahan, and Samuel Caldwell.

By the year 1807, fewer than one hundred families were living within the town of Russellville. An election to select Trustees for the town was held, and the following persons voted:

Jno. Adams	Robert Clendenning	Aaron Lewis	Wm. Parham
Alex. Alderson	John Cross	Isaac Lewis	Jack Phelps
Curtis Alderson	Spencer Curd	Jeremiah Lewis	John Phelps
Josiah Anderson	Harry Cyrus	Thomas Linebaugh	John Roberts
S. T. Anderson	James H. Davidson	G. A. Martin	James Rollins
Jno. Andrews	Amos Edwards	Richard Maulding	John K. Smith
George Baker	Robert Grimes	Tyler Maulding	Joseph Steele
Ban Barner	Nat. Harris	West Maulding	Fred Waller
Jno. Brewington	Henry Hauzy	R. A. McCabe	G. W. Whitaker
Alex. Brown	Edward Hockersmith	Alex. McLaurain	Wm. W. Whitaker
George Brown	Samuel Jackson	Christ Meller	Wm. Whitsitt
David Caldwell	Walter Jones	Jno. P. Oldham	

The candidates in the election were: James H. Davidson, Aaron Lewis, Josiah

Wilson, Joseph Steele, and William W. Whitaker, who were elected, and Walter
Jones, Fred Waller, and William Orr, who were not elected.

Methodists in Middle Tennessee

Rev. Jeremiah Lambert was probably the first preacher to carry the Methodist
doctrines into what is now Tennessee. In 1783, he was one of seventy-six members
of the "Holston Circuit." He died soon after his return from missionary service in
the West Indies. His death was reported at the General Conference of 1786.

The General Conference minutes of 1784 show that the Rev. Henry Willis was
assigned a charge in the Holston Circuit.

The Georgia Circuit first appears in the minutes in 1785 when the Rev. Beverley
Allen was sent from the Conference to that section. There was a Beverley A. Allen
in Robertson County, Tennessee in 1797. On 4 March, Bazel Boren of Robertson
County, for love and affection to children Ann C. Allen, John H. Allen, Mary Allen
and Beverley A. Allen, and Sarah Allen, transfered to Bazel Boren all interest in
the land Beverley A. Allen bought from James Bulgin of Charleston, South Carolina
and Isaac Herbert of Richmond County, Georgia.

In 1786, Thomas Humphries and John Majors were sent to Georgia, and the Broad
River circuit was opened under the care of Stephen Johnson. The same year, three
ministers, Mark Whitaker, Mark Moore, and James O'Kelly, went to the Holstein
circuit.

A Barnard Majors, living in Charles City and Prince George Counties, Virginia,
had a son John. The will of Barnard Major, dated 4 April 1777, was probated in
Charles City County Court on 3 September 1777. The land "I live on" was left to his
son Barnard; land purchased of John Stokes to son Samuel; and the remainder of the
land to son John. The following were also mentioned: daughter Mary Emery; daughter
Joice West; daughter Martha W. Carrable; son-in-law Stephen West "until his eldest
child is of age;" grandchildren Betty Major West, Sarah West, and Stephen West,
children of Stephen West; son-in-law Thomas Griffith; grandchildren Harwood and
Joice Major; Elizabeth, daughter of Barnard Major; grandson Turner Jackson; and
granddaughter Sarah Jackson. Son Barnard Major was named executor.

In 1787, the Kentucky Circuit and the Cumberland Circuit appear in the minutes
of the General Conference. At the same time, the Nollichuckie circuit was born.
Jeremiah Mastin and Nathaniel Moore were sent to Holstein; Thomas Ware, Micajah
Tracy, and James Hunt (elder), to Nollichuckie; Thomas Williamson and Wilson Lee,
to Kentucky; and Benjamine Ogden, to Cumberland.

The next year, the Holstein circuit reported having 360 members and two preachers, Jeremiah Mastin and Joseph Doddridge. Daniel Asbury was assigned to a new
circuit, the French Broad.

Daniel Asbury was a native of Fairfax County, Virginia, born on 18 February
1762. When he was sixteen years of age, he went to Kentucky where he traveled as
a Methodist minister.

Benjamine Ogden went to the Brunswick Circuit in Virginia. David Combs and
Barnabas McHenry were sent to Cumberland in his place.

Rev. Ogden was the first Methodist Missionary to preach in the vicinity of Nashville. He came in October 1787, aged 23, and set up the Cumberland mission, which
included Nashville and all the forts and settlements on the north side of the Cumberland River from Gallatin to Clarksville. The first year, Rev. Mr. Ogden's labors
resulted in reporting "sixty-three members, four of whom were colored persons."

After traveling and preaching for a number of years, Benjamine Ogden located in
Caldwell County, Kentucky. He was there in 1834 in which year, on 8 November, he
made his will. In his will, proved in December of the same year, he named his wife,

Nancy, children Stephen Ogden and Mary Harpersing, and grandson Benjamine Harpersing, son of Asbury and Mary Harpersing.

In his pension application, dated 20 August 1832, Benjamin Ogden stated that he was then sixty-eight years of age, born at Baskingridge, New Jersey in April 1764, and that he lived there till 1778-9. In 1783, he moved to Baltimore, Maryland and lived with his brother, Col. Amos Ogden, till 1784. In 1785, he became a Methodist Itinerant Preacher. His original application is on file in the National Archives.

In 1789, John Baldwin and Mark Whitaker were in the Holstein circuit. Julius Conner was sent to Holstein, and at the same time, a new circuit was created which placed John M'Gee, John West, and Thomas Bowen (elder) among the Greene County, Tennessee people. John Sewell replaced Rev. Julius Conner in 1791.

In 1792, Salathiel Weeks and James Ward were at Holstein, and Stephen Brooke and Wm. Burke were in Greene County.

There is no mention of the Cumberland Circuit in the General Conference minutes for 1790-91 or 1792, but in 1793, Henry Birchett was down from Kentucky, John Simmons and Stith Meade arrived to serve the Holstein, and Samuel Rudder and John Ray were placed in Greene County.

Henry Birchett was a native of Brunswick County, Virginia. He was evidently the son of Edward Birchett or Birckett of that place, whose will, dated 16 February 1790 and probated the same year, names children Edward, Henry, Theodrick, and Agnes Walker.

Elizabeth Birchett (Birkitt) is mentioned as one of the heirs in the will of Judith Thweatt, dated 12 November 1770-3 in the same county.

Rev. Birchett reportedly died in February 1794. It is believed that Cumberland was probably without an itinerant minister (circuit-rider) for the rest of that year, for the minutes of the conference for 1794 do not mention the Cumberland circuit. However, Francis Acuff and John Lindsay went to Holston, and William Kavanaugh and Lewis Garrett went to Greene County.

Rev. Birkett was a guest at the home of James Hoggatt when he was in the Cumberland. James Hoggatt was a wealthy planter. On 6 January 1784, he purchased land in Davidson County from Daniel Oglesby, son of Elisha Oglesby of the 96th District in South Carolina. On 3 July 1787, Julius Sanders sold James Hoggett 980 acres on Big Harpeth, twenty-four miles from French Lick.

In April 1784, James Hoggett "being sworn declares to best of his knowledge it was the 7th of July past that he and Abednego Lewellen arrived at the settlement on the Cumberland River, and he is certain that Abednego Lewellen was not in the settlement a month or more before and he does not believe the said Lewellen could be the father of the two bastard children which he is charged by oath of Mary Tramel."

John Hoggatt's estate was divided on 25 February 1829 (Davidson County, Tennessee Will Book 8, p. 286). His wife Diana (her will, W.B. 9, p. 218) left items to Agnes W. Hoggatt and her infant Sandife Hoggatt by his guardian for the purpose of Albert Ward being the heir of John H. Hoggatt, decd.; to heirs of Abraham S. Hoggatt, deceased; to heirs of James W. Hoggatt; and interest to Rhoda Clopton. She also mentioned Mrs. Rhoda Clopton, Amanda F. Hoggatt, son Sandifer Hoggatt, and named son James W. Hoggett executor, 9 July 1828.

The Old Hoggett graveyard is located on the Clover Bottom farm in the Stones River bottom.

About 1795, a Methodist Church had been organized about two and one half miles south of Brentwood and named "Liberty Hill," by Rev. Green Hill. It was in Rev. Green Hill's nearby home that Bishop Asbury and Bishop McKendree stayed in 1808.

Major Green Hill was born on 11 November 1741 in Bertie County, North Carolina, where he resided during the Revolutionary War. He was the son of Green Hill, who was born on 20 November 1714, and Grace Bennett Hill, who was born on 26 March 1721. The elder Hills were married in March 1739.

Major Hill was married twice, first in Bertie County about 1763 to Nancy Thomas, who was born on 26 July 1745. He married his second wife, Mary Sewell, about 1793. By his first wife, Major Hill had five known children: Jordan, who was born on 17 October 1765; Hannah, who was born on 28 May 1766 and married Thomas Stokes; Nancy, who was born on 25 January 1768 and married Mr. Wynne; Martha, who was born on 2 October 1769 and married Jere Brown; and Richard. By his second wife, Major Hill had a daughter Martha.

Martha Hill married Jeremiah Brown, who was born on 22 April 1765 and died on 20 January 1790. Their daughter, Nancy Thomas Brown, was born on 8 November 1790, died on 8 February 1881, and was married on 17 December 1807 to Joseph Johnson, who was born on 24 March 1782 and died on 11 June 1863. They had a daughter, Mary Johnson, who died on 26 September 1855 and was married on 30 July 1834 to Thomas Anderson, who was born on 14 September 1813 and died on 15 May 1895. Thompson Anderson and his wife were the parents of Joseph Johnson Anderson who married Jessie Gardner Houston on 19 October 1886.

Rev. Green Hill was one of the Representatives from Bertie County, North Carolina in the Provincial Congress which met at Newbern on 4 April 1774. He was a member of the Hillsboro Congress which met on 20 August 1775 and of the Halifax Congress of April 1776. He was a member of the first and each succeeding Provincial Congress of the state and was State Treasurer for a while. When the Revolutionary War broke out, he was the first to enlist. He served as both a Major and Chaplain. Toward the close of the century, Major Green Hill moved to Tennessee and settled about fourteen miles from Nashville, where he spent the remainder of his life. He died on 11 September 1825.

About the same time, or a little earlier than Rev. Green Hill located between Nashville and Franklin, Strother's Meeting House was organized in Sumner County, a hand-hewn log structure in the woods, about seven miles from the site of Gallatin, near the spot where Cottontown is now. It was first recorded as a preaching point in the Cumberland circuit in 1800 and was very likely named for Richard Strother, who was living in the vicinity at the time.

Mr. Strother had settled in Sumner County before 1791, in the community where Cottontown was later situated. Richard Strother is named in several deeds in Sumner. In his will, dated 23 September 1809, he named his wife Susannah, a son James, a son Robert, a daughter Susannah Pitt, a daughter Nancy Hollis, and a daughter Betsy McConnell.

In 1803, East Tennessee was placed in the Western Conference with John Watson, presiding Elder. His district included the Holstein Circuit with Thomas Milligan and John Adam Grenada; the Nollichickie Circuit, placed in the charge of Henry Smith; the French Broad Circuit, under the care of Louther Taylor; the Powell's Valley Circuit, assigned to Benjamin Young; the Clinch Circuit, with Moses Black as their minister; and the New River Circuit, given to Learner Blackman.

John Adam Granade was born in Jones County, North Carolina. He taught school in 1799, and in 1800, he attended the quarterly meeting of the Methodist and preached. After several camp meetings in the Holston, he was sent to New River Circuit. In 1803 or early in 1804, he was in Kentucky. He returned to Tennessee in 1804, and the next year, 1805, he married Polly Wynn. He died on 6 December 1807. He had a grandson, the Rev. Herve M. Granade of the Arkansas Conference.

The first Granade in America is thought to have been one John Granade, who located in North Carolina. It is believed that he married a daughter of Elizabeth Ward of Onslow County, for in her will, dated 1767, she mentioned Ann Granade among other legatees. Some of John Granade's children were: Joseph, who had a wife named Margaret; Martin, who had a wife named Susannah; and another son who married Mary Johnson, daughter of Collinson Johnson. Johnson's will, dated 1795 in Jones County, North Carolina, names his wife, Leah, and children, including Mary Granade.

I am told that there is a record in North Carolina which says, "John Granade, father of John Adam Granade, had advanced the children of a first wife their inheritance, and that the mother of John Adam, Anna, Elizabeth Sanderson and Ann was named Ann."

Joseph Granade, Senior of Jones County made a will, dated 1799, in which he named his wife, Margaret, and children, Stephen, Nancy, Sally, Joseph, John, Elizabeth McAllister, Barbara Wood, and Celia Wallace.

Martin Granade left a will in Anson County, North Carolina in 1802 in which he mentioned his wife Susannah, a daughter Eliza Thurman, another daughter Nancy Thurman, and a nephew Benjamin Granade.

William Granade died in Smith County, Tennessee, leaving a will in 1818 in which he mentioned son Silas, grandson William Wilson, son-in-law Ephraim Wilson, daughter Nancy, and son Forque.

Several branches of the Granade family came to Tennessee. Most of them settled, at least for a time, in Smith County, Tennessee. Members of the Granade family intermarried with the Fortescue (Forscue) family in North Carolina, which accounts for the name Fortescue being frequently found among the descendants of the Tennessee Granades. Both Granade and Fortescue are French names.

By 1803, the Kentucky district had eight circuits with William McKendree as Presiding Elder and the following circuits: Limestone, Wm. Burke; Miami, Elisha W. Bowman; Scioto, John Sale and Stephen Timmons; Hinkstone, Hezekiah Harriman; Lexington, Samuel Douthat; Danville, Lewis Garrett and William Crutchfield; Salt River and Shelby, Benjamin Larkin and Ralph Lotspeich.

The Cumberland district with John Page as Presiding Elder had four circuits: Nashville, Thomas Wilkerson and Levin Edney; Red River, Jesse Walker; Barren, James Garvin and Jacob Young; Natchez, Moses Floyd and Tobias Gibson.

James and Samuel Douthit (also spelled Douthat) were Methodist preachers. It is believed that they were brothers, the sons of John Douthet, who died in March 1812 in Rowan County, North Carolina. John and his wife, Eliner Davis, had seven or more children, including James and Samuel.

John Page, a Methodist minister, died in 1859, probably at Smith's Fork in Tennessee.

Moses Black, aged 40 years, was a native of South Carolina, born near the city of Charleston. He died in Carter's Valley, Tennessee on 3 February 1810.

Elisha W. Bowman was born in Virginia, the son of a local preacher. His father moved to Kentucky, and Elisha became a minister there.

Tobias Gibson, was born in Liberty County, South Carolina, on the Great Pee-Dee, on 10 November 1771. He was admitted to preach in 1792. He died on 5 April 1804 at Natchez, Claiborne Parish, Mississippi.

Rev. Jesse Walker, a native of Buckingham County, Virginia, was born on 9 June 1766 and married Susannah Webly, a wealthy woman. He traveled throughout North Carolina, East Tennessee, and later into West Tennessee (now Middle Tennessee). He served in the Nashville Circuit. Long before he became an itinerant preacher, he was a local minister. There were many attempts made to persuade him to enter the itinerant ministry, but he refused on the grounds that it would not be fair to his wife. His refusal continued until death claimed two of his children. In 1802, he was received into the Western Conference, and he served the Tennessee and Kentucky circuits until 1806. He then went to Illinois and may be considered the "father of Methodism in Illinois." He went as a missionary to the Missouri Conference, which then embraced all of Missouri and Illinois. Rev. Jesse Walker's son-in-law, James Walker, was also his nephew. James Walker married Rev. Walker's daughter Jane. James Walker was a native of Tennessee and served under General Andrew Jackson at New Orleans. After the War of 1812 and the removal of his family to Illinois, James Walker became a Methodist minister.

In 1804, the Western Conference opened the Wilderness circuit, which was being served by Jacob Young. Cumberland reported seven circuits, with Lewis Garrett, presiding elder: Nashville, Leven Edney; Red River, Ralph Lotspeich; Barren, Anthony Houston; Wayne, Wm. Crutchfield; Livingston, Jesse Walker; Natchez, Moses Floyd, H. Harrison, A. Amos, and Tobias Gibson; and Illinois, Benjamin Young.

Leven Edney's name is associated with Edney Chapel at Pasquo, Davidson County. On 9 December 1808, Alson Edney of Davidson County deeded one acre of land to the Trustees of the Methodist Church, Francis Hodge, William Gower, Levin Edney, Aquilla Sugg, and Alson Edney. The land lay in Davidson County on the east branch of Richland Creek and was to be used for "building a meeting house subject to the use by ministers and preachers of the Methodist Episcopal Church."

There is also a deed, dated 3 September 1807, wherein Leven Edney, Aquilla Sugg, and Wm. Roach, trustees, also Newton Edney of Davidson County, and Leven Edney, Aquilla Sugg, and Wm. Roach, Trustees, one acre of land on Trace Creek of Big Harpeth for the site to build a house of worship. The transaction was witnessed by Richard Hart and Hardy Mitchell.

The will of Newton Edney, dated 14 July 1834 and proved April 1835 in Davidson County, directs that the heirs of son Edmond Edney, his son William excepted, receive a tract of land "whereon I live, 178 acres on Trace Creek." It also mentions two daughters, Dorcas Jones and Nancy Davis; son Samuel Edney; grandson Jesse Lee Edney; Parmelia Bray; wife; grandson Isaiah Newton Jones; and grandson Isaiah Newton Davis. Brother Leven Edney and friend John Davis were named as executors.

The administration and list of sale of the estate of Alson Edney, recorded in Williamson County, names Polly, the wife of Alson Edney.

Major William Mills, who was born in Virginia in 1744 and died in 1834 in Rutherford County, North Carolina, married Eleanor Morris. Their children were: Sarah Mills, who married Asa Edney, brother of Rev. Samuel Edney, Methodist minister; Eleanor Mills, who married Rev. Samuel Edney; John Mills, who married Sallie Robertson of Chester or Camden County, South Carolina; Merville Mills, who died in 1849, aged seventy-seven years, and married Mary Chambliss; Elizabeth Mills, who married George W. Jones of North Carolina; Phalby Mills, who was born on 24 September 1780 in North Carolina and died in 1854 in South Carolina; and Mourning Mills, who married Mr. Overton or John Graves Lewis of Virginia.

Samuel Edney was born in Pasquotank County, North Carolina in 1768 and was admitted to preach in 1791. He is said to have been related to Sir Isaac Newton. One source lists his children as James M., Maylis, and a daughter who married Isaac B. Sawyer. Another says that he and his wife Eleanor had Bayliss M., Rufus, Tom, James, Allison (Alson), John, Elizabeth, and Mary Kelly. Rev. Samuel Edney is said to have been the first Methodist Minister to cross the Blue Ridge Mountains.

Also of this family connection, one John Morris Edney married a Miss Fall of Augusta, Georgia.

Rev. Mr. Garrett was retained as presiding elder in the Cumberland for 1805, but numerous changes took effect among the circuits: Nashville, William Crutchfield and Fletcher Sullivan; Red River, Miles Harper and James Axley; Barren, Ralph Lotspeich; Wayne, Asa Shinn and John McClure; Roaring River, Richard Browning; Livingston and Hartford, Jesse Walker and Joshua Barnes; Natchez, Learner Blackman and Nathan Barnes; and Illinois, Joseph Oglesby.

Learner Blackman died in 1815, drowned in the Ohio River.

William Crutchfield became feeble and died on 6 August 1812. He was born in Brunswick County, Virginia. His father moved to Tennessee and settled near the mouth of Red River. The senior Crutchfield was killed by Indians when William was about seven or eight years old.

Rev. Fletcher Sullivan ceased to travel at the close of 1812. He settled in Cage's Bend, Sumner County where he lived for several years. He later located in Wilson County. Rev. McFerrin is in error about Rev. Sullivan's moving West, for he left a will in Wilson County, Tennessee, dated 1816, in which he named his wife, Nelly, and children: Amy Laton, Rachel Monnette, Peter Sullivan, Fletcher Sullivan, Jr., Clemmy Sullivan, Polly Sherrill, Nancy Moon, and Sally Chandler. Rachel Monnette was the wife of Rev. James Monnette, a local Methodist preacher who moved from Wilson County to Mississippi. The Monnette Family History says that James Monnette married Mary Kinedine in Maryland. However, the husband of Mary Kinedine was probably an uncle of Rev. James Monnette. Rev. Monnette was born in 1782, according to his tombstone in Mississippi. Some of his descendants claim that his wife was Rachel Fletcher, related to the Sullivan family.

Rev. Fletcher Sullivan was instrumental in establishing a number of churches in Wilson County. In a deed at Lebanon, dated 13 March 1830, Benjamin Nichol of Carroll County, Tennessee deeded one acre to the Trustees of the Methodist Episcopal Church. The land in Wilson County was for a church on the north side of Pond Lick Creek where Geliad Meeting house now stands. The witnesses were Lee Harrison, Lee Hancock, James Wynne, and Samuel Hancock.

In another deed, dated 12 June 1834, Aaron Ruyle, for the consideration of $5.00, deeded a lot to Joseph Fite, Leonard Fite, John M. Bennett, Edward Robinson, and William S. Anderson, all of Wilson County, the Trustees in Trust for a Methodist Episcopal Church. The land lay in Wilson County on Pirtle's Creek within thirty yards of the Main Road, in a tract of land belonging to Panathan Turner. This church became known as "Pirtle Creek Church."

In still another deed in Wilson County, dated 24 July 1829 and proved by the court in September 1830, George L. Swann (Swean ?), William Gill, Wm. Seay, Samuel Springs, Wm. Sear, John Seay, Sr., Trustees in Trust, confirmed the four acres in the First District of Wilson County on the west side of Dry Fork of Round Lick Creek, the southwest corner of Goodhope Meeting House. The witnesses were Solomon Caplinger and Benjamine Springs, Sr. The building erected on the property was known as "Abner Springs Methodist Church."

Rev. James Axley and his wife, Cynthia, lie buried about two and one half miles from Sweetwater, near the Athens Road. He died on 23 February 1837, aged sixty years. He was born in Cumberland County, Virginia, the son of James and Lemuanner Axley, and moved to Kentucky in 1799. Rev. Axley was admitted to the Western Conference in 1804 and located in 1822.

Rev. James Axley had two brothers and two sisters. The brothers, Pleasant and Robert, were converted near their home in Salem, Kentucky in 1802. Pleasant Axley was a local preacher for may years but did not attain the celebrity of his brother James. It is said that James Axley had no school training and no advantages in youth. James Axley married Cynthia Earnest, who was born in 1800. She was a sister of Mary Ann Earnest, who was born in 1789 and married John Lotspeich, Sr.

In 1806, Rev. William McKendree was presiding elder of the Cumberland District and its eight circuits: Nashville, Zadock B. Thackston; Red River, Thomas Hellum; Barren, Joshua Oglesby; Roaring River, Benjamin Edge; Wayne, Wm. Ellington and Henry Fisher; Livingston, William Houston; Hartford, Jesse Walker; and Illinois, Charles B. Matheny.

The Mississippi District was created with Nathan Barnes, Thomas Lasley, Caleb W. Cloud, Wm. Pattison, and Elisha W. Bowman assigned to travel to the inhabitants.

Rev. Joseph Oglesby was born in Virginia on 3 July 1782 and died in 1852. He served in the Missouri Conference during most of his latter years.

Elder William McKendree was born in King William County, Virginia on 5 July 1757 and died at the home of his brother, Dr. James McKendree, in Sumner County, Tennessee on 5 March 1835. When Bishop McKendree died, he left a will, executed on 24 January 1833 and probated in May 1835 (Will Book 2, folio 191) in Sumner County. In it, he devised items to his friend, Dr. Henry Wilkins of Baltimore, Maryland, his two sisters Dolly Harris and Nancy D. McKendree, his brother James, his brother-in-law Charles Harris, his friend Joseph T. Elliston, esq. of Davidson County, his friend M. R. W. Hill of Nashville, his friend Elijah Boddie of Sumner County, and the remainder of his estate in trust to Joshua Soule, including all manuscripts and papers to be disposed of with the assistence of Thomas L. Douglass.

Bishop Soule, mentioned above, was a native of Bristol, Maine, born on 1 August 1781, and licensed to preach at the age of seventeen.

Elijah Boddie was born in 1788 and reared in Nash County, North Carolina. He moved to Sumner County, Tennessee, near Gallatin about 1815. He married Maria Platt Elliott of Sumner County on 24 December 1816. She died on 10 November 1846. Mr. Boddie was the only child of Elijah Boddie, Sr., who was born in 1765, died in 1788, and married Elizabeth Taylor in December 1787. Elijah, Sr. was the son of Nathan Boddie, a native of Isle of Wight County, Virginia, who was born on 22 February 1832 and died on 7 December 1797, having removed to Nash County, North Carolina where he left a will. His wife, Chloe Crudup, was born in 1745 and died on 16 September 1781. Nathan was the son of William, the son of John Boddie, the son of William Boddie, American immigrant.

Elijah Boddie and his wife Maria Elliott had eleven children: Charles Elliott, who was born on 14 August 1818 and was married firt to Eveline Douglass and second to Susan Haney; Elizabeth Blackman, who was born on 26 August 1820 and married Wm. Robert Elliston; Mary Elliott, who was born on 27 February 1823 and married Rufus K. Cage; George, who was born on 14 October 1825 and died on 1 September 1846; Mourning Hilliard, who was born on 26 January 1828 and married Alfred Douglas; William Summerfield, who was born on 4 May 1830 and died on 11 June 1833; Micajah Thomas, who was born on 26 April 1832 and died on 29 June 1833; Gulieme, who was born on 26 November 1834 and died on 13 June 1835; Ella Douglas, who was born on 15 June 1836 and married Henry Craft; Van Buren, who was born on 14 December 1838 and married Anna Jewell; and Maria, who was born on 5 February 1841 and married Carrington Mason.

The Missouri Circuit was added to Cumberland District in 1807, and Rev. John Travis was placed in charge. The other circuits were: Nashville, Jacob Young and Hezekiah Shaw; Red River, Zadock B. Thackston; Barren, Abbott Goddard; Roaring River, Miles Harper; Wayne, Moses Ashworth; Livingston, David Young; Hartford, Benjamine Edge and Samuel Sellers; and Illinois, Jesse Walker.

Five circuits now composed the Mississippi District, Learner Blackman, presiding elder: Natchez, Wilkinson, Claiborne, Cohitta, and Appalousas with Caleb W. Cloud, William Pattison, Nathan Barnes, John Tarver, Thomas Lasley, and Elisha W. Bowman in the various circuits.

Benjamine Edge died in 1836. Thomas Lasley, a native of Virginia, son of Monoah Lasley, a local preacher, was converted in Kentucky and entered the conference in 1804. He died at the home of his son-in-law, M. McMillen, in McMinnville, Tennessee on 20 June 1857. Rev. Thomas Lasley was the father of Rev. Wm. Lasley and Rev. M. N. Lasley, both Methodist ministers.

In 1807, William Burke was presiding elder of the Kentucky District. His assistants or circuit-riders were Abraham Amos, Samuel Parker, Hector Sandford, James Ward, George Askin, Joseph Williams, John Thompson, Wm. Hitt, Joseph Bennett, Frederick Hood, and Joseph Oglesby.

Rev. Samuel Parker later went to Missouri, where he died four years later, in 1819. He was born in New Jersey in 1774 and was married in Kentucky to Alethia Tipton, the daughter of a local preacher.

In 1808, Rev. James Ward replaced Bishop Wm. McKendree as Presiding Elder of Cumberland District, which had added two more circuits under McKendree. The following were serving with Ward: John McClure, Joseph Oglesby, David Young, Thomas Lasley, Peter Cartwright, William Vermillion, James King, Sela Paine, Abraham Amos, Thomas Stilwell, John Cragg, and William Lewis. John Clingan was sent to the Illinois circuit; Edmund Wilcox to Missouri; and Zadock B. Thackson to the

the new Duck River circuit.

Rev. David Young, a Virginia, was born on 7 March 1799 and died in Missouri in 1858. Edmond Wilcox remained in Missouri only one year.

Zadock Baker Thaxton (or Thackston) was a native of North Carolina. He came to Middle Tennessee in 1791 or 1792.

The presiding elder of Cumberland in 1809 was Miles Harper, who served only one year. Illinois and Missouri had been made into districts. The remaining circuits were: Nashville, Elijah W. Bowman and William Vermillion; Red River, Frederick Stier; Barren, Joseph Bennett and John Lewis; Roaring River, Zadock B. Thackston and John Travis; Livingston, Thomas Kirkman; Hartford, Samuel Sellers and Jacob Turman; Elk (a new circuit that year), Thomas Stilwell; and Dixon, William Lewis and James Gwinn.

In 1810, Learner Blackman was presiding elder in Cumberland. Two new circuits, Henderson and Flint, were added and new circuit-riders: Thomas Hellums, James Gwinn, Isaac M'Kowen, Jacob Turman, Peter Cartwright, John Cragg, John Lewis, Josiah Crawford, Thomas Stillwell, William Lewis, and Jadidiah McMinn.

In 1811, many new ministeres were added to the list in Cumberland, among them: William B. Elgin, Samuel King, Marcus Lindsay, Lewis Anderson, Thomas A. King, John Manley, and John Phipps. Those retained another year were: James Gwinn, Peter Cartwright, James Axley, John Cragg, John Page, Thomas Stilwell, and Thomas Kirkman.

About this time, the old stone meeting house on the Public Square in Nashville was torn away, and the Methodists worshipped for a time in the County jail. Edward D. Hobbs, the jailer, was an ardent Methodist. The new church at Church Street and Printer's Alley, in the original plan of Nashville, is identified by the records in the Davidson County Court House. There were only two lots between Fifth and Sixth Avenues on Church Street. They were Lots No. 102 and 90. Lot No. 102 on the corner of High (now 6th Ave.) and Church Street was sold by the Trustees of Nashville to Dr. Valentine Sevier in 1792. Lot No. 90 on the corner of Sumner (now 5th Ave.) and Church Street was owned by James Shaw. In 1817, George Poyser gave a plot, 43 x 60 feet, for the erection of McKendree Methodist Church. The Shaw lot was the location of Dr. Leon Brockman's Infirmery in 1866.

The third church in Nashville was the principal church in the city and the scene of many revivals, according to the records. Such noted men as Dr. Thomas Maddin, Dr. Robert Paine (later Bishop), Rev. A. P. Green, and Dr. John B. McFerrin were among them.

Dr. A. L. P. Green died in 1874 and lies buried in Mt. Olivet Cemetery in Nashville. Rev. John B. McFerrin died in 1887 and is also buried in Mt. Olivet Cemetery.

Peter Cartwright was the celebrated "Backwood preacher." In 1846, he ran for Congress from Illinois against Abraham Lincoln.

In the pension records of the National Archives, there is a statement by Rev. Peter Cartwright, written from Sangamon County, Illinois and dated 19 November 1852. In it, he stated that he was the son and only surviving child of Peter and Christian Cartwright. He testified that his father had entered the service from Amherst County, Virginia about 1777 or 1778 and died in Caldwell County, Kentucky, 1809-1810. Peter said he had heard his father say that he was in the Battle of Brandywine, where he lost two brothers, and that he married Christian Garvin in Amherst County on 27 February 1787. They moved to Kentucky in 1791. Shortly afterwards, their home burned, and the family Bible was destroyed. They had the following children: Rosanna, Peter, and Polly. Neither of Peter's parents ever applied for a pension. His mother died in Caldwell County, Kentucky on 23 December 1838. On 18 October 1852, Mrs. Sophia Wilcox and John Rucker testified that Peter Cartwright was the son of Peter Cartwright, the Revolutionary soldier, and his wife, Christian Garvin and that the elder Peter's other children, Rosanna Vineyard and Polly Pentecost, and his widow, Christian Cartwright, were deceased.

Marriage Records, 1763-1800, Amherst County, Virginia, by Wm. Montgomery Sweeney, p. 17, shows Peter Cartwright, bachelor, and Christian Garvin, spinster, married on 27 February 1787. William Cartwright was the surety. Consent was given by Christian. There also appears the marriage record of John Cartwright, widower, and Martha Patterson, spinster, 31 July 1779, with George Calaspie as surety.

An inventory and administration of a Peter Cartwright, dated 16 June 1809 and 5 February 1810, names wife Christian and son Rev. Peter Cartright, in Caldwell County, Kentucky (Will Book A, 1809-1834).

Red River Missionary Baptist Church was organized near the line of Montgomery and Robertson Counties in 1791. Its records are found in the Tennessee State Library in Nashville. Ministers of the Presbyterian Church served at this Baptist Church in 1799: Elders McGready, Hoge, and Rankin. Two ministers belonging to the Methodist Episcopal Church, Elders John McGee and William McGee, held a sacramental meeting, at which a large congregation was present.

It is a matter of record that there was a Methodist church in Montgomery County as early as 1817, for a deed of conveyance from Thomas Rivers to Wm. O. Roberts, Nicholas M. Gilmer, John T. Gilmer, Edward Taylor, and John Brodie in Trust for the Methodist Church, one acre of land, was proved in the court of 20 October 1817 by the oath of Alexander Martin and Peter H. Cole, as witnessed.

The oldest Methodist Episcopal Church in Robertson County is Mount Zion, formed in 1798 by Jesse Walker, who later went to Illinois and Missouri. Among the traveling preachers who visited this church during its first years were Peter Cartwright, Bishops Morris, McKendree, and Payne, Lewis Garrett, and many others. Thomas and James Gunn, Patrick and Thomas Martin, and Jesse Walker were some of the local preachers.

Miller's Creek Church, near Turnersville, was organized at an early date, perhaps as early as 1815, but went out of existence before 1886. The Glovers, Ellises, and Jameses were among the first members.

Andrew's Church was formed about 1824 and continued as an organization for about thirty years. William Andrews, Darden Luter, James Atkins, Elisha and Wiley B. Gossett, and Elisha Luter belonged to this church. It was situated in the western part of the county, near Brush Creek.

Ebenezer Church was organized about 1833, near where Cedar Hill is now, to which place it was removed in 1860. Mark Settles, Jefferson Gooch, James and John Long, Rollin Ward, Thomas Spain, William Thomas, James Byrnes, with their families, and the Gunns and Martins constituted the early membership.

The church at Martin's Chapel, about three miles southwest of Coopertown, was organized by Patrick Martin about 1845.

After 1825, the church at New Chapel was organized at the house of Peter Fisor, in the Eighth Civil District.

Pleasant Grove Church was originally organized about three miles south of Cross Plains in 1821 by Parsons Edwards and Jernigan.

The first circuit-riders in the county were Black, Browder, William and Simeon Peters, Brown, and Evans. Some of the first members of the Methodist Church in the county were the Jernigan and Edwards families, Susan Gilbert, Lucy Cunningham, Nicholas Covington and wife, and Stephen Cole.

Salem Church, in the Seventeenth Civil District near Sandersville, was organized in 1843 with the following members: Robert Mitchell and wife, Robert Shanklin and wife, James T. Gunn and wife, Thomas Williamson and wife, H. Sadler and wife, Richard Qualls and daughter, Tabitha Williamson, and W. R. and Elizabeth Sadler. The first minister was Rev. Dye.

Among the original members of Wartrace Church were: J. B. Culbertson, James

Culbertson, Margaret Culbertson, Elizabeth Bell, Rev. Charles Crawford, Lucy and Margaret Crawford, Lucy J. Lemaster, and William Wynn and wife. A house was built in 1846, in which Charles Crawford preached the first sermon. The first pastor was Jesse J. Ellis.

In 1852, New Salem Church was erected upon land donated by Matthew Willis. Among the first members were Matthew Willis and wife, Aaron Ellison and wife, C. W. Warren and wife, Jesse B. Tapley, Betty Deur, Henrietta Davis, Thomas and Frank Willis, and Harrison and Pheobe Clayton. The first minister was William H. Browning. Other ministers were William P. Hickman, F. S. Petway, Cato B. Davis, William Randall, and G. M. Saunders.

Barren Plains Methodist Church was organized in October 1883. Dr. J. T. Scott, John R. Dunn, and John R. Long were the trustees.

The Methodist Church at Springfield was organized some time in the 1830's with Daniel P. Braden, Thomas J. Ryan, John S. Hutchison, George C. Conrad, Henry Hart, Thomas Martin, and Isaac England as trustees. Among the other members were Joachin Green, Marshall Jamison, Dr. Archibald Thomas, Mrs. John E. Garner, Mrs. R. K. Hicks. The church's lot, No. 37, was purchased from Dr. Thomas in 1837.

Major Richard Bibb, a member of a distinguished and wealthy Virginia family and a pioneer Methodist preacher, lived in Kentucky, near the Tennessee line. The Gunn Brothers no doubt visited and exhorted in his home and locality.

The progenitor of the Bibb family in America was Benjamin Bibb. He was a French Protestant who came from Wales to Hanover County, Virginia with his wife and three sons, William, James, and Thomas. Some of the descendants of the family settled in Georgia and Alabama. One John Bibb was born in Hanover County in 1703, the son of William. John married Susannah Bigger, commonly called "pretty Suckey" Bigger. They had sons and daughters. Their three sons were William, Thomas and Richard. William went to Georgia, and Thomas went to Alabama. Each became governor of their adopted state and also United States Senators. Each of them had a Bibb County named in their honor.

Richard Bibb was intended for the ministry of the Church of England, but, with the Revolutionary War coming on, he entered the army and attained the rank of Major. After the Revolution, he represented his county in the Virginia Legislature. He migrated to Kentucky about 1799 and settled at Lexington. He did not remain there long, before he moved to Bullitt County. While in the latter location, he owned and operated the Salt Works. It was not long until he made his final move and located at Russellville, Logan County, just above the Tennessee and Kentucky line.

Major Bibb was a man of unimpeachable character and one of the wealthiest men in Western Kentucky. Major Bibb's will in Logan County provided, "I do hereby emancipate all of my slaves from and after the first day of January next after my death, and desire that all of them, who have not wives or husbands in bondage, be sent to Liberia." He left them $5,000, all his stock, farming tools, wagons, carts and crops, and all his lands in Grayson County, plus "The land in the county of Logan conveyed to me by Benjamin Tompkins, Ralph E. Nourse and Robert Nourse is to be divided among them at the direction of executors, and also the land in Logan conveyed to me by Mark Hardin and about thirty acres adjoining it." He specifically mentioned "my Aaron" and "my woman Clarissa." The directions set out in the will were not entirely carried out. The manumitted slaves were mostly settled on the wild lands in Logan County, some of them remaining on the lots in Russellville.

Major Bibb was married twice, first to Lucy Booker, by whom he had three sons and three daughters. His second wife, Alice Young Jackson, widow of John Jackson of Woodford County, Kentucky, bore Bibb no children.

One of Major Bibb's sons, Richard Bibb, died at Russellville. Another son, John B. Bibb, was an officer in the War of 1812 and represented Logan County in the Kentucky Legislature. He married Sarah P. Horsley, daughter of General Samuel Horsley. John B. Bibb died in Frankfort, Kentucky at the age of ninety-four years.

George Bibb, the third son of Major Bibb, was born in 1776 in Virginia, educated at Hampton-Sydney and at William and Mary. He graduated from William and Mary in 1799. His wife, Martha Tabb Scott, was the daughter of Col. Charles Scott. In 1809, George Bibb was Chief Justice of Kentucky. He resigned in 1815 to become United States Senator, elected in 1829. He served as Secretary of the Treasury under President Tyler from 1835 to 1844. He was also Chancellor in Louisville. Mary Bibb, one of Major Bibb's daughters, married Gabriel Lewis, the son of Lawrence Lewis and his wife, Nellie Curtis. The other two daughters of Major Bibb married Dr. B. Roberts and Thomas S. Slaughter.

In Rutherford County, Tennessee, there lived four brothers: James, Thomas, Gideon, and Bennett Rucker, natives of Bedford and Amherst Counties, the sons of Benjamin Rucker, a wealthy and prominent citizen of the day. The four brothers married four Read sisters and moved to Tennessee a few years before 1800. These Virginians purchased large tracts of land then in Davidson County but later in the newly formed Wilson, Rutherford, and Cannon Counties. All four of the Ruckers were ministers, each of a different denomination. Each organized a church on their own land.

Rev. James Rucker, a Methodist, was of local rank until the Conference of 1812, when he was ordained as an itinerant. Sometime prior to 1810, however, he had established a Methodist Church on his land in Rutherford County, about four miles north of Murfreesboro, near the site of the present Veteran's facilities. Rev. Rucker, his wife, and some other members of his family are buried there. Rucker's, as it was called, was formally organized in 1812 and thrived for a number of years. After the death of Rev. Rucker, the congregation moved about a mile and consolidated with the Emory Methodist Church and continued until that building burned.

I am proud to be the possessor of two Bibles which belonged to Rev. Rucker. In one of these Bibles, Rev. Rucker recorded the names and birth dates of all his children. Rev. and Mrs. Rucker were my great great-grandparents.

Memorials of Methodists by Bennett, p. 233.
Min. of Metho. Conf., 1773-1813, by Totten, 1813.
Sketches of the Pioneers of Methodism in N. C. and Va., by Moore, 1884, p. 167.
Nashville Banner, Magazine section, Nov. 28, 1937 "150 Years of Methodist Preaching" by Florence Wilson; Jan. 17, 1941; June 25, 1943.
Methodist in Ky., by Redford.
DAR Magazine, 1935, p. 438.
Sam Davis, Confederate Hero, by Edythe Whitley (Thweatt family).
Sketches of Pioneer Methodist in Tenn., by McFerrin.
Hist. of N. C., by John H. Wheeler, Chapter 9, pp. 64, 78, 81.
The Heart of Bishop Asbury's Journals, by Ezra S. Tipple, D. D.
DAR No. 107060, 125992, 26320 (1926).
"Methodist Memento," by Louise Davis, Nashville Tennessean, March 2, 1947.
Hist. of Tenn. Conf., by Carter, p. 546.
Methodist Movement in Northern Illinois, by Almer M. Pennewell, 1942.
Holston Methodist, by Price, p. 228.
Clendenning and Related Families, pp. 167-168.
Monnette Family History, by Monnette.
History of Sweetwater Valley, Tennessee, by W. B. Lenoir, 1917, p. 50.
Annals of Metho. in Mo., by W. S. Woodward, 1893, p. 8
Boddie and Allied Families, by John Thomas and John Bennett Boddie, 1918.
Life of Lincoln, by Barton, Vol. 1, pp. 277-278
Amherst Co., Va. in the Revolution, by Sweeney, 1951, p. 112.
Goodspeed's History of Tenn., Montgomery Co., 1886, pp. 796-799.
Register of the Kentucky Historical Society, Vol. 1 and 2, pp. 43 and 44.
Collin's History of Ky., Vol. 2, p. 772.
Rucker's and Connections, by Edythe Whitley.
Davidson County, Tenn. W. B. 1, pp. 3, 65; Min. Book A, 1783-1791, p. 14; Deed Book c, p. 33; Deed Book G, pp 383 509
Smith Co., Tenn. records Misc.; W. B. 1, p. 261
Wilson Co., Tenn. Will Book 1814-1819, p. 308; Deed Books C, p. 224; E, p. 626; H, p. 134; M, pp. 162, 471; N, p. 270; P, p. 530; O, p. 30; P, p. 530; O, p. 30; P, p. 318; R, p. 464; T, p. 395; V, pp. 121, 579; W, pp. 6, 202.

152

178

184

Trumbull, Wm. 48
Tucker, Daniel 131
  Gray 120
Tull, William 134
Turbeyfield, William 129
Turman, Jacob 143
Turnley, —— 23
Turpin, Solomon 120
Tutom, William 120
Tuton, William 120
Tygert, Robert 131
Tyler, ——, Pres. 146
  Robert 20
Tyre, Wright 133
Tyreell, William 121
Tyrrell, W. 116
  William 111, 113, 119, 120
  Wm. 121
Tyson, Henry W. 78
  John 78
  John P. 78
  Peter R. 78
  Uriah 134
  William 78
  William H. 78

--- U ---

Ury, George 133
Ussery, Edwin M. 56
  Eugene E. 56
  Frank 56
  George 56
  Ida 56
  John R. 56
  John W., Dr. 56
  Maud H. 56
  Norman 56
  Robert L. 56
  Sarah E. 56
  William 56

--- V ---

Vance, John 121
  Sarah 54
  Samuel 79, 124, 130
  Samuel, Capt. 79
Vanderfield, William 121
Vaughan, —— 75, 82, 133
  J. P. 7
  John 23, 24
  Lucy 23
Vermillion, William 142, 143
Verrell, William 121
Vick, John 129
  Roland 131
Villiers, Harriett 61
  John 61
Villines, Calista 78
  Charley 79

Eddie Lee 38, 79
J. W. 78
James W. 78
John 79
Lizzie 79
Lydia K. 78
Mary 78, 79
Mattie 79
N. J. 78
Nancy J. 78
Nannie 79
Robert M. 78
Sallie 78
Susan Hollis 78
T. J. 78
W. H. 78
William 78, 79
William E. 78
William H. 79
Vineyard, Rosanna 143

--- W ---

Waddleton, James 86
  Margaret 86
Wade, Andrew 121
  Macijah 74
  Micajah 74
Walker, —— 79, 95
  Agnes 137
  Alfonso 80
  Allen 121
  Andrew 131
  Buck 34
  Caroline 80
  Catherine 80
  Eliza Jane 81
  Elizabeth 80
  Eneas 80
  Enos 80, 81
  Ephraim Foster 81
  Gennett 80
  George Bunn 81
  George W. 80
  Georgia 80
  Georgia Bunn 81
  Hattie 80
  Herschel 80
  Isabella 37
  Jackson L. 81
  James 37, 45, 139, 140
  Jane 139
  Jas. O. 81
  Jeremiah 22
  Jesse 139, 140, 141, 142, 144
  Jno. Bell 81
  John 80, 81
  John A. 80
  Joseph 77
  Malinda 37
  Mary Ann 80, 81
  Martha 81
  Martha House 81